MAMA 'N' 'EM

Louis Gardner

iUniverse, Inc.
Bloomington

Mama 'N' 'Em

iUniverse books may be ordered through booksellers or by contacting:

iUniverse
1663 Liberty Drive
Bloomington, IN 47403
www.iuniverse.com
1-800-Authors (1-800-288-4677)

Because of the dynamic nature of the Internet, any web addresses or links contained in this book may have changed since publication and may no longer be valid. The views expressed in this work are solely those of the author and do not necessarily reflect the views of the publisher, and the publisher hereby disclaims any responsibility for them.

Any people depicted in stock imagery provided by Thinkstock are models, and such images are being used for illustrative purposes only.
Certain stock imagery © Thinkstock.

ISBN: 978-1-4502-9332-7 (pbk)
ISBN: 978-1-4502-9333-4 (ebk)

Printed in the United States of America

iUniverse rev. date: 06/22/2011

Preface

In the process of writing these memories, I must confess I was inspired by my older siblings Lillian, Mabel, Cecelia, and my brother, Ralph Jr. Along with other family members, they filled me with the history and stories and convinced me they needed to be told for the generations to come.

The stories are centered on the facts and revelations of an extended family. They were touched by the lives of their ancestors, yet undocumented, who became free men and contributed to a freer society of black people. This family spoke of those who volunteered and risked all for the redemption of those yet enslaved. They again surrendered themselves in World War I. They found economic advancement in the roaring twenties that followed the war. Then came the Great Depression to take away the many hard earned but meager job advancements. Progress became a struggle. World War II brought about a necessity for all to become involved. The war affected all our lives immensely. We continued to struggle for racial progress throughout our times. We were affected by wars, the economic times, and the prejudices of our governing bodies. We were affected by our lack of schooling opportunities, by our racially conscious leaders and ministers, and those who opposed any progress of our race. These are the stories of the experiences of one family. As the author, I have attempted to relate as much of the life and times as they were. Being the middle child of a ten-sibling family, the stories in the end become more autobiographical, yet the life and times of Mama 'n' 'Em are alive in this book.

Acknowledgments

First, I want to thank from the bottom of my heart the circumstances that led me, a retired city employee, to write these memoirs. My brother, Ralph Jr., diligently researched the family history so we could accurately describe our heritage. My sister, Cecelia, urged me to write of the struggles, the dedication, and the love it took to survive the Great Depression in a neighborhood of unpardonable whites.

I would also like to express my good fortune in having the help of Vaudine Long in the early days of writing these pages. Her guidance in literary correctness encouraged me to continue the first meager attempts to tell of the past. My thanks and greatest appreciation go to the following friends and relatives, who assisted in the construction. First Janice Able, then DeAsha Long, K'Yon Gardner, Marva "Toni" Johnson, Carmen Collins, and Navee Lynn. Then there is that large group of people who contributed, sometimes unknowingly, through their reminders of past events and places while they breathed life into daily conversations with their recollections.

1904 RAlph (PApA)

It began when the dashing young Will Gardner (reportedly from South Carolina) met and won the love of Della Forney. Will took the position of sharecropper while distinguishing himself by singing and playing music at the local church. Della Forney was one of the two daughters of Alfred and Harriet Forney. The Forneys lived on a large tract of land covering the top of one of the many mountains around Union Mills, North Carolina. The land was covered with southern pine trees and home to an abundance of wildlife. The Forneys survived and prospered on this land deeded to them two or more generations in the past.

Will and Della married, and while struggling on a shared farm, they produced two children. The first was Ralph and then Lola. Della passed way tragically after that second childbirth. The two children went to live with their maternal grandmother, while Will went on sharecropping. Will soon remarried and had two children, William Jr. and Lucy Gardner. Will prospered and was able to purchase a small plot of land for his growing family. It was then he decided to go back to Alfred and Harriet Forney for his older children. They would be a great help. The story of Ralph Gardner and Ada Williams Gardner, the mama and papa that would stretch the Gardner family to ten, begins here. Let Papa tell it.

I remember so well as we left the schoolhouse, Professor Gillen hung the big padlock on the door. Why? Why would someone break into a schoolhouse to steal a McGuffey reader? We called him Professor Gillen. As the old folks said, "To give him respect, give him his due." We all knew the teachers were not paid as the others and were kept in their so-called place. That's how the white folks kept their order.

This was early in the year, before spring. Professor Gillen had spent much of the winter and up to the end teaching the new sciences. He explained as much as he could about electricity and the telephone, which none of us had at home. When he got to the steam engine, we understood more of how it worked. Steam was in everyone's home. When he started talking about the automobile, it took a bit more time to get the details. I got excited and gave it all attention. "These gasoline-powered engines are used in the larger cities around the world. London, Paris, New York, and even Chicago," he told us.

In the future, these engines would replace horses. Professor Gillen was good at drawing parts on the blackboard to explain. I was thrilled with thoughts of this automobile, powered by a gasoline engine. Someday I meant to see one up close, see how it really worked, test the engine and drive the automobile. I would have my own. Having come to my grandma's at the age of 4. I have now grown to be 12yrs old I have finished school. Reading, writing and simple arithmetic is all that is needed on the farm. As Grandma Forney stood in the doorway with Aunt Pearl, I could tell someone was coming up the path. I knew who it was when I heard the raspy voice. It was my dad. He rarely came to the homestead since my mother passed away eight years ago. He told my grandma and Aunt Pearl of his past, his church involvement and choir directing, and the small farm he had on the road to Charlotte. Now with a wife, one child, and another child on the way, he wanted to unite his family. He wanted me to be a part of his new family.

I stacked the last of a bundle of firewood beside the big fireplace and went to my daddy. Quickly I noticed I came up to his shoulders. He pulled me to him, putting one hand on my shoulder. He remarked about how I had grown and how happy he was to hear of me being mannerly and attending school so regularly. As seldom as I had seen my daddy since losing my mother, I felt drawn to him. Still, I loved dearly my times spent with my Grandma Harriet and the one who stood so faithfully behind me, my mother's closest sister, Aunt Pearl. As soon as school was out, I went to go to live with my daddy. I remembered the things he said and what he didn't say. He didn't say he missed me.

The Decision—Ralph (Papa)

At my father's there was no schooling. The summers were long. Daddy along with some of our neighbors and two of his choir member's stepped in to harvest the crops and store for the coming winter. We had feed for the livestock, one cow, two hogs, and some chickens. Susan Francis my step mother had worked hard as well canning and preserving food. She was good to me as well. We tried a small field of tobacco for the first time with some success, though they declared we were not paid the going price for our crop. All and all we had a great year with our neighbors complementing our success. Daddy called and rewarded all who helped with one exception. This was my third year with my daddy. I had learned to do every chore yet I was passed over without a word. Winter is here I thought, but when spring comes I will be gone.

In the spring of 1906, I made my quick good-byes and then walked to Union Mills where I could catch a train to Ashville. The scenery on the way to Ashville was quite like I expected, though I had never been so far from home. When boarding the train alone, I took a bench seat at the end of the aisle. I made sure to sit behind the colored-only sign. I stared out the window to avoid the stares of the white passengers up front. They sometimes would look back, as if intimidated by the presence of the few colored passengers. I stood six feet one inch and weighed one hundred twenty pounds when I left school at the age of twelve. I was now fifteen and likely the most intimidating figure on the train.

I moved as close to the window as possible and covered my face with my hands. I gave a quick prayer for a safe trip, then continued to stare out the window. The scenery changed to a more flat terrain as we finally left the mountains. The farms were much larger than any I'd seen. The mules were in teams. I saw a steamboat for the first time. I saw no colored people.

Darkness came quickly and many began to nod their heads and position themselves to sleep on those hard seats. I pulled my one bag closer to me. It had a change of clothing and a sandwich from my Aunt Pearl. She alone knew my plan and had prepared me with advice. I was to ask for directions to the home of her older brother, Mills Forney, who lived in Cincinnati. I had the address written down.

When I finally reached Uncle Mill's house, he was already gone to work for the day. The summer season for concrete work had already started. My aunt Maymie, his wife, fed me and I rested up for the following work day. I was anxious.

The next day, I carried water all day long for the men and cement mixers. The hours were long and tiresome but necessary. Like the men who followed him on the job, I began to call my uncle Sup, because he was our supervisor. I admired my uncle for the way he operated his business and the family life he lived. He'd built his own home on a corner lot. His children, Rozwell and Everlena, were the greatest. He and the children regularly went to church on Sunday where he was a member of the official board and superintendent of Sunday school. Like most of the labor force I was thankful for the day off, and used it for a much-needed day of rest.

As the days of summer began to shorten I noticed the intensity to get as much work done as possible. The reasoning came to me as I noticed Uncle Sup daily watching the morning temperatures. They would be unable to pour concrete when the temperature went to freezing. The freezing temperatures would not allow the cement to set or harden without cracking. They knew no way to avoid this. They would complete as many basement foundations and sidewalks as possible before shutting down until spring.

I was not prepared for a winter in Cincinnati. I'd saved a good bit but was not ready to burden my uncle and his wife until spring. I decided to go home for the winter and tough it out. At home I learned that the railroad was coming right through my hometown and they were hiring. I quickly applied. They looked at my size and they hired me. I was sixteen, so they gave me the job of water boy. I thought the load would be light, but they drank heavily and often used the water to pour over their heads and sometimes their feet to cool themselves from the heat. As the train tracks went through and beyond Union Mills, the water had to be carried a longer distance and over hills. I could hardly keep up.

I stayed with those hardened railroad men. Those guys were something. We slept in a shack several times but mostly in boxcars. They fed us then deducted the cost from our pay. The men slept like they worked. Hard. They cursed heavily. On weekends they seemed disgruntled. Maybe it was from being away from their families. They cursed constantly while drinking themselves into some kind of a stupor. They often fought each other without a real reason when drinking. It was hard for me to take.

When the tracks we laid began to take us well beyond Union Mills, I became more and more uneasy with the railroad workers. It did not take me long to make the decision now that the winter was over. I would go back to Cincinnati in a little bit better situation than I was before. This time I was going to get a full-time job.

At the Crossroads—Ada

Ada went to the window to open only the top pane. She then pulled the shade, as the front room at 3539 Irving Street stood only a few feet from the front sidewalk. It was an early hot summer night, and the windows were open. She lit the lantern on the table before the window. She took the *Union* (the colored newspaper) to the table. The night was young. The fireflies were finished and the crickets had nearly finished their nightly chorus. Then came the noises from the Cincinnati Zoo which was just across Forrest Ave. It began with the lions and they were joined by the sea lions barking into the later night hours.

"What keeps you up so late?" asked Hattie.

"Oh, I don't know, I guess it's the many concerns I have about my future. I've determined to give my future life in dedication to he who gave his life that we might live. I want to be an example as the great Sojourner Truth was. Yet I can't see my way. What church will send me afar? I can't change my church. I can't do that," said Ada.

"Then why do you sit there reading that *Union*?"

"Oh, I feel an obligation to do my share. I don't want to be a burden. Our parents are gone to that farm now, and it's best for them, but we have to take care of this place ourselves. I'm looking for work to help pay my share. I'm looking here at these ads. Stay on the place, no children, no pets, comparable wage. These ads are in the *Union*. Some even say colored may apply and some say colored preferred."

"Well sister," replied Hattie, "it's pretty much as described. I have had my experiences, and that's why I'm a cook. You see, when it says 'colored may apply,' they are expecting you will accept less. 'Colored preferred' means they are paying so little colored are the only who will accept. 'If hired will pay for interview carfare' means

6

nothing. Forget that—they consider it their discretion to pay or not to pay. Don't build your hopes on those people. They are totally unpredictable and unreliable. They can be very cunning. What they say at the interview can be easily misunderstood. Within the family you might be called upon for services of any kind, sometimes even onerous ones by the males and you don't want that. Be a cook, stay in the kitchen and prepare meals and bag lunches, and leave after dinner and you'll likely get more in pay.

"I've noticed you have less and less talk these days for the usual neighborhood friends. Boys, that is. That Ralph seems to be 'it.' Oh don't say nothing, sister, I know my people. He has become 'it,' at least around here. He shoots pool—he's the star player at Avon Oaks. The big bopper, I hear he's a hard hitter. He's the best on the team at the bat. You go faithfully to the games. You are there when they return and he looks for you when he passes the house. Anyone can tell. Now come on, Ada, he's tall. What you call a treetop lover. And where you say he's from, Carolina? This don't tally up. You're going to his games and to his store to eat his ice cream as a gift? What do you think? You are accepting him. Coming from the backwoods as he is he might be a little raw but who is perfect? His young energy can give you protection, and I'm sure he will get work that is long lasting. You, Ada, my beloved, have the better schooling. He needs your learning.'

"Do you know that Bessie Smith is coming here to this town? She is gonna be at the Cotton Club. I have got to be there. She's mesmerizing. She's not known around yet, but the white will soon hear and she will be playing the famous Cottage Grove, Palisades, Castle Farms, Beverly Hills, and those places. This may be our only chance to see that girl, she'll be crossing over. Oh, we may get her record when she makes one and you've got something to play it on. You and that treetop, you say Carolina special, better plan one of those good ones. Go get a couple of tickets and get yourselves together and go on down there to the club. You will never regret it."

They could hear the group of employees coming from Castle Farms after a long night in the kitchen. "Oh my goodness, it must be near daylight. Good night love," said Hattie.

Ada

The day finally came. We planned a short gathering at the house. Already licensed by the justice of the peace and with papers in hand we were ready. The vows by the Reverend Pendleton would finish this thing. The February weather was cold. We wanted to gather at the church, but so few would have come. Those closest to me were there, thankfully. They stood in their coats in the small living room that was short of seating. We needed a short service for them. Mom and Dad sat patiently waiting with approving eyes, having come from Woodlawn on the streetcar. The reverend came from Walnut Hills, also by streetcar. I attempted to judge the feeling of the neighbors in the standing group. I knew this would be topic one in the coming months.

Standing before Reverend Pendleton I felt the missionary zeal slipping away from me. My dream of the past three years of following my idol was stymied. Ralph seemed to take a firmer grip on my hand, which was unnecessary. I felt no real fear, just a feeling of great change overtaking me. I had not given this enough thought. "Oh, hogwash," my dad would say. "Let's just listen to the Reverend and get his message." In the silence I can feel the 'it' as Hattie described. I've accepted this man wholeheartedly. I was going to be a married, wholesome woman who knew no other man. I was happy and proud. This would be a great force in keeping a Christian marriage. We would keep our home a Christian home. I'd like Ralph to spend more time at church, maybe in Bible study, even if it means less time at home or even a little less income. I accepted this as the Lord's will. We would rejoice in the Christian faith and he would make a way.

The guests applauded at the end of the ceremony. A few neighbors wished us well and began to leave. The preacher started to lecture us on what our parents had taught us much earlier. Then I started off with "I Am on the Battlefield, for my Lord" and was joined by all who remained in the crowd. I could tell by the expression on Ralph's face that he did not think the song fit with what the reverend had been lecturing. Then moments later I could see him realizing after all it did have relevance. I was uplifted.

As soon as the neighbors departed, on cue Marie and Fannie went to the kitchen and shortly returned with a tray of cookies and a tray of tea spiced with lime. Hattie had prepared this earlier and now stood at the front door assuring all that the wedding was over.

Ralph

S he came into the store again today with her sister while I was stacking the shelves. I knew it was her sister because they look so much alike. I don't know their names. Surely wish I did. I've been told it's not proper to ask since I'm a clerk at work. They are not as friendly as the girls at home who would have had something to say. They have stout bodies and they seem to know what they are about. The one has long hair in a wrap, hair that needs only a comb and brush. I like that.

My Uncle Sup rented this place and made a store for the neighborhood. "We need a store close by, and it'll give you something to do in the evenings, Ralph," he said. Right now it's been nearly a year we've been here. He's put a lot into the store since we started. So much that's needed, including canned goods, potatoes, onions, needles and thread, candles, some school supplies, and candy for the kids. We have no meat. Uncle Sup plans to have dry ice later so we can have ice cream this summer. Just for the kids and the neighborhood, he would say. He is the superintendent at that Mt Zion Sunday school.

Since I've been here I've walked Vine Street, though only a portion both ways, as it is the longest street in the city. I've been to Bucktown. What a place. So different, such a mass of Negroes like I've never seen before. I watched the river from its high points. I fished there. I saw the ferry but did not ride it. No use, I've got no reason to. The hills here were nice, but not like the mountains at home. We had more mountains way back into the distance. Along Fourth Street I'm fascinated by the line of gasoline-driven automobiles. The drivers take their seat behind the steering wheel in such a proud way. They pass each horse and buggy they see in a bossy way then look back and sneer. Oh, by golly, I'm gonna find the place they say automobiles race each other. That's gonna be the most fun.

On so many days boredom overcame me at a store. I was glad to be called on one of Uncle Sup's construction jobs. At seventeen I fall in line with those who have been at that work for years. It's good to know where I stand and that there are options. I'd rather there was something steadier with regular days and hours. Those days of uncertainty gave me too much time to think. What's my future?

In my quiet moments, I think about home. I think about the one mountain range where my ancestors are and have been as far back as any one family member or any others can recall. There is nothing like that place. At times I could catch the first train there to rush open arms once again to be with my folks. I will always reflect back on those past and glory days when I'm blue to uplift my spirit. Some days I do become so down. Oh, but one day I will return to show them that I have had success. I must have an automobile to prove it, and that's still a dream.

My heart goes out to those souls back home so tied up to the earth, their very existence tethered to a piece of ground and dependant on nature and the almighty for survival. I've promised to love all and spread caring ways to the fullest, then pity the rest. And that I will do.

A Long Talk—Ralph

This town is now a thriving city, the home of our President William Howard Taft. Advanced new construction is everywhere. A new bridge now crosses the river, connecting us with cities in the east. The canal connects the northern cities. The Negro population is increasing, and we have a newspaper and a recent graduate from the prestigious University of Cincinnati. The state integrated the schools some years ago, though most of ours were pushed aside into two all-colored schools. There has been progress for those who have ventured out and into the foundries, the tanneries, and some construction jobs. Progress is being made because of the need. The city is growing by leaps and bounds. The wealthy that moved to the hills around the city are now moving beyond. Migration from Europe's overflow through New York is affecting this city. Now the Jewish people are taking over from the Germans and Catholics. Here in Avondale, the largest suburb of the city, there is a Negro arm of progress. We are mostly domestics, but there is a feeling of progress for the race.

I like the community feeling of our neighborhood. I like the neat entrance rooms to these newly-built two up and two down frame houses. Most houses have a pot-bellied stove, a cotton-stuffed chair or two, and maybe a seat for two under the front window. I like those wallboards with marriage licenses and pictures by the door. There were pictures of their past, and our past. There were pictures of Booker T. Washington, Fred Douglas, and others. There were pictures of family members old and new. Some have pictures of jockeys in uniform at a racetrack. At Ada's house I see a picture with men in the blue and gray uniform of the civil war and one in the navy uniform.

This community, nestled between the hillsides of Avondale and Clifton, harbors a conclave of Negroes. Many of them are domestics serving the needs of the wealthy citizens, who are mostly Jews. In Madisonville and Dunbar, they serve the massive homes of Indian Hill. Blue Ash has its Hazelwood and Hyde Park has Obryonville.

I walked alone on the way to the house on Irving Street, my whole being excited by a sudden realization of having progressed so much in my first year here. I loved this place; it gave me so much energy, like nothing I had ever felt before. If I were at the bat I would hit the ball to somewhere in Alabama. I felt just that great. The fulltime job helping my uncle Sup gave me a chance to make my life what I want it to be.

At Mr. Miller's house on Irving Street, where the big catalpa tree stood covering much of the sidewalk, I could hear Ada's voice singing. It stopped me in my tracks. I wanted to stand there and listen, but not in front of Mr. Miller's house. I saw two of the Turner brothers carrying some ice to their house down the street. *So strange*, I thought.

Ada explained they were preparing for a rent party. Of course, I begged for an explanation. "A rent party is a party to raise money for the rent," she told me.

"But this is not the beginning of the month," I said.

"Yes, Ralph, but what does your ball team do when they need money for equipment or transportation?"

"We have an extra game and pass around the hat."

"That's just what they are doing. It gets that way. Sometimes I think it's just an excuse to party. They do it on a regular basis like an unlicensed business."

Without a couch, we sat on two wooden chairs beside the small table next to the window. We talked the many hours to midnight and far beyond. Having been away from my people for so long, it nearly brought tears to my eyes when I told her some of the memories of my people and their hardships. I told her how white kids sometimes threw stones at our little schoolhouse for no real reason. We had a hard time understanding that until we learned many whites feared that the education of the Negro would produce a generation that would compete with them and their positions would be threatened. It's not at all like here, where most all get at least eight or nine years in school. "We need that," I told her.

"It's a beginning," she replied.

I was stunned by her family's past. Her grandpa passed away in that soldier's home in Dayton, Ohio, a veteran of the Civil War. Her grandma was a full Indian from Versailles, Kentucky. Her stern face and long hair explained that. Daddy was from Kentucky, near Lexington, where the family owned land and were horsemen. "My daddy came to Cincinnati, and he along with Mills Forney, who is your Uncle Sup, was employed by the contractors who paved Irving Street years back. He has not told you that. Let me tell you something. You know that frame building where the store is? That building was put there when the city was paving the street. In the beginning it had a large blueprint on a table at one end. On the other end they stored their tools, shovels, rakes, and brooms. Outside they had a faucet for drinking water and they washed the tools there. Then the building was abandoned, and stood empty awhile. My daddy took it upon himself to get scrap lumber and divide it into rooms and rent it out. Your uncle later thought we needed a store, and then he rented it. That's before you came. They once worked on the Alms and Doepke building together. They later subcontracted concrete work on those apartments on Northern and Hearne. Daddy and Sup, as you call him, dug basements together. Sup built his house at Dick Street and Tallant as well as a few others in the neighborhood, mostly using Sears's blueprint construction. Now Daddy has bought and moved to a farm on Grove Road in Woodlawn. They call themselves retired, though they did this for my mother's benefit at her doctor's advice. My mother was named Jessie after my grandfather, who we honor for the example he has been to all of us. He lived a life of dedication for his people. I too want to be as honored as he is," she said.

Only a great determination to do what was expected of me pulled me to my feet for the journey home. These, my people, were forging ahead, and I too must play my part. These people here are no different than my people back home in their goals to improve the lot of the Negro. I must and will evermore devote myself. I love everything that's happened to me since coming from home (North Carolina). At eighteen years old, I was at the most exciting point in my life.

Close Quarters—Ada

Woodrow Wilson and his congress have declared war on Germany. It was expected by all, especially in Cincinnati, where we have been getting so many of their immigrants. Jobs are good and now are expected to increase. Many will be drafted, leaving more jobs for fewer men. I don't like to see so many of our boys going into the army to defend our country, or more correctly protect the wealth of the whites here. But we are part and parcel of this country; we have no other country to defend. Judge Parker and some of the others Ralph drives for on occasion declare he will not be called up. I'm sitting here expecting our third child, that's why. Six years have gone by so fast. We should have had our own home by now. I've enjoyed the years and count each child a blessing, but there is just too little space. This is the family home, and Mom and Daddy allow us to stay here for the upkeep, but we are obliged to allow family members to stay who are in need of housing. Even the thought of this happening makes me feel uneasy.

My once dream has faded; I will always serve in some manner. I love each child passionately. The family life is wonderful, but Ralph and I will have to talk about this soon. We must have the space.

It was the end of summer when they came to an already-crowded house at 3539 Irving Street. It so shocked me when they knocked on the door at midday as I had not seen even a picture of either of them. I could tell they had been traveling by their bags, their tied-up boxes, and the way they were dressed. Immediately the man's voice caught hold. It was Ralph's daddy and the children of his marriage to Susan Francis, his two young brothers. They did not look as strikingly like Ralph as I would have imagined, but the southern voices made clear their identity. I gave my best effort to welcome them with sincerity, which seemed to find favor with them.

I began to feel a spirit of togetherness, a family tie, and even a loving connection. These boys were the second family of the marriage of Mr. Will Gardner and Susan Francis. Will Jr. was called Bill, and Fred was the younger one. They grouped themselves in the small living room soon after Ralph returned from work. I sang the refrain, "Standing on the Promises of God" from the kitchen while preparing a meal. Mr. Will, facing the boys, pulled a harp from his vest pocket. He gave one quick, sharp blast from the harp. Then, with one finger extended from the right hand, he gave a quick striking motion. Out came a harmonizing never before seen by my children. A spiritual display of southern culture struck them. The household responded with extreme joy and appreciation. It is just what was needed at this time. Love abounded.

Why?

(Small story passed down by my older sister Lillian Gardner)

One fall evening, Papa's friend Teddy stopped in front of the house at 3539 Irving Street. When he called out, Papa went to the front of the house to talk with him. Teddy related to Papa that the last racecar meeting at Sharonville's racetrack would be held on Sunday and that there would be no more races for the season. They had to go! They went.

They both enjoyed the races tremendously. So much so that they were saddened to be reminded there would be no more races until spring. They lingered as they were leaving. On approaching the exit gates, they saw some of the cars they had previously seen in the races standing side-by-side on the pavement. "Look," said Teddy, "you could buy one of those cars if you had the money."

"Well, then I can," said Papa.

"You're dreaming," said Teddy. "You've got too many kids. You'll never have anything." Papa was shaken. How could his friend say such a thing? *I'll show him*, thought Papa.

Now Papa and Mama had been saving for the express purpose of buying their first home, for there were now five children. Still, there was a fire inside Papa to prove to his friend once and for all he was the man, that he had the finances and was in control. Papa took all of the family savings, without anyone knowing, returned to the track, and purchased the winning car of the final race. Papa paid cash.

Mama refused to get into the car because of what it represented. The car was a racecar, something some might want to be seen in, but it was not for her. She would not get in that contraption. Papa, however, was elated to drive and to be seen driving that racecar, the finalist of the season. He felt like a celebrity as he raced here and there. In a show-off manner he often improperly parked, even double parked. As luck would have it (as they say) one time he double-parked, and the fabulous racecar so adored by Papa—and such a symbol of idolatry by Mama—was destroyed. It was hit by a tractor trailer making a legal turn. There was no one to blame or to file a claim. This was a serious setback for the family.

Norwood

When the Chevrolet plant opened in Norwood in 1923, the city already had its share of industries. The US Playing Card Company, Globe Wernicke, Strobridge Lithographing Company, and American Laundry Machinery, to name a few, were there.

There were more jobs than citizens to fill them. The city became widely known as a source of jobs. People commuted from Cincinnati and beyond into neighboring Kentucky. The city swelled by day with commuters, yet strongly held to its past having a majority of first and second generation Germans, Catholic, and Protestant citizens. Mixed in were some other Europeans, mainly Italian, Polish, and Irish. There were no Jews, Hispanics, or Asians. The Germans were the skilled machinists ran the factories. They were the schoolteachers, the butchers, and the bakers

At city hall they enforced good government, parks, and safe playgrounds. They involved themselves in every city endeavor, including the Norwood Day parade. They brought their thrifty teachings to the schools on a weekly basis. Their thriftiness and steadfast ways allowed the city of Cincinnati to annex all its surrounding areas. Being completely surrounded by Cincinnati, the mix of people began to slowly change. The city's reputation of jobs and excellent schools continued.

Even after the Chevrolet plant closed in Norwood, the showplace city hall and the magnificent churches remained. So did the huge veteran's memorial in Victory Park and a few of the factories. The modern expressways did not divide any of the city. Montgomery Road still goes through the city as in the past. Many now go through thinking of it as just another suburb of Cincinnati, unless they get a speeding ticket.

The memory of school children standing on the steps at city hall at Christmastime singing Christmas carols haunts me. The blond and blue-eyed were placed near the sidewalk. All sang the choruses in German.

Let us go back to the Negro family who had just moved from 3539 Irving Street in Avondale to 1709 Hopkins Avenue in Norwood. They were Ralph and Ada Gardner and their children Lillian, Mabel, Cecelia, Francis, Ralph Jr. and myself (Louis).

That could be one of them on the steps of city hall, singing. "Yes, and he looks like a fly in a glass of buttermilk, if you ask me," said another, gazing at a picture in the Norwood Enterprise.

The Move-In

It was early 1925 when Mama and Papa moved into the house at 1709 Hopkins Avenue in Norwood, Ohio. They had six children.

Lillian (Lil) always held fast to her position as the oldest child. At home she refused to be beaten at anything. Many did not like her aggressive attitude or wondered why she did not dance when she was so athletic, yet they marveled at the wit and wisdom of her explanations. She was tall and slender like Grandma Williams, with the same gingerly arm-swinging walk. She could repeat a Sunday school lesson for her younger siblings, then follow up with appropriate stories or even jokes. On her age level she was a leader. No one challenged her.

Mabel was a good student and picked her friends well. Not nearly as outgoing as Lil, yet she was quick to put people in their place nicely. She was particular about her clothes and style. She was ladylike at all times, and looked like and embraced much of Mama's ways.

Cecelia (Cel) was the quiet and reflective one. She clung to her older or younger brother or sister. She had one best friend at church and another best friend at school. Cel was also particular about her hair and clothes. She was racially proud and had studied her heritage, and she stood ready to explain it. She also liked sports but was often too laid-back to participate. She also limited herself to certain dances.

Francis (Fran) was small for her age from birth. She entered school late and was challenged academically. She seemed to try but came up short. When, after failing the second time, it became clear she was struggling mightily. Her classmates began to sympathize with her rather than cast her down. She was quietly appreciative of them. At home, Fran began to be motherly to her younger sisters until the day two teachers from the school came over to declare they had done all they could for her. They told mama to train her to be a housewife, which mama did with great success.

The girls gave Ralph Jr. the nickname Barney when he was a toddler. They named him after the cartoon character, because he was the first boy. Ralph entered school much like Lillian, having one other Negro boy in the school. He did extremely well in all of his classes and excelled in math. At home he did all the outside chores. He raked the leaves, cut the grass, shoveled the snow, and carried out the garbage. When the yard man where Papa chauffeured for the Dernham sisters became ill, Papa took over the job for another five dollars per week. He did much of the work on Saturdays and through summer vacations. Most people saw the studious side of Ralph Jr. and encouraged him. He carefully selected his friends at church and at school. His friends were the elite. He liked to dance and could teach it. He was a sprinter who wanted to name his position in other sports. When turned down he went to his after school jobs. He helped one friend in his father's furniture store, and worked in a men's clothing store where he helped tag merchandise. He then settled in at Stone's Bowling Alley where he set pins. Ralph seemed to be at ease in all social settings, yet in a sense he walked alone.

Mama was expecting Della when moving. She was born on April 15 and named after Della Forney Papa's mother. There would be three more girls to follow.

Though papa was chauffeuring steadily for the prosperous and kind Abe Dernham, some delay arose in the negotiations for the sale of the house. So instead of the normal deed, a lease was signed. The move-in went well, with most of the belongings being hauled in the Ford touring car Papa bought little more than a year ago. Only the iron beds, the living room chair, couch and table and Mama's most precious first pieces of furniture were hauled in Uncle Sup's truck.

Though the house was clearly too small for the family of eight, from the beginning Papa had his grandiose plan. The house would be rearranged or expanded to somehow fit everyone, with even a garage added later for his part-time car repair business. The house became a source of pride. There were never overnight visitors. Not even relatives. There was only one exception and that was my uncle Fred.

In September, the four girls enrolled in school. Lillian was twelve. They all did well in class, but Lillian led the way academically. The Williams (no relation to Mama) and the Shans family who lived next to them on Webster Street were the only Negros with children living in Norwood. For some unknown reason, the Shans moved away before the end of the school year. The girls, having previously attended North Avondale School, were accustomed to a majority of Jewish students, with less than five percent Negro students. The Jews did not mix but were not antagonistic, either. The girls quickly caught on to the ways of a very different group of people. They were cordial with the teachers and won their respect, and later would go to some of their homes to help with cleaning or washing and ironing. Having attended North Avondale herself, Mama prepared them well. They paired or grouped themselves to and from school. Francis, the smaller and youngest of the four, was protected. At home they did homework while they discussed the ways and attitudes of the teachers. They had their special classroom friends they talked about at home, though the rest of the family never saw them. While at Sunday school they let their guard against prejudice down. They socialized to the max, fully enjoying each day. After Sunday's dinner, the family went each week to visit the Waller cousins in Woodlawn where the joy continued.

This seemed to be the culmination of Mama and Papa's dreams, an uplifting environment with a chance of a better education for their children. They were happy.

The Beggar

Louis was the youngest and not yet two when the move was made. For two summers he had thoroughly explored the house and yard. He now anxiously awaited the return of his elder siblings from school, with wild-eyed anticipation for the stories they would tell. His excitement would build with each story told about life beyond the house.

When his day finally came to go to school, Cecelia was assigned to take him to his afternoon kindergarten. They were first in line at the courtyard door. Mabel, seeing her two siblings, came over to tease. When they noticed a white woman go with her son to the locked door, then stand first in line, Mabel spoke out, as Cecelia would not have done. The woman then took her rightful place with a look of indignation.

Louis was thin and underweight. The family sometimes called him "puny" or "poor." The teachers also began to talk about his weight. They questioned him about drinking milk. There was no milk at home. It was only for the baby. All children need it, they said. It's the perfect food. They bought him some at recess and he later spewed it up. When they noticed this they asked what he ate for breakfast, then sent him home. It took those teachers a year to accept that the milk they gave him made him sick.

It was the last of those days of being sent home that Louis began to see his little sister getting most of his mama's attention. He began to stick close and follow her around the house.

Louis went to the basement adjoining the kitchen. Mama knew he was safe and near. He looked at the huge baby buggy standing in front of the stack of hand-crafted shelving that held jelly jars candles and containers Mama had used when she sold kerosene lamps to neighbors in the old neighborhood. This all represented a new beginning, a passing on, a joy in progress. The agony, pain, suffering, and tears would likely follow.

With a younger sister he did not get the attention he had been accustomed to, so he sulked and despaired. When he messed his pants and was scolded he vowed it would be the last time as he felt his mother's attention slowly drifting from him. He now longed for more adventure. He found it in his father and longed for him daily. He would rush to the garage to meet Papa whenever Mama and the weather permitted. As soon as Papa sat on his old wooden chair in the kitchen, Louis would climb on his leg. There he could feel a connection with that great outside would so unknown to him. A world he longed to hear about and one day hoped to face. He explored everything he could. He spent hours watching from the windows and toyed with insects, catching them in his hands or in glass jars, sometimes pulling their wings. He was sometimes bitten or stung but continually explored all things possible in the small yard where he lived. Louis never took part in any household chores, for that wouldn't be like Papa. The winters brought more extreme weather conditions. He listened when Mama questioned his older brother and sisters about their schoolwork. He especially listened on Sundays when they were questioned about Sunday school and the sermon on Sunday. He sometimes remembered parts of what was said and repeated portions later to the surprise of the older family members. Still, he was bored, so he ran the stairs, turned on and off the lights, and flushed the toilet for no reason. Then, staring out the window, he gave a description of what he saw, whether it was a bird, a squirrel, snow, rain, a car, or a truck. When Papa's younger brother came to visit, they sat up late and talked of their days in North Carolina. Louis listened to every tale and longed to have their experiences. Then, falling to sleep, he was carried to bed, eventually to awake again in Mama's care, bored. He grew and learned day by day. He wanted to be a help to Mama. He especially wanted to explore, to venture beyond the confines of the old house and yard. He couldn't go with Papa, even on Saturdays. He was too little and too wild.

One day Mama was washing clothes in the basement. She could see out the kitchen door, so Louis ventured outside. He couldn't carry hot water; too dangerous. He couldn't turn the hand crank on the wringer; he's too little and too slow. He stepped outside, saw a manly figure coming toward the door, and retreated back to where Mama was washing. He screamed, "Mama, a man, a man!" Shocked and afraid, he grabbed Mama's skirt with both hands.

"Let me see," she said. The man stood outside the screen.

"Please, ma'am, I am hungry. Can you give me anything to eat? I have not had a bite in three days. I'd be so much obliged for whatever."

"Wait just a minute," said Mama. "You caught us at a bad time, but I'm sure there is some food here for you. Do you eat greens? I'll heat some up."

"No," the man said, "they fine just as they is."

"You can sit on the steps there," said Mama. Soon she handed the man a plate of cold greens containing a small piece of bean bacon and a large piece of cornbread. Louis stood close inside the door watching bug-eyed, observing everything. He yearned to travel and was excited to learn of anything that was happening beyond that house. This man was disheveled far beyond anyone Louis had ever seen. He had a messy beard, uncombed hair, a big mouth, and dark teeth. His shoes were large and seemingly not in tune with his other clothing. They were work shoes, but he wore a suit faded and worn thin.

Mama gave Louis a mason jar filled with water. "Here, give this to the man." Louis handed the water to the beggar with caution. He looked at the man's dirty hands and smelled odors recognizable by a five year old, like train smoke like coming from the furnace. He also smelled body odors, instead of the tobacco smell of Papa. Mama took the empty plate and asked if that was enough water.

"I'd like some more, ma'am," he answered. He drank the second pint jar of water then said, "Ma'am, I thank you. I'm so blessed to have found my own people. If there is anything I can do I would be much obliged, anything I can do to show my thanks. If there are any leftovers or just a piece of that cornbread I can take along, I would be grateful."

Mama wrapped another piece of cold cornbread in a piece of bread wrapper. "Here you are," she said. "You're more than welcome. I do wish there was more."

"Thank you, thank you. May God bless you," was his reply as he turned toward the street. Louis stood still, watching intently. He had never seen a more wretched and humble person, yet the man had a childlike look of innocence. He was happy to see the man leave, because he had felt as if he had to protect Mama. Yet he was fascinated knowing the man had come from someplace far away by train.

While Louis stood bug-eyed, watching the man as he turned toward the street, the man turned to look at Louis as if to show appreciation or attempt to remove the puzzled look from the boy's face. "When you see the world, you will see it differently," said the beggar. Louis was completely baffled. He found no meaning in this. When the man turned onto the sidewalk, Louis noticed things he had not noticed before. The man wore a tattered suit so far outdated it could have been worn in the days of Abraham Lincoln. The suit was clearly made for a far more full-bodied man. The shoulders were tight, yet the rest of the coat was much too broad and too short, making him look like a big chicken. The pants were long enough only to reach his high shoe tops. He had clearly picked up a suit from a rummage sale or even a trash bin, a suit meant for a short, fat man, when he was slender with slim hips. Then Louis could see the man was still chewing on that piece of bean bacon and Louis remembered his experience with that chewy bean bacon. *You can never chew it up*, he thought. He smiled as he returned to the kitchen to hear Mama's words. "But for the grace of God goes I," she said. "And that means you don't laugh at someone else's misfortune."

"Yes, Mama," replied Louis in total acceptance, yet not nearly understanding.

J.J. Elcho

As a gesture of friendship and a welcome to the neighborhood, the Elcho family came to 1709 Hopkins in the early spring of 1925. They had one child with them, Dorothy, who was just two and a half years. Mr. Elcho led all of the conversation. An Italian immigrant, he had a strong accent and was sometimes hard to understand. He had his convictions of the neighborhood, its needs, and its problems. He explained how natural gas lines had been put in on Hopkins Avenue, down to where the railroad crossed over the street. This was only one hundred feet from his house, and it was his nagging complaint. He could only get an extension if all signed a petition for the service to his house and beyond. His house and beyond would include fourteen houses. To Mr. Elcho, who had a landscaping business, this new gas line was of great importance.

Having recently moved from a house with only candles and kerosene, the Gardner's were elated to have an electric light in each room. Natural gas for cooking would save time and it would mean better cooking and a cleaner kitchen. But could they afford it? Somehow, there was always paper and wood to start a fire. This house had a coal furnace, so mostly there was coal. Ralph Jr. got up early enough to get the stove going. Oh, but Mama had decided Louis was old enough to begin taking a turn to make the fire. Making a fire in a cook stove was not difficult or strenuous. What was difficult was facing the freezing temperature of an unheated downstairs. Mama helped Louis on the first morning, even though Ralph Jr. had instructed him thoroughly and he had made fires in the woods by the park. The temperature in the kitchen on a winter morning was awesomely bone chilling. So Louis had a plan. On the evening before, as soon as water for washing the dishes was heated, he went to work and got wood, paper, and coal. He carefully laid material for the fire in the stove and went to bed happy. All he had to do in the morning was light the paper under the wood.

Rising with the sound of the alarm in Mama's room, Louis got up, dressed, and crept down to the kitchen. He grabbed some matches and went to the stove and opened the door. He found nothing. There wasn't a sign of the preparations he had made the night before. "Mama, Mama," he said, "It's all gone! I made it last night and it's gone."

"Well, we've got to have a fire."

"But I made it, Mama, I made one," he said through his tears as he quickly began to prepare another fire. Before he went to bed, Louis had unknowingly placed the wood and paper on the hot coals, which burned the paper as he slept.

Penny Up

In the year 1930, the country and the world was experiencing a depression like nothing seen before. There were encouraging words and even promises that better days were coming by the White House and its politicians, yet wages and prices held at their previous lows. In many cases, employees were forced into reduced hours, thus enabling employers to hire and help some of the many without jobs. In the Gardner family, Papa's wages were average or slightly above for an African American family. The problem was they had a family that reached to ten children, a house payment, a car, and a telephone, all of which were necessary for Papa's extra jobs.

On a hot summer day in 1930 Mama gave Louis eight pennies. She instructed him to go to the new store called Pay-N-Takit, where a pound loaf of bread was eight cents. The walk to Pay-N-Takit was long, but that was no matter to Louis. When he passed the ice house he saw a penny in the mud between the sidewalk and the curb where someone had likely dropped it while loading the ice. Louis happily walked on to the store and picked up the one-pound loaf of bread. He placed the bread on the counter and reached into his pocket for the pennies, when he heard the young clerk say, "Nine cents."

Shocked to hear this, Louis meekly uttered, "My mama said it's eight cents."

"That was last week," said the young clerk. Louis knew as well as the clerk that nine cents was still the lowest price in this town, so he put up that lucky penny.

Upon arriving home, Louis placed the bread on the kitchen table turned and addressed Mama. "Mama, Mama, you told me it's lucky if you find money. I found a penny, then I had to spend it, that ain't lucky."

"Yes, it is, Son, 'cause if you came home with eight cents and no bread, I would have given you another penny and you would be on your way back to Pay-N-Takit. Isn't that lucky?" As his mama always said, "You can't spend what you ain't got. You can't lose what you never had."

Halloween

Halloween came. Louis was unprepared, so he resorted to putting on a dress, which he hated with a passion, but he had to go. There were those who wanted to get in as many treats as possible. In addition, there were those who wanted only to play tricks. On this night, Louis got together with some of his schoolmates from across town. They came out to play tricks and were well prepared. They came with dog feces in paper bags with the top folded down. They carefully placed the bags on unlit porches and rang the doorbell. Then, quickly setting fire to the bags, they ran when someone came to the door. They were sometimes able to see the resident stomping the bag before realizing they had dog feces on their shoe. The angry residents would scream out vulgarities and sometimes threaten to call the law.

Abe L. Dernham

At the turn of the century, most of all the horse-drawn streetcars were gone. Few horse-drawn wagons climbed the hills. The trolley car became the mode of transportation to and from anywhere you wanted to go. Travel by foot was the means by which most got from home to work, school, church, or anywhere for that matter. Cincinnati was a walking city. Children climbed the hills to schools like Hughes, Clifton, and Purcell. At eight cents per ride, the cost was too much for many of the lower income. However, things were sure to change. In France and Germany, there was great competition to produce a gas-driven automobile. They competed for show style and speed all while improving performance safety and endurance of the automobile. Henry Ford in Detroit had his ingenious idea of a car for the working class built on an assembly line. He soon built a stream of automobiles in an unbelievable fashion with great success. They appeared in increasing numbers around the country as service stations sprang up along main streets and highways.

In Cincinnati's west end along Dayton and Findley Streets were the many homes of the wealthy. They previously had stables, horses, and wagons with coach houses and hired horsemen. The coach houses continued to serve as quarters for chauffeurs. There was a changing of the guard, however, as many horsemen could not become drivers of those automobiles. They did not understand the gear shift, the clutch, and the choke.

In Avondale, the problem was not drivers but a place to store the automobiles. Only a few houses were built with coach houses. Few of the others could be fitted with a garage, as a garage and drive would destroy the curb appeal of their expensive homes. They wanted an automobile but needed some alternative.

Someone soon came up with the right idea, which was a service garage where an automobile owner could store his automobile for the night. The owner could drive to the garage, whereby a garage person would take them home. Then, if needed, for a fee, they could be picked up the next morning. While in storage, the automobile could be serviced or cleaned. Such a service garage was built in Avondale on Northern Avenue.

"Ada," Papa said as he settled in at the table. "As I was leaving the garage just a while ago a middle-aged man stopped and said he needed a chauffeur and asked if I would I be willing. He gave me a card with his name and phone number. I told him I would let him know tomorrow. He said he would be obliged to pay me at a good rate."

"Then what's the drawback?" questioned Mama.

"Well, this man Abe is a younger man than the judges I worked for when I last drove. These young folks are out nights. He's downtown, and there's the traffic and parking problems. He's from Germany and has never had a chauffeur before, and I don't like those clown uniforms these people want their men to wear. I'm just afraid it won't work out."

"Ralph," said Mama, "I know you don't like change. You like the people at that garage. How soon we forget—last winter you and Ed had that shop together. You got pneumonia and were down for more than a week, you were advised not to go back to lying under cars in that cold shop. You were blessed to get back at that northern garage. You want to be independent, I know, but what about these kids? It's going to take sixteen years for them to be gone. The Lord provideth, we have all been blessed. That man seems to want you as his first choice. You should talk to him and tell him what you think. I'm sure he will have some good things to say as well. We need to be stable, Ralph. A slow dime is better than a quick nickel," said Mama.

Papa sat on a leather chair, a chauffeur's cap in his hand. Abe was on the phone, having been interrupted several times in his conversation with Ralph. Ralph was noticeably impatient. Dropping the phone, Abe said, "Now what were you saying?"

"Gosh darn, if I knew you wanted someone to work Sundays."

"Now, Ralph," replied Abe "no, this was not discussed because I did not expect this. This is not something that is going to happen every week. This trip is extremely important to my business. Would you want me to call your wife and explain? I know that's the reason."

"No," answered Ralph. "I'll make that decision. As you say, this is sudden, and it's important. I'll go." Papa had more than one reason for not wanting to work on Sundays or even late on Saturdays. He often worked or made livery trips on the weekend in town and might lose more than he would gain on the trip. He also knew if Abe had called Mama, her answer would have been yes.

Overall the trip to Chicago was uneventful. Businesswise it fared no better. They talked sports, baseball, boxing, auto, and horseracing, and vowed to go to the racetracks together soon. They smoked the same cigar brand and seemed to have a terrific understanding of each other as well as both being family oriented. Being one Negro and one Jew they had to get carry out, or Abe would eat in and bring Ralph's dinner to the car. On reaching Chicago, Abe was dropped off at the Palmer House and Ralph went to the south side and registered at a rooming house where he called and gave Abe the number. Thus went the dreaded trip for Ralph. Not good, but not really a disaster. He dropped Abe off at his apartment and went home at a late hour.

On Tuesday morning, Abe did not call. He was not at his office. Neither was he at his apartment. Ralph was deeply puzzled. As evening came, he received a call to pick up Abe at the Jewish hospital. As Ralph approached the hospital, he could see Abe. His head was down and he looked pale. He knew right off that something was wrong. Abe was in deep despair. "What's wrong, boss?" asked Ralph.

"Haven't you heard the news?" Abe asked, and that was all he said. After taking Abe to his apartment, Ralph rushed home to read the newspaper with Mama. The headlines and picture told the story. There had been a terrible disaster. A street car conductor had lost control on Vine Street causing injuries to everyone aboard. Most were hospitalized due to shock and the difficulty of getting them from the wreckage. Flora and Eva were on the list of passengers. They were the younger sisters of Abe who had only been in the United States from Germany five months. Flora would die in the hospital and Eva would spend the rest of her days in an institution. She never completely recovered from the severe shock. Abe had sent for and provided them an apartment. He showed them around the city. While on their own they were finding their way saving Ralph and Abe the time and inconvenience. This terrible tragedy affected the lives of this family forever.

Abe sent for his two other sisters, Sarah and Julia. Though he knew they would not be able to help with any arrangements, he knew this to be a comforting move as they would be able to know the full circumstances of the tragedy as well as visit Eva. As went on Ralph came to know Julia and Sarah. He first had great sympathy for them, but as time went by he could see them becoming more dependent. They seemed to think that because they stayed home, they were not getting their due from Ralph. Ralph did not object to any trips given to him by Abe, but when either of the sisters requested a service of any nature his face showed his discomfort.

"After you pick up the car, Ralph, would you come back into my office?" asked Abe. Again, Ralph was in that leather chair in Abe's office.

Ralph said, "Abe, it has been two years since we made that trip to Chicago, and I know it's something you do not want to do, yet there is no one to really do this but you. This is really important to me and the business. Indianapolis is a much shorter trip. Do we really have to spend the night?"

"Well," said Abe, "I would have to set up so early for the seminar that would also make our trip so late as to mean an all-night drive. That's just too hazardous, Ralph."

"Okay, then" he agreed.

While on the way to Indianapolis and both smoking, cigars Abe said to Ralph, "If I knew a little more about these potential clients it would really help. Ralph said nothing but continued to ponder what Abe had said. They continued on to Indianapolis. Abe checked into a downtown hotel while Ralph went to an address given to him by the hotel clerk. He found the address to be a rooming house, but it was a better than expected Negro operated business. He had to park curbside, and while doing so observed other chauffeurs cars as he walked toward the building. He also saw lights in the basement and noticed that there was a pool table. Just as he had hoped, he was early and there was time for a few games of pool and some talk with his contemporaries. Ralph knew chauffeurs to be a proud lot. Other chauffeurs were so proud that they often bragged that their boss Bob Bartlett or whomever was CEO or general manager or president or whatever of such and such company. Ralph could not write all this down but he had an uncanny ability to retain this seemingly trivial talk. Abe was overjoyed with the information given to him by Ralph. He used it to his success in Indianapolis as well as later in Cincinnati. This turned out to be a very successful trip for all. This prompted Abe to lightly increase Ralph's stipend. Ralph tried hard not to mention family matters because of that very tragic streetcar accident. But not thinking, he said, "Why is it that your sisters never married?

Abe answered, "We, as Jews, believe the older girl should be the first to marry. She is not the glamour girl as you can see, though she was supposed to have had a suitor aboard that ill-fated Titanic. I was here at the time and did not know him. The girls may have talked of these things with our parents but never to me, so I don't really know, that's what I think. Certainly I would like to see them all married. When Flora and Eva came here they were so joyful, dashing here and there I thought they would surely marry. But that damn streetcar."

"I'm so sorry," replied Ralph.

In the coming months, Abe thought more and more about his parents back in Germany. Why were they not heeding his urgent messages for them to come? He expected them to be a little hesitant because of their age, but there were bad times ahead for his people in Germany. Abe became more concerned as the months passed. A trip to Germany was explored as a solution, but they determined it to be impractical. Abe was never to learn of their whereabouts or their fate.

A steady stream of progress had been made since Abe Dernham had first come to Cincinnati just before the turn of the century. The city was spreading above and beyond the hills. A new government existed at city hall. Prohibition was still in effect. Great improvements were made in the school system. There was the zoo, a general hospital to serve all, as well as professional firefighters and the first professional baseball team. Progress of all kind could be seen in many forms, with more in the planning stages. Abe was as much a part of the city's progress as he could be, continually trying to pump more and more energy into the business community. He became a driven man. Fewer were the days of relaxation at the Cincinnati club. Trips to the race track or ball park were gone. Abe was a caring man and his contemporaries as well as Ralph wondered what was happening in his private life. Seldom was there an opportunity for anyone to go to his apartment, but when they did the evidence was there. Another cluttered desk, piles of notes financial sheets, balance sheets, stock market analyses and notes, notes, and more notes. Abe was working as hard at home as he was at his office. His doctor's advice was not shared with anyone and apparently ignored by him.

When one day he was suddenly taken to the hospital from his office, everyone feared for the worst. The worse they thought was some time away from the office. When the news came that Abe had suffered a massive heart attack they all were stunned. He died within twenty-four hours. This small man had such an immense knowledge of the business world and he was a salesperson supreme. This compassionate person saw success only for what success he could garner for others. The City of Cincinnati was greater for having had him. His family, Julia and Sarah, for sure know they lost a most loving and caring brother. This great man, who was regularly seen chauffeured in an automobile driven by a large Negro, would no more be seen and no one would know the gratitude owed him by that Negro's family.

The Great Depression

Before the depression there was the Roaring Twenties. It was a time of prosperity that followed the end of World War I and lasted until The Great Depression. The crash of the stock market in late 1929 marked the beginning of the hurt and desperation that would last until World War II. Many of the wealthy lost all they had with the stock market crash and became penniless. Some jumped from tall buildings and bridges, unable to face reality. Others joined the ranks of the suddenly unemployed, becoming vagabonds, drifters, beggars, and the like. Some traveled, hobo-style, from train to train across the country in search of any type of work that would sustain them. They were known to sleep in barns, basements, or the outdoors as they went through colder climates. Among them were some who simply abandoned their families in shame and then found survival for themselves a challenge. There were soup kitchens where one could get an occasional hand out but were not expected to return daily.

In our churches, where once they had fundraisers to pay off the mortgages, they were struggling to meet the mortgage deadline. They had constant cookouts. They had singing groups, who accepted any type of gift, including food and shelter through the time of the event. They had rummage sales. People tried on shoes and left the old pair left behind.

There existed no form of welfare for the poor, and many veterans were among them. Though there was sympathy for veterans who received no pensions, they fell to the same destiny as others.

When listening to the radio, we learned of the Bowery in Lower Manhattan, New York and skid row on West Halstead Street in Chicago. These were places where homeless derelicts survived. Generations of abandoned people without jobs were left to fend for themselves with little sympathy. The unemployment rate fluctuated at forty percent. We wondered what would happen to the Negro.

In Cincinnati, Negroes were accepted as caretakers of larger apartment complexes. They stoked the furnaces in winter. They kept the hallways clean and free of garbage. They kept the building free of pests. They tended the lawns in the summer. When and if there were children, the children would be accepted at the local school. The state of Ohio had integrated schools years before; however a form of de facto segregation existed. In the depression this was seen as progress.

Because of the depression, whites ventured into jobs formerly viewed as colored jobs. "I'm going to get me one of those white chauffeurs," was a joke repeated by some well-positioned Negroes. Then two of our more successful celebrities did just that. They were pictured in the newspapers with their chauffeurs. The view from the streets was changing, yet ugly.

On the well-kept lawns of the wealthy there often stood a molded figure of a black-faced jockey, whip in hand. These figures were not intended to intimidate. In earlier days this was the norm at race tracks. Negroes were thought to be the best at handling, training, and riding horses. Stables were almost exclusively operated by Negroes. The depression, however, changed things, giving the higher paying jockey jobs to whites. New clubhouses were built, and the colored jockeys became extinct.

At home there were daily reflections of this great depression. When Mama said, "Clean your plate," she didn't mean take it to the garbage can and scrape it. She meant clearly for you to eat every morsel of food on the plate. Mama would hem or alter clothes to fit. She seemingly did the impossible, in which case we called the product Mama-make. Mama became doctor and nurse-mom with her tea, liniments, rubs, hot-toddies, and castor oil. When in need of the smallest amount of change for a program or field trip at school, you went to Mama. When she answered, "I'll look into it," there was a chance for you to get it. If she answered saying, "If something comes up," it meant just that, an extra income or good fortune by

Papa or your own endeavor. If she said, "Don't hold your breath," you had just better forget it.

Meanwhile, Papa became a kitchen barber for all ages, male and female, with his skin-pinching mechanical clippers. He stepped up with his shiny pliers to pull that first set of teeth. Papa was also plumber, electrician, or handyman. He said if he failed, the cost would not be any different had he called a professional.

Julius and I sat on the low wall in front of Papa's garage, which ran to the sidewalk. We talked of many things, most of which reflected on this Great Depression, which we only partly understood. We expressed our opinions of attempts by the neighborhood people to unite and share both black and white. Mr. Elcho, the florist, sold to neighbors at a lower rate. He raised strawberries and his kids sold them cheaper in the neighborhood. Mr. Bauer, on Webster Street, worked at their family-owned bakery and on rare occasions had bread to give. We ran errands for the players at the ballpark. All or most all of the neighbors shared information on ways to survive this depression.

The area along Victory Parkway from Hopkins to Xavier University was heavily wooded. We often went into the area to pick from the wild apple trees, gather dandelions, or find anything edible or of value. On occasion, we saw couples casually walk off the sidewalk and on to the bridle path that ran the length of the woods and beyond. We called them lovers. The man often carried a rolled-up newspaper under his arm. Hand in hand, they would walk beyond the ragweed and shrubbery to a grassy spot concealed form the path or street. Where we had picked dandelions they spread out the newspaper. Not knowing or not caring, they proceeded while we watched from a position of advantage, as we knew the area like no others. What we saw was another product of the depression. It was shocking and it was ugly.

Miss Ann

Snow-filled winds swirled in a maddening fashion, pouring sheet-like billows of snow across the landscape before and beyond the house at 1709 Hopkins. Clear visions of the street below come and go between the vicious winds and gusts of snow. Della standing and Louis kneeling on a chair placed against the door are wide-eyed with amazement. Coming home from school, there had been just a hint of snow only two hours before. Now winter was here with a vengeance. Papa's not home yet. *He'd better get home quick,* they thought. Snow continued to swirl, and as it did, the children could see car wheels spinning while they tried to climb their way up the hill. Some go sliding to the curb. Some go beyond the curb. The children ooohed and aaahed at the sight of each driver's mishap.

While Mama sings "What a Friend We Have in Jesus" as she prepares supper, the steam from her cooking circles the room, settling on the kitchen door window. This, along with the children's steamy breaths and the plunging temperatures outside, causes ice crystals to form on the window. The ice thickens and covers the window. Suddenly they are gripped by a feeling of isolation, shut out from the world outside into this cubicle of a kitchen. The sound of cars outside seems to fade away. The wind, however, worsens to a threatening sound that seems to say, "Be glad you're inside, and you'd better stay." Is this punishment to the world for some evil deed or what? Mama's songs are comforting in times like these. "What's that I hear?" asks Mama.

Louis and Della ran upstairs to a front unfrosted window. Looking out into the still-swirling snow, they could see Papa shoveling snow from the garage to the house. In unison they shouted, "Its Papa, Mama!"

In these times the cancellation of school is unheard of. There are no school buses and no real means to notify families. A large wooden box containing ten to twelve pairs of goulashes in various sizes is pulled from beneath the basement stairs. Each family member is obliged to pick a pair of these high toppers to wear for the winter. Getting the best fit is important. A poor fit or leaky sole could mean disaster. After displaying their winter gear, hats, coats, and gloves for approval, each is given a spoonful of that dreaded castor oil. Lillian, the oldest enjoys these times when she is given charge. She marches "the little ones," as she calls them, past Mama's room to give each a chance to say, "Goodnight, Mama." All is normal, Mama sitting and rocking the baby. The baby under a warm blanket, nursing a bottle or being breast fed, seems so comforted and is the envy of those who yet remember being there in that position. These comforting thoughts and reminders hasten their sleep.

Papa's employers, those wonderful sisters Julia and Sarah, continually come to mind for what they had done for this family. They had made financially possible the addition of two rooms and bath, a conversion of the old coal furnace to gas, and a hot water heater. This addition not only changed the home, it changed the way the family lived. The new bedrooms gave twice the space for sleeping as well as storage. The bath gave privacy as well as much more comfortable bathing. The hot water tank provided more hot water for washing clothes and dishes. They now had two basement rooms as well, each the size of the rooms above. Because of some bickering between Papa and Mr. Newmark, the general contractor, the basement room floors were not cemented. They would remain dirt until money was available to complete the work.

In the spring, the family was given four baby chickens, called bitties. Baby chicks were available by mail order, seemingly a ridiculous thing, while raising chickens was restricted within city limits. The mail ordering of baby chicks was discouraged and later banned. The Gardner's had theirs. They were so cute, so cuddly, bound by a corrugated paper box. Beautiful pets, harmless, a joy to the children, yet unknowingly at least to them, this was future food. These babies grew rapidly. They also developed diseases and two died within weeks. When school was out, the two began to develop serious wings and thus could not be trusted outside, so Papa fenced them in on the dirt basement floor. Soon after this another chicken died. Papa told us the last and only chick was a girl. A farm boy himself, he probably knew.

The children learned much from this experience. Chickens will eat anything they can swallow whole or peck into pieces small enough to swallow. This girl seemed to swallow without hesitation anything thrown before her, bread of any kind, vegetables cooked or raw, as long as she could swallow it. Bits of meat, gristle, fat, seeds, grape, apple, and cherry, all within her reach, were quickly consumed. Though she had survived while the others had died, she looked frail and sickly. They had not properly provided water along with her food. When Papa asked had she been fed, the answer was always yes. By the end of summer and beginning of October this poor chicken was frail. She had survived neglect and mistreatment by some stroke of luck or the grace of God. While Papa sized her up for the dinner table the children were yet finding pleasure in tormenting her.

Della, at the dinner table, was not happy with the dress given to her to wear at a special school party. She said, "I can't wear this dress. It don't fit me anywhere."

"Put a hem in, some tucks or gathers, or whatever you need to do. It's yours to wear. Who do you think you are, Miss Ann?" asked Papa. They all laughed all around the table. This was an expression Papa used often when confronted in this manner.

Following dinner, as usual bits and pieces were taken to the chicken. On this day however, for some unknown reason she refused to eat what was given her. She strutted back and forth along the back of her pen. Even bits and pieces were thrown directly in her path were refused. The children were puzzled and became quite silent. Then Betty, the youngest one present, said, "Miss Ann." They all had a good laugh. From then on the chicken was called Miss Ann.

Days later Papa decided the chicken was ready for cooking. She was beheaded, cut up, cooked, and dished out, but none stuck a fork in Miss Ann.

The Spuds

One-book Tony, that's what his family members called him. Not wanting to be criticized or made ridiculous by his lack of interest, he would always carry one book. That one book was usually the speller, the smallest. This he tucked beneath his belt. Hands-free was his way. He walked some, he ran some, skipped and did handsprings, rolled on lawns, and ran through lawn sprinklers. He was free, no books, no speller. All had been checked in. His industrial arts project had been taken home on that last day. His gym shoes were already at home. With all the joy and excitement one child could hold, he ran alone the last few blocks toward home. Suddenly, he saw the garage doors in front of his home open. He smelled gasoline. Papa must be inside.

Papa had wisely built this garage, or had his Uncle (Sup) Forney build it. It was a simply constructed two-car garage. There were two windows, one on the east side, and one on the west. It had no running water or electricity, only a crude work bench, handmade from lumber extracted from leftovers or demolition. There had to be a drain in the floor for washing cars. The only provision for the work he had to do in cleaning and servicing cars. On cold days he laid whatever was available on the floor when crawling beneath cars. Whenever knowing of this, Mama would complain, and say, "You must remember, Ralph. That's how you got that pneumonia and spent a winter unable to work."

Papa was finished washing parts of the '35 Ford that belonged to his friend, Ed Miller, a friend and a former co-worker from his short time employment at the "Mill," which is what they called the Cincinnati Milling Machine Company. Mr. Miller was also from Papa's beloved North Carolina. They both could easily turn to a conversation that touched each other's heart and past. Anyone who could connect with his past would easily become a friend and confidant of Papa. These thoughts filled Papa's mind as his son, one-book Tony, popped into the garage. He greeted his son and went directly into explaining what he was doing and its importance. The crud and build-up caused by low octane and un-burnt fuel choked the system, piston walls, head, and valves. "In order to have a fully-performing engine, the air, the gas, and the electricity from the battery must flow freely," Papa said.

Papa was aware of his shortcomings. He had been taken to his maternal grandmother when his mother died when he was four years old. Being a stepson, he was not given the educational opportunities his uncles enjoyed. Nonetheless, he passed on what he had learned to anyone willing to listen, especially his children. He would stop what he was doing, take a piece of wrapping paper or brown paper bag, and draw a diagram of pistons or gear shifts. He could make clear the function of mechanical parts. On one occasion this had resulted in an "A" in science for one-book Tony. Papa's instructions were lasting.

Papa wiped the engine head with a large blackened rag after pulling it from an old shallow metal baker's pan he used for cleaning parts. He leaned over the left fender in order to place the engine head over the block to center it. The sweat flowed profusely from his face. He tried to wipe with his shoulder and arm, but unable to do this while holding and placing the motor head onto the block, he simply blew from his mouth, blowing sweat that dripped from his nose, thus preventing its entering his mouth. While sweat was showering him, one-book Tony said nothing, he was so engrossed by the day.

While the depression was forcing itself upon the mind, body, and soul of the nation, there was a fighting back, and dealing with its realities. Papa felt a need to point some things out to his son. "In life you must play the hand that's dealt you, Tony. It's more difficult for some, 'cause you have to start from where you are. You must carry on to the end, for race, family, and the Lord. Some say we need to stick together and support one another, and I say yes, but we need to be strong individually first."

"Papa! Mama said you named me Louis."

"I did," answered Papa, "There was a Jewish fella whose car I serviced a lot. His name was Louis. He was the kind of person you admire, and I wanted you to be like him. So I gave you the name. There came another young Jewish man when you were two. He liked clothes and drove a sporty car. I thought you would be really more like him. They called him Tony."

Papa completed the motor overhaul. He started and checked the timing of the engine by listening to its rhythm. Then he stood in front of the window while steadily cleaning the grease and grime from his hands with a well-used and spotty rag. One-book Tony could see a handsome man dressed in virtual rags. A life dedicated to the family he had spawned. Suddenly, Papa blurted out, "What is that?" He pointed to something growing in the window well on the garage's east side. "That's a potato growing there." Indeed it was. One-book Tony realized what he was seeing. Yes it was some of his doings. "That's a potato growing there, and I believe you must know about it," said Papa. "Potatoes are food and that's something I don't take to—wasting food. I won't stand for that, boy."

"Uh huh, Papa. Lacy, and me we was gonna cook out. When it started to rain and Lacy didn't come, I put it in that window under some leaves I'd forgot."

One-book, not knowing what Papa's reaction would be, was greatly relieved when Papa remarked, "Well long as you were going to eat it and things went wrong, I ain't too much against it."

Grandpa Gardner

Louis was lucky to be sitting at the big table at all, being the child number six. Cecelia, Louis, Ralph Jr., and Mabel sat around one end of the table filled with some of Mama's fried chicken, sweet potatoes, mixed greens, and mashed potatoes. There was apple cobbler and most of all there were plenty of homemade rolls, a very special treat. They would eat pans and pans of these light and tasty treats. They were treats because they only surfaced on very special occasions.

Having heard Grandpa was coming, Louis was expecting Grandpa Williams. It turned out to be Grandpa Gardner, Papa's Daddy, whom Louis had heard of and might have seen before, yet did not remember. He watched Grandpa Gardner as he came up the walk. He was not nearly as tall as Papa. He walked with an air of importance and he was noticeably well dressed. When he greeted Mama, Louis noticed his voice, a golden tone, heavy but mellowed from singing. It was a beautiful voice that compelled one to listen. His pinstripe suit fit perfectly, and his shoes were unscarred. A very close look revealed a neat haircut, and perfectly matched suit and tie colors, with cuff links and a stickpin. Louis thought, "This is the person I want to be like. I want to be like my grandfather."

At The Campaign Site

In these days of hard times, local political campaigning was reduced to a level of actually speaking from temporarily and hastily-built platforms. Usually on vacant lots, they attracted many of the residents, including some quite young. When the campaigning began, it presented a unique opportunity for some devilish boys who were there to have fun. The boys ran around among the crowd, screaming at each other in a make-believe game of tag. The game plan was to be as disturbing and annoying as possible. The response was quick, there were calls of, "Cut it out, stupid kids, go home!"

Suddenly, a gentler voice called out, "Hey you kids, come here." At first the boys were apprehensive, then seeing this prosperous-looking man reach into his deep pocket, they approached him, smiling. "This is no place to play. Here! Go get yourselves something at that store," said the man as he handed some change to the closest boy. Louis would rather have pocketed his share and gone home, but the store was on the adjoining lot, and that left little time for debate. Once the storeowner had the money, there was but one move to make. Order up. "Root beer," said Louis. Louis had tried homemade root beer before, but this is his first from a store. He liked the sound of root beer. What most struck Louis was he and he alone would stand there in front of the store and consume the whole twelve-ounce bottle. Being part of a large, close-knit family where sharing was survival, Louis could not do this without a small measure of regret.

BYE BYE BABY BROTHER

Years of scientific research and discovery have determined, and psychiatrists agree, that the most grievous and painful loss is that of a mother losing her child. A mother losing her child inflicts more pain and grief than the loss of a husband or wife. Loss of a sibling would be second. A tragedy of this severity struck this family on July 19, 1927, just seven days after the birth of Ada Gardner's eighth child, a boy. This was the first of her children to be born at home. There was a midwife and an assistant in training, Ada's sister, Hattie Webster. From day one, Ada felt something was wrong with her child, so on the third day she summoned a doctor who assured or tried to assure her nothing was wrong with her child, he would be fine. Having had seven successful births, which she carefully observed and nurtured to a healthy toddler, she still had a sense that something she could not define was happening to her baby. She suffered mightily in pain. While others accepted and relied on the doctor's words of reassurance, Ada was not satisfied. Her experience in childbirth and infant care were all she needed to know something was seriously wrong. Another doctor was called who came and left, leaving with not the same assurance as the first, but not really describing a condition or giving a prescription for the baby's care. Ada brought her children to the crib to visit their baby brother. All would remember this pink-faced baby, who would always be remembered and spoke of as baby brother. In less than twenty four hours, this eighth child of Ada Gardner died. Ada was gripped with pain. Why had this happened? Why? From the beginning, she knew something was wrong. She had asked for help. She had prayed. Everything she knew to do she had done, yet she alone could see this baby slipping away. No one would explain his tragic misfortune. A life lost without explanation.

In this year and beyond parents were given a time frame of days to give or add a first name to an infant's birth certificate, usually on the child's first check up. The child, having died before its first check up, presented a problem. When questioned for a name, Ralph blurted out in desperate frustration, "Ralph," and the name was added to his birth certificate. Now there are three Ralphs. One Junior, one Senior, one plain Ralph, though always and affectionately remembered as baby brother by all.

On many occasions there was talk as to what happened to the child and attempts to place blame for the tragedy on the midwife, the two doctors, and even Aunt Hattie. Ada, wanting no animosity, quieted those by saying, "The Lord giveth and the Lord taketh away. Blessed be the name of the Lord."

Baby Brother's Birth Certificate.

LACY

"Louis" said Lacy, "you said you don't know who Frederick Douglass is. I can't believe you! Who's the head of the NAACP, then?"

"I don't know," said Louis, "really! I don't know about Marcus Garvey or George Washington Carver," said Louis.

"You don't know anything about your own people, then," replied Lacy.

"I do know about my own people," said Louis. "My papa is from North Carolina and my mama is from Cincinnati. My uncle Lesley was gassed in the Great War. Papa was exempt, too many kids. My mama's uncle and grandfather were in the civil," he said, referring to the Civil War.

"At Douglass School you would fail the first grade not knowing your Negro history," said Lacy.

"If you are going to go to my school, you better know about George Washington instead of Booker T., and all those who signed the Declaration of Independence," answered Louis. "I'd be glad to see you in my school, though," said Louis, "you might like it." They sat on a three-foot-high retaining wall in front of the two-car garage at 1709 Hopkins Ave. The wall was brightly lit from a lamppost across the street, yet not visible from the house where Louis lived, or from 1707 where Lacy lived. Earlier in the day, at this same location, they had tied a tin can on the tail of a stray cat. They now laughed about that, and referred to the cat as lucky because they could not find a match to light his tail. Louis was older than Lacy by about a year, and Lacy showed him respect. Louis, in turn, felt a need to be more daring. "That's Alice, my sister, calling me," said Lacy. "See you tomorrow!"

Louis, thinking he had the right to stay out longer than Lacy, because he was older, stood on the sidewalk, watching as Lacy went to his home. Then, turning and looking up the street beyond the railroad overpass, he could see two figures in the dark. They were Richard and John Lackey, gesturing and talking to one another. Louis could not guess what they were up to, so he had to walk the four hundred or so feet to see. As he approached the two, he could see John was eating some kind of pastry, taken from the truck parked across the street. While rapidly, chewing on an apple turnover, John pointed toward the bakery truck sitting across the street. "Get your own," he said. While not answering John's remarks, Louis and Richard looked at each other. Then raced across the street together, thus committing themselves to thieving. They retreated quickly to the dark spot beneath the railroad overpass. Just as quickly, their loot was consumed. There was little conversation between them. They went to the same school and sometimes met and played together at the ball field. Louis was African American and John and Richard were white cousins. They were the second generation of the Lackeys from Somerset Kentucky, near the Tennessee border. The Lackeys were probably the least-respected family in the neighborhood. Though this neighborhood was not as closely knit as some, it was a poor neighborhood. This being the depression, a survival mood existed within the community. Cooperation and unity was expressed on many an occasion.

"Oh, hell!" said John as he peered up the street. He could see his big brother, Carl, walking at a fast pace, suddenly approach the group huddled under the railroad overpass.

"You think he'll tell?" asked Richard.

"He'll spill his guts," said John. Richard and John's fathers were brothers. Their mothers were sisters. These were onerous, oppressive, dominating fathers. The wives, who were seldom seen, were likely quite controlled. Louis spoke to Carl as he passed, and Carl acknowledged him in a subtle tone. Louis felt sympathy for the two as they slowly walked the short distance to their homes.

At 1709, Louis could see a light in the living room, but he did not notice a nearly new car parked in front of the house. The kitchen door was open, as usual, in the summer. He entered through the open door. Climbing the stairs to the living quarters of the house, he felt uneasy. He was suddenly confronted at the top of the stairs by Papa with, "Just sit there, son. I'm gonna see you before you go to bed."

Papa was clearly disturbed, if not deeply angered by something. Suddenly, Louis wondered if Carl had come to the house and told Papa what he had seen under the railroad overpass. He must have. Yes, Papa was deeply disturbed. Stealing was forbidden. Louis suddenly had hurtful, painful feelings. He sank slowly from a standing position to a sitting one. With his head in his hands, he listened and could gather that a car salesman was attempting to sell Papa a new car. The salesman had heard and Papa was embarrassed by that. Louis must pay. He was in mental torment. The physical would follow. When it was finished there was no conversation. Papa knew this son would never steal again.

Collards Turnips and Tony

When gathering in the living room, a pecking order had evolved. Papa sat in the big side chair, close to the radio. Mama sat on the end of the couch. The older girl claimed the seat next to Mama. They followed in line, age wise. The younger one sat at her foot. The two boys had a choice, on the floor in front of Papa, or in front of the girls. It was always like this. My spot, your spot, like at church. My pew, your pew. Beside Mama, on a small table, she kept the hairbrush and the comb, and, most importantly, a jar of pomade positioned so she could go into braiding hair at a moment's notice. Papa alone turned the radio dials. "Hush! Hush!" he would say when afraid he might miss hearing something.

Then Mama would say, "Don't let me have to run you out of here . . ." which she never did. When there were guests—though this was very rare—the same format was used. The Victrola would be pushed farther into the corner and some straight wooden chairs would be brought from the kitchen and placed along the wall, where the guests were obliged to sit. This was how things were in 1930.

At the kitchen table it was quite the same. Mama was at the table in front of the stove. Papa sat beside her. On Mama's side, it was the oldest to the youngest. This was convenient for Mama, as she knew whose plate she filled, even though they were not at the table. The table had one leaf squeezed in. Beside that was a folding card table with unmatched chairs, presenting extremely crowed conditions. On hot days, the place was sweltering. From the mismatched and even backless chairs, Louis found a stool a little higher than the chairs. He was allowed to use it because it allowed just a little more space for getting around the table or passing through the kitchen. His position at the table was directly opposite the entry door, where he could see clearly to the street in front. By the grin on his face you could tell he loved that.

Just as Mama placed the last bowl of food on the table and turned to Papa, she nodded for him to begin blessing the food. Louis could see Uncle Sup coming up the walkway. He stopped just before the door. Afraid of a scolding for interrupting, Louis bowed his head and said nothing. Uncle Sup, hearing what was happening, stopped and waited. When Papa was finished, Uncle Sup knocked. Uncle Sup was a builder contractor who in his early days as a cement finisher was often left in charge of his coworkers. His home, which he had built at Dick and Talent Streets in Avondale, occupied two lots, one of which was a beautiful vegetable garden. Since his children were now grown, he came to give away some of his turnips and collards.

After a fond greeting by Mama, Papa, and all who remembered him, Uncle Sup's response was, "Well, what you want me to do with these?" He held a large sheet-like cloth tied by the corners containing a good bushel of those greens.

"Son, get a tub and put some water in it," said Mama. He did. Louis's stool was pushed even closer to the table, barely allowing space for the tub to be placed on the kitchen floor. All bade farewell to Uncle Sup, and just as quickly as the tub was half full, all were back at the table. Then, as quickly as one two three, Louis pretended to slap at Della, who was sitting next to him. Papa, while standing, backhanded Louis, lightly grazing him. To avoid the hand, Louis fell backward off the stool, landing backside first into the tub! He looked like a turtle stuck on its back, unable to get a hand or foot onto the floor. Struggling mighty, he soon was back on the stool. His whole package was soaked and dripping, when Papa said, "Boy, you don't do that—not even playing."

Louis thought Papa must have sensed he was playing with Della. Sitting high on the stool, Louis looked around at his family. Seeing comforting, sympathetic smiles he thought, *I love my family, you too, Papa. Sorry, Della.*

Heartbroken

M ama thoroughly instructed Louis on what she needed before sending him to the store. A can of Calumet baking powder, with the red Indian face on the label. She gave correct change, for Mama was thoroughly up on her prices. He begged off from the note, saying he was now nine and knew how to go without an old note. Mama gave Louis the money, and while he stuffed the money in his pocket, she pushed the note into his other pocket with the cautioning words, "Lest you forget. And by the way, I'll need that baking powder as soon as you get back. Be careful, son." This always made Louis feel proud and important. He would be proud again when he returned, knowing the whole family was waiting and depending on him. Yes, he would hurry, and he ran out the door down to the sidewalk. He noticed a light drizzle as he ran. Being the month of October there were neither winds nor lightning, and no downpour was threatening.

Looking up the street he could see his friend Lacy. What a coincidence, Lacy was doing the same as he, a trip to the store for an important addition to the dinner menu. Stopping abruptly, Louis cupped his hands in the fashion of a megaphone and imitated the sound of Tarzan from one of those movies. Or his best try at that sound. "Aaah oo aaah-aaah ooo aaah." Lacy did not stop, but turned and motioned for Louis to come in a hurry, as he was in a hurry too.

Lacy's first words were, "Was that supposed to be a Tarzan yell? Sounds more like a Jane or the monkey. Your voice is high." There was silence for a moment as they quickly walked in the drizzling rain. Then Lacy said, "Slick, yeah Slick, they call you that."

"No, no," said Louis. "They used to call me that, but I don't like it, and they don't call me that no more."

"But that's what I heard, and I heard it yesterday. I'm going to call you Slick."

"Cut it out, Lacy I told you I don't answer to Slick. You first said I sounded like that monkey, then you called me Slick. I'm through."

Realizing they might have taken more time than expected of them, they ran nearly in silence from the store to their homes. Then they slowed enough to plan on asking Mama and Alice, Lacy's sister and guardian, if they could sit outside while dinner was on the stove. Permission was given and they met again and set on the steps of Lacy's front porch. The same steps where they had planned their Halloween pranks weeks before. Lacy began the conversation by telling Louis about his trip to the YMCA with Leo Stone. Surprised to hear this, Louis listened carefully as Lacy related the events of his trip just the past Saturday. Louis at first did not want to believe Lacey. Why would Leo Stone take Lacy on such a trip when he himself had known Leo Stone long before Lacy came into the neighborhood? As Lacy described the YMCA, Louis felt from his description of the indoor track, the gym, and the indoor swimming pool that Lacy was not lying.

Leo Stone was a young man just a few years out of college who had established himself in business and managed his mother's property, consisting of a duplex where he lived with his mother, and the house where Lacy lived. The YMCA was in the west end of Cincinnati, in a predominantly Negro neighborhood. Leo was a successful young Negro, and as expected he became a member and intended to hold an open house by bringing someone. Nonetheless, Louis, with his narrow-minded selfishness, could not accept this. He was deeply disturbed. Louis turned to Lacy with self-pity in his look as well as his voice and said, "Leo never took me. I've never been there. Leo used to rent my papa's garage, and he took you? Why?"

Lacy, showing no sympathy, returned, "Well, Alice said it's because I don't have a daddy."

"Lacy, you know everyone has a daddy," Louis shot back.

Lacy looked straight ahead into the drizzling rain, seeing nothing but the hillside of trees across the street. It was the early fall, so the sun still held back the night. As Lacy stared into the trees, he was not really seeing the trees. His stare let you know his mind was far, far away. After a short silence, Lacy began again. "My mama said Daddy always had his way until that judge had his way. My mama saved her money to go to that Columbus jail, but when she got there he was already gone to one of the worst jails in the south, where he will get the worst kind of treatment. I have never seen my daddy and they say I never will."

There was another long pause as Louis gazed intently into Lacy's face, trying to judge Lacy's emotions. The drizzling rain, along with his intense stare, did nothing to hide Lacy's expression of hurt. Then he began again. "I see you meet your daddy when he comes home and ya'll go into the garage and do things together. I hear laughter coming from your house like ya'll playing games. I see you and your daddy go in y'all's car. Sundays ya'll go to church. I see you sometimes go in that big car, your daddy's work-lady's car. I ain't got it nothing like that, Louis. That day when it was thunder it was lightning, your daddy came to the school and picked you up, and I walked in all that mess. It was pouring down raining. Then when I get home I have to clean shit from my sister's little kids."

Louis could see Lacy's anger and feel his pain, and wanted to say something to break Lacy's intense stare and anger that seemed to be near a breaking point. Then he decided to hear Lacy out without saying anything. Lacy gripped both hands into a fist and placed his fists on his thighs just above his knees. Louis could see Lacy's face was like chiseled stone, now with a somewhat protruding lip that showed a quiver. "My mama works hard for me and my sister Alice. I know. Last summer when school was out, when her work lady, Ms. Wilson, was gone on vacation, Mama took me to Ms. Wilson's house. I saw the swimming pool. Mama said, 'No, son, the neighbors might see you and Ms. Wilson would die.' Mama took me to the kitchen. She made me bacon, eggs, and toast, as much as I could eat, and good orange juice. Oh it was so good. The house was big. We went up to her room in the attic. The room was small with only room for a few clothes. She carried a pitcher of water and put it in a huge bowl. The water she would drink from if she was thirsty, but in the morning it was for her to wash up. She had pictures stuck into the mirror of her small dresser; one of Father Devine, that minister of healing in Detroit who was her savior. One of them was a picture of a large gathering of people, one of which was my father." Lacy's voice seemed to break and he paused again, then continued, "I could see his teeth and knew he was smiling. I don't know if he looks like me, but it must have been one of the few happy days in his life. She had pictures of Booker T. Washington and Frederick Douglass. She showed them with pride. She said to be like them and not like my father or Jack Johnson. She had another picture that showed a large gathering of Negroes, some even former slaves some years into freedom, mostly Mama's family and her as a child. They all stood in front of a tin-roofed log cabin with a falling brick chimney and cotton fields to the end of the picture. Their faces showed painful distress, disillusion, and sorrow.

'These people gave their all,' Mama said. 'You must not despair, you must make the best of this opportunity given to you by the pain and suffering of those people, your people, who have given their all that you can have freedom and opportunity to live a higher life right here in this country. I'll always do all I can for you and Alice to have better,' she said. That night I slept with my mama and I-I-I cried."

Louis and Lacy II

"Son," called out Mama, "come and see if you can open this shutter." It was the only window in the house that was shuttered. Being low to the ground and in the master bedroom, these shutters were usually opened only at the time of spring cleaning. After opening the shutters, Louis climbed outside to latch the shutters to keep them from flapping when the wind blew.

Suddenly, the whole package of spring was everywhere. The embankment between this window and the house next door was filled with honeysuckle vines, which were like a thick blanket decorated with a myriad of tiny yellow and white flowers that filled the air with their once-yearly dousing of a very special fragrance. The lilies of the valley and other annuals were showing early growth, if not buds. The scene was heavenly. "It's pretty out here," said Louis. Mama said nothing, just continued her work while singing, "What a Friend We Have in Jesus."

Louis was excited, expecting Lacy to be coming out of the house next door at any minute. He was anxious. He and Lacy had made plans the day before. They were going on a hike. They would take food along to be cooked later on the trail. Louis knew it would be a monstrous task to get food to take out of the house. *Mama's in a good mood*, he thought. He had opened the window for her and she was so happy singing that song. Louis followed Mama into the kitchen as she went to prepare breakfast for the kids. It was Saturday, there was no school, and Papa was gone to work. "Mama," said Louis, "Lacy and I are going on a hike. Can I take my food with me?"

"What food?" asked Mama.

"My egg," answered Louis.

"How do you know you are getting a whole egg? I take what's there, scramble them, add a little canned milk to make them fluffy, then they are on the table," said Mama.

"Then can I have tomorrow's egg?" asked Louis.

"Tomorrow's not promised" was Mama's answer. Then Mama said, "Do you mean that you are not eating breakfast?"

"Yes Mama," said Louis. Mama accepted Louis's outgoing, adventurous ways. When no one was present or observing, she gave Louis the egg. She gave him a small bag as well. He then asked for a potato, which he knew was a given. Then with his potato, his egg, and a biscuit, he was quickly off to the house next door to wait for Lacy to come out.

Suddenly, Lacy appeared, coming out from the kitchen door carrying a small bag. They were on their way. As previously planned, they were going to the end of Bloody Run. Bloody Run was an underground sewer that carried waste from a shoe factory, among other industries.

The dyes and chemicals from the shoe factory would color the sewage red. When the spring rain came, the water, with the sewage, would spill into a normally dry creek. They called the creek Bloody Run Creek.

"What did you bring to eat?" asked Louis.

"I've got a peanut butter and jelly sandwich and an apple," Lacy said.

Louis replied, "I thought we were going to cook."

"Alice didn't trust me to cook," answered Lacy.

Louis said, "I got a potato, an egg, and a biscuit. I'm going to cook. When you're on a trail for real, you gotta cook." They walked to the ballpark. They crossed the ball diamond and the field beyond. Upon reaching the creek bed, they looked for the best location to climb down the embankment.

Then, partially descending and partially sliding, they reached the sandy creek bed. The large puddles of water were discolored, with a mixture that showed a red cast. There were no tadpoles or minnows. There was little life between the embankments. They followed the creek bed, leaping some puddles and bypassing others as they traveled. Louis, with a stick, was more observant. He poked into puddles and overturned rocks with his walking stick. He poked into holes, hoping to stir some life as he went. He turned over rocks with his stick and observed certain insects that would quickly go back down under the rocks. The same insects placed on his stick would always go down the stick when he pointed it toward the sky. When he pointed the stick to the ground, they would turn and go down. Then, taking other types of insects from trees, he found something different. These insects would always go up. Placed on his stick they always went up. When he pointed his stick down, they turned around and went up. He found nature to be more and more interesting. They came to a point where the creek narrowed into a large pipe that went under a street. They walked up and over the street only to find another street to cross. Then climbing down to the creek bed again, they soon found themselves in a position of having to retreat to the street and go around, or leap a broad section of the creek. Louis probed the large puddles with his stick; he found it to be knee deep. It was very thick and with a very ugly color. This portion of Bloody Run, seemingly bypassed by the spring rains, was the color of an Easter egg dyed blue. It was dark and ugly. It had a green, foam-like covering and it had horrible garbage-like odor.

Lacy, an unusually physical person for his age, loved a challenge. He tossed his bag of food and leaped across this mess. Barely clearing the water's edge, he was exuberant. "Come on Louis," he said. Louis looked back with a disgusted frown. First he tossed his stick, then the tomato can he hoped to use to broil his egg. He carefully placed the egg in his pocket over the biscuit. He leaped. Suddenly, feeling the egg break in his pocket, he slipped and landed on one knee and both feet in this gooiest of goo.

"Shit!" Louis cried out as he attempted to wipe the goo from his body. Then, walking toward his stick, all he could see was Lacy's mouth wide open, laughing. Lacy had his hand on his knees and laughed and laughed until Louis said, "Shut up, Lacy." Lacy said nothing, then slowly stopped laughing. The annoying grin was still on his face. Louis's heartfelt pride was turning into anger as they again walked the creek bed. Soon, coming upon another impossible point, they stopped. Louis, with his egg broken, his pride reeling, and his wet, stinky sneakers was ready to give up the trail. Lacy was not. Then there was the sound of dogs barking. While contemplating if the dogs were tied up or behind a fence, there came a light rain to spoil this beautiful spring day. Louis and Lacy had known each other only a few months, yet they had bonded with each other. They both knew it was time to turn back.

They left the creek bed and traveled better-known paths to the ball park. When they reached the park, the rain stopped. They ventured under a large oak tree, where Louis reached into his pocket and came out with a pocketknife. "Let's play mumbly peg," he said. The two sat on the above-ground roots of the huge tree while playing. Louis was confident; he always won in this type of game. He would stop Lacy's annoying grin once and for all. Feeling better as they went through the game, Louis relaxed. To his surprise, Lacy won the game. "Louis," said Lacy, "you made me get that peg with my teeth last time. You get it like I did." Lacy, in his attempt at revenge for the past, had driven the peg into the ground in an impossible position for Louis to pull with his teeth, as the loser should. Louis slowly picked up the pocketknife, folded it, put it in his pocket, and slowly walked across the cinder path toward home. Lacy followed, saying nothing. Standing on the corner about three hundred feet across the street they could see Roger, Lacy's little brother calling, "Lacy, Lacy, Mama wants you."

"Go home and tell Alice that Lacy is not coming home," said Louis. Louis was attempting to use humor to ease the pain of leaving his friend while he was angry. Lacy, however, saw nothing funny and was ready to fight. "You're just trying to get me into trouble," shouted Lacy.

Lacy rushed Louis with an anger he had never felt before. Louis was taller and could use his reach to defend himself, but this time Lacy was beside himself with anger. They fought for several minutes before Louis was on the ground with his back pressed hard against the heavy, cinder-laden track. Lacy tried to pummel Louis while Louis twisted and turned to avoid the blows. All the while, the cinders on the track cut through his thin shirt as he tried to right himself. Suddenly, unknown to the two of them, Pete Lackey came up with a bottle and struck Lacy on top of his head. For a moment, Louis and Lacy did not know what had happened. The rush of blood from the crown of Lacy's head covered his face and hand. They both jumped to their feet to see Pete running away. Lacy rushed home. Louis was stopped by the first neighbor and questioned. He could say what happened but could not explain. "You and Pete have been around for a while. Pete probably thought he was protecting you from the new kid," said the neighbor.

Lacy was treated for his wound. He was scolded, but due to the injury escaped further punishment. Louis was visibly hurt by what had happened, because Lacy had become his friend. Now he had no friend. Pete would never be his friend again, that white boy had destroyed everything.

Louis walked into the house quietly and cautiously. He did not want anyone to notice his dirty and foul-smelling clothes, nor his puffy eyes or swollen forehead. He went to the table in the living room, got a magazine, and then retreated to the front porch. He had read the magazine more than once, yet tried hard to pretend reading. As it came time for Papa to return from work, he retreated to the kitchen where dinner was nearly ready. "Boy, you stink," said Lil. "Mama, you smelt this boy?" she asked.

"What happened?" asked Mama. "Look at your face, boy, what have you been doing?"

"Me and Lacy, we been climbing trees," was Louis's reply.

"Go take a bath, son, you smell like garbage," said Mama.

Later, at the dinner table, Lil said, "Look at your face, boy, that's what climbing trees will get you. You are a sight." Louis, however, was not greatly disturbed by what she said, nor did his bodily aches and pains overwhelm him. The pain of losing a friend hurt the most. He grieved and wondered about the future.

Two days later, Louis saw Lacy by the chrysanthemum bush at the end of their walkway. Louis quickly and cautiously walked up to Lacy, and asked, "Are you okay, Lacy?"

"I'm okay," said Lacy, "but we are moving, and a long way, too. We are going to Colorado to live." Lacy sounded sincere, yet Louis was hoping Lacy was wrong.

Louis asked in a small voice, "Will you be back?"

"No, only to visit, maybe," was Lacy's answer. There was a long silence. There were many thoughts and many unanswered questions going through their minds.

"That Richard Lackey, I'm going to make him pay," said Louis.

Then Alice's familiar, high-pitched voice rang out, "Lacy! We got more packing to do." Louis and Lacy slowly turned in the direction of their homes. They waved to each other as they went. They never saw each other again.

Hard Times

L ouis knelt beside the kitchen chair, quietly watching as Mama picked and washed nearly half a bushel basket of greens. Leaf by leaf, she inspected them for worms and cut away any brown spots or thick stems. Then she washed them in a water bucket and pressed them into her largest cooking pot. "Is that for supper, Mama?" Louis asked.

"Yes," said Mama.

"What kind are they?" asked Louis.

"These are mustard, those are collards," was Mama's reply as she pointed to each kind in turn. "Yes, these greens are supper along with a pan of cornbread. I do wish there was more, but this will have to suffice for the day. Now that your papa is out of a job, like so many more, we must face this depression thing head on."

"The whole country is in a mess and we all have to sacrifice and pull through," said Papa.

Then Louis replied, "We'll have a new president next year, and he'll make things better."

"Yes," said Mama, "if the Lord is willing."

"Mama, Mama," said sister Francis as she came into the kitchen, "Ms. Stone wants Louis to go to the store for her. It's important. She needs him now."

"Can I go, Mama?" asked Louis.

"Of course," was Mama's reply, "as I said, we all must pull together to get through these times. Go and do what you can." Louis was happy to go, mostly because it pleased Mama, who he loved deeply, and felt honored to please, as she so well understood his feelings. Ms. Stone was appreciative of the things Louis did for her, though he could not understand her way of showing it. She sometimes paid five cents, and sometimes pennies, and upset Louis most when she forgot to pay, knowing he was forbidden to ask for money.

Ms. Stone gave Louis a note and money wrapped in newspaper, tightly bound by a rubber band. He placed it in his pocket and carefully listened to Ms. Stone's instructions. "Give this note to the druggist at Shapiro's. He will give you my medicine and any change. And please be careful, son."

At this point Louis had no concern for the pay he would receive for his chore. His only thought was about Shapiro's drugstore, more than a mile away. This must be one of the cases where Mama said, "This is God's blessing, and they don't come easy." He walked along with Ms. Stone's dog, Spot. Having full confidence that his mother's prayers were with him, first he passed the German bakery. Hans Frey was the name above the door, but it was mostly called Hans's bakery. There were chocolate éclairs, pies, and cream puffs in the window, which he had never tasted but longed to try. Then, passing the small neighborhood store, he saw fruits and vegetables in baskets out front. The apples looked inviting, and the candy store in the adjoining building was just as inviting, but he had no time to lose, for Ms. Stone needed her medication.

He then passed the ice house and the Schneider grocery store with more apples. Then he passed a large apartment, where a longtime Negro resident of Norwood was caretaker and lived in the basement. Then there was the magnificent Shriner's building with its huge pillared entrance, and the Geek Orthodox Church and finally Montgomery Road, the mainstream. Not stopping to gaze as he went, he passed the Buick dealer, the library, the bicycle shop, Linder's ice cream store, Peter's Restaurant, Norwood Building and Loan, Thom McKann Shoe Store, and finally, Shapiro's drugstore.

The druggist made the prescription and sale, and gave Louis the medicine wrapped tightly, with the change inside the bag. "Thank you," they both said, and Louis began his long walk home, mission accomplished. Now his thoughts returned to his mother's words. He did not fully understand the meaning of the depression and pulling through those hard times as she had expressed. He didn't even know why there was a real shortage for the main ingredient of the meal, or why and how the president could make such a difference in one's life. In earnest he stopped, sat on the steps of the Greek Orthodox Church, and pondered the situation. There was one constant, his mother's prayers and her constant belief in him. Or was she saying their shared love and belief in her prayers was really enough to carry them through whatever they faced?

He gave the bag, complete with medication and change, to Ms. Stone. "Wait a minute," she said while opening the bag. She counted the change twice, and then with two fingers reached out to hand Louis a small coin saying, "Thanks, son."

Louis looked at the shiny new dime, saying, "Thanks" with his biggest smile. This was the most he had ever received for an errand. Louis turned and ran, as he was anxious to show Mama. Mama took the dime in her hand while stirring the cornbread mix. Then she explained to Louis how much it meant to her that he was a good and understanding child, how much Ms. Stone appreciated his efforts, though she sometimes was unable to pay, she was most appreciative. She explained how now he could contribute to the family needs like all the older ones had done. He was disappointed when he thought of the things he could have bought for himself with the money. Then Louis was shocked again when Mama turned to him, saying, "For these greens to taste like anything, they must have a piece of meat of some kind, bean bacon or salt pork. Take this and go to the store on Madison and Montgomery and tell the butcher what you need. He knows you are my child."

When leaving the house at 1709 Hopkins, Louis felt happy because he was pleasing his mother in a very depressing time. However, as he progressed along the route he had just traveled, he became depressed. He did not look as he passed the bakery window nor did he look into any store windows. He was trying hard to understand what was happening hard times, the depression, and no jobs to pull through. What did it all mean? As things went for him, everything was not bad. Papa was not working, and had more time for him while working on cars. He was not one to be idle. Mama, on the other hand, greatly appreciated anything done on her behalf, or anything done for a member of the family. She also believed they were stronger as a family, and should stand as a family and go up or down as a family. No one was to have more or less than any other. Sharing was a must.

Louis now marched toward home with that neatly-wrapped piece of bean bacon carried in one hand, sometimes changing hands, even tossing it in the air as he continued on his way. Somewhat tired of the walk and suddenly feeling the loss of his friend Lacy, Louis began to feel sorry for himself. He had no other friends in the neighborhood at the time, and the white friends he had at Allison St. School never ventured into his neighborhood. That dime he so joyously planned to spend was gone. Why? He had always done his share, ran all the errands for the family and anyone in the neighborhood, did all the chores at home as instructed by Papa. On Saturdays and summer when school was out he, cut grass, raked leaves, and watered flowers without any pay. He gathered wild apples, berries, and wild greens from the woods, which Mama cooked for all.

Those were his thoughts as Louis entered the kitchen, placing the package containing that ten-cent piece of bacon on the table in front of where Mama was mixing Kool-Aid. He glanced at Mama and attempted to smile while continuing on toward the back door when suddenly she said, "Son." He returned to the kitchen and sat beside the table where mama was still stirring the Kool-Aid. Louis, at this age, stood as tall as Mama and offered to sit in front of her so as not to look intimidating. He looked into her face—the wide mouth, deep brown and wide eyes with the long, tied-up hairstyle. He knew Mama was not the disciplinarian Papa was, and with the slightest inkling of pity in a smile she was as harmless as a butterfly. With words face-to-face and a message heart-to-heart she began, "Son, I saw the look on your face when you walked in the door. You don't look like that for nothing, what's the problem?"

"Oh, nothing," Louis answered, not wanting to say anything to upset her or show disobedience. He really wanted to please, even though he thought his psyche was a little ahead of hers. But that was no matter; her will was his to obey.

Again she said, "You don't look like you looked for nothing, what's the problem?"

"Well, I do miss Lacy since he's gone, and I did want to spend that dime. Well maybe not all but some."

"Well, son, as I've said we are in a depression, and maybe you don't properly understand. We must survive. No one should want to walk around with money needed for survival when others are virtually starving. We all are doing whatever we can, and we will survive. I know." There was a pause while mama lifted the lid on the greens to see how that piece of bacon was taking its hold on those greens. Then she slightly opened the oven door to peek at the color of the cornbread. All the while Louis sat, thinking, "It's not time for Papa to come home, the dinner is not finished, and Mama's not finished with me." He could see it in Mama and he could feel it.

Without any kind of threatening way, with a voice deeper than most, she began again. "You are not here on your own; you are blessed to be here as we all are. Life is like a journey, and as you pass through this earth you are being judged on the things you do. You don't do things for people only for what you can get out of them. You do it because you care and it's the right thing to do. Do you understand?"

"Yes, Mama," answered Louis.

Mama's Club

Mama looked into the living room as she made her last preparations for her club, The Norwood Avondale College Hill Social Club for Change. The roses were in that one vase that had been around forever. The three roses, now two days old, have changed. The bud was in full bloom. The full bloom had wilted. They were, however, perfect for the setting and still holding some of their fragrance. They now sit in the middle of the one table centered beneath the ceiling light where tea and cookies will later be served. Suddenly, I could not restrain myself. I must tell Mama how it all came about that I got those flowers. I knew she assumed that they had been gathered in the woods or that someone like Mr. Elcho, the florist neighbor, had given them to me for some errand. "Mama, Mama," I called out, "Let me tell you!" So excited was I to get Mama's attention that I had difficulty getting started. "Oh, Mama," I said. "When we turned onto Courtland Street going to school, there was a big horse lying in the street. His leg was broken. The man was on his knees. The wagon was gone—they took it around the corner. The man petted the horse but it would not get up. I think it couldn't, Mama. The one man stood and watched the huckster make the sign of the cross and kept looking into the horse's eyes. He begged the horse. 'Please, Nellie, please,' he kept saying. 'Please get up and show you are not lame. I need you, Nellie, say it ain't so.'

The other man said, 'She is indeed lame, her leg is broken, see how she holds it.' They said she would have to be put down. Put down means she has to be shot, Mama. The huckster made the sign of the cross again and pleaded with the horse. 'We've been through a lot together. I can't make it without my Nellie.' When two more men came, he began to know the horse would not rise. She would surely have to get shot. They told us kids to get along to school. They did not want us to see the horse get shot.

"After school I rushed to the same spot. But there was no horse or wagon. There was no blood on the street, even. While standing there I turned and saw this large trellis of roses just up a few steps from the sidewalk. I could not resist. I went up to the roses for a closer look and to smell them. While bending before the trellis of roses I was surprised by the woman who lives there. She did not come from the kitchen; she came around the side from the front of the house. I was trapped. I froze, Mama. I could have run, I can out-run anyone, Mama. But you don't run when you are trapped. That causes suspicion. 'Do you like flowers?' she asked. I told her I did. 'Would you like one?,' she asked. I said I would, for my mama. 'Oh, well, then let me see.' She carefully picked an older bloom, then a fresh new bud. 'These are American beauties,' she said.

"She reached into her apron and pulled out a piece of old newspaper to wrap the thorny stems, then gave them to me. I took them in both hands. I looked into her face for the first time, wondering what kind face went with that high-pitched but kind, pleasant voice. That elderly white woman had many features I don't like, Mama." A skin so white, she changed like a chameleon as she talked. Her hair was straight and limp, she had deep blue eyes, and none of the makeup seen on teachers at school. Living in one of the better and well kept homes in the area, I expected more. Her haggard appearance made me feel sorry. I nearly dropped the roses backing away from her. I said thanks.

"Oh! You are quite welcome," she said. She smiled what was to me the most genuine, caring smile I had ever received from a white woman at that age. She was no longer the wretched person I had first saw.

"Now I know, mama, there are good and bad people, and you can't tell by their face."

As usual, Mama's words were, "You are blessed, my son."

I was out of school with that dreadful whooping cough. Della had contracted the illness just after me. She was better, but not as far along as I, and we would soon be released and back to school. Today, though, she was asleep from the days of her persistent coughing. I was nearly one hundred percent recovered. The meeting had now begun. I rushed to my position at the top of the stairs. The door was always kept shut, preventing Della from falling down the steps. It also kept the club from knowing I was listening.

This would be my finest hour, listening to the meeting and especially the many comments. I would learn to imitate most members. I listened intently, trying hard to remember, even repeating comments to myself while listening. I felt great joy hearing Mama's hearty laugh when she heard me repeat imitate the members.

There first was a prayer by none other than that penny-pinching Ms. Stone, for whom I so often ran errands. The planned purpose of the club was repeated, then their business, which I could not really follow. I remember talk like, "These cookies are delicious."

"Yes, homemade," said Mama.

"I'll need several to satisfy this sweet tooth of mine," said one woman.

"Sugar is expensive these days, fifty-nine cents for a ten-pounder, "said Mama. "But do be pleased."

Another voice said, "Reverend, since you live above the church, I know people always come to you for food and all. What do you do, how do you handle that, you and your wife?" "Well," said the Reverend, "We do have that benevolent fund, which is never enough. Then we do as you do when your insurance collector man comes. Lock the door and act like nobody's home." They laughed.

"Now, down in the west end," said one "you've got your own stores, doctors, and lawyers, even. That's progress you can see right there in the west end."

Another voice said, "We're making progress all around, for sure, but some in the west end are waiting for jobs that are not coming. Move out, move up I say.

Another voice, "Now I'm the president here. We're just trying to hash things out. We will have different opinions and we all need to be heard. We have many problems. There are many places we can make a better life for others."

Another voice, "Well now, could we all go to the Cotton Club one night? Helen Humes, that great singer from Louisville, is coming. She is fine, she's jazzy."

Another voice, "I like her singing as well as that house band. But now with family—I support them yet I decline. I don't want to go there. I don't want to be cut up."

"Oh that's not the way it is," answered another. "That don't happen all the time. We go a lot and have no problem. There is that other element we are not proud of, sure, but those are our people still, they are in the forefront of the world of music."

Another said, "Just let me know when that Fisk Jubilee Choir comes to town. I'll be ready. When they sing those spirituals they just warm the heart so there's not a dry eye in the house. Their recordings are so hard to find. I hear the record company, Victor, limits the production because of race. That way we don' get to hear our own, they don't even get played on the radio."

Another said, "Does anyone get the *Chicago Defender* or the *Pittsburgh Courier*? We all need the information. We need to keep up. Bessie Porter tells me she gets the *Chicago Defender* always yet she never has one to share. I think she lies."

Mama said, "Ralph gets one at least bi-weekly mostly, and we share. Next time we have one I'll save it for the meeting."

Another, "Good, but let's save some money and all go to that Colored Orphan Home in Walnut Hills. It's right at the top of Wehrman Avenue. Reverend Harris would be glad to have any kind of help or just someone who cares about those kids. We don't sing but we can do something." None mentioned the walking distance to Montgomery Road, the nearest streetcar stop, or the walk from Gilbert Avenue to the orphanage, which included a hill that would surely tire these sisters. I listened and could see at an early age their desire to contribute to a rise from earlier beginnings. They could see progress and wanted to play a part.

The Norwood Avondale College Hill Social Club for Change closed its meeting with a standing prayer. Not a long, Uncle Jake-like prayer but a good one only dampened by that proper voice of Jennifer Twitty, who seemed to be teaching proper diction as she went.

After the "Ah-men," my mouth began to water as thoughts of how many cookies would be left entered my mind. Della was asleep now it was just Mama and me. I could eat a bunch. No one seemed to be anxious to leave, however and they continued in conversation. Now in two and sometimes three separate conversations they made eavesdropping difficult. The talk that followed the meeting was just as much fun as the meeting itself. I tried hard following one conversation and then another until I heard, "What did it make you feel like the first time you knew you came from slavery? Yes, tell me. Tell me," the voice repeated, "How did you feel?" I took these words to heart as if they had been asked of me. I immediately recalled sitting in Eva Klump's class, book open, looking at a picture of slaves. I saw men, women, and children picking a field of cotton. Ms. Klump explained the need for such an act as slavery, yet never mentioned its cruelty or admitted its inhumanity. Admittedly, even though I was often the only African American in the class, I often forget I was different. I quickly looked around the room at the others, trying hard not to draw attention to myself. At Allison Street School, the vast majority of the children were second generation Europeans. There were no Asians, Hispanics, or American Indians. I looked down at my arm and realized how much I stood out from the others. There were no words to express my feelings. I was crushed, like the Great Wall of China fell on me. Intimidated, like facing an eight-hundred-pound gorilla. exposed, like a turtle stripped of its shell. Pride swept away by a tornado. In just a few words I was changed for life. I now saw all whites as oppressors. The whole world changed right there in freedom's land. This would remain with me forever. However, I would not let it blot my destiny. *We do have a long way to go*, I thought.

"Those who suffered the pains brought the gains," is what my sister Mabel said later, which was of little comfort to me.

Lillian

"I like being the oldest child in the family, and being a girl gives me a feeling of closeness to Mama" said Lillian. We can have a heart-to-heart talk as she calls them. They make me feel proud and closer to her. I love the feeling. Maybe it's because she trusts me with her precious ones. I know now with little Betty, her eighth child, she surely needs my help. And what would she do with the little ones when they are out and about? Because of the early rain and flooding this year, Allison Street School's trip to the zoo was canceled. The money was not returned, they just gave everyone a ticket to be used on any later summer day. So that's how I got stuck.

First, Mama paired us off. Each older one had a younger one to care for. Now, I was nearly sixteen, and I was not only charge of the group, but also the most difficult, unruly child. Papa would load us all up and take us to the zoo, then return to pick us up outside the front gate. Most of the animals would be fed at five o'clock after which we would gather, all eight of us, and head for the front gate. Papa had the only watch in the family. We followed our instincts. Any sign of nightfall triggered a faster-paced move toward the exit.

This day I had my fill with the zoo. I could hardly wait to get home. We were at the back of the zoo, way back by Forrest Avenue. You know, where the buffalo range is. We stood in front of that split-rail fence and all that heavy rain left a huge puddle of mud on both sides of the fence. The buffalos were grouped together up on the hill. We watched them, then before you could say "scat," That Louis was over the low rail of the split-rail fence and the other side of the mud. He was mimicking twisting himself, saying, "Yeah, yeah," with his arms all out.

It scared me bad. I hollered at him, "Get your heinie back over here boy," but he did not stop until I screamed, "The bull is coming after you!" He looked back and saw the bull with its head down, pawing at the ground. That boy's eyes were big and I could see he was scared. Right through that mud he came and dove over the bottom rail onto the ground. I was embarrassed before a crowd of people. He was a sight, dirty with mud to his knees. One sneaker was stuck in the mud. "That's what happens when you don't tie your shoes right," I told him. I made him go back and get his shoe. He didn't want to, but I was not going to bring him home without it. "That's what happens when you act all crazy," I told him.

When we got home, Mama said, "Come here son. What happened at the zoo?" Louis only shrugged his shoulders. "Did you have fun?" asked Mama.

"She wouldn't let me," he answered.

"Well, I wasn't having any picnic with you, either, buster," I told him. "I should have let you come home like you was, all covered in mud." I was still mad, but I could tell by the look on Mama's face that my little brother was going to get off the hook again with this one. She just don't treat those two boys like she treats us girls.

BROTHERS

In the year 1930, one year into the Great Depression, a dentist was given permission by the city and the board of education to check the dental care needs of elementary children. Allison St. School was found to have an extremely large percentage of children needing dental extractions; nearly one hundred percent of those at the second and third year level. Extractions would be free. Parents had only to sign a waiver. All were examined. Cards were printed, charting each child's exact extraction needs. Parents were notified of the date of each child's extraction. This news of free extractions was not alarming to Papa. This would save him nothing. He had several pairs of pliers that would do the job of extractions. "Now that don't hurt," he would say. "Go get yourself a drink of water, you'll be okay." Papa was now behind on this job, and I was a prime candidate for extractions.

My sister Francis would always say, "Boy, they took all your teeth out, don't you remember?" But I do remember. My extractions were right after lunch. When school was finally out, I began that long walk home. I felt terribly weak and overheated from blistering summer sun. I knew I was not going to make it home. Maybe I had not eaten. Maybe I was dehydrated. Maybe it was a loss of blood from the extractions. The blistering heat seemed to draw all the energy from my body as I cut through lawns, trying to get as far as I could go.

Finally, on a grassy lawn beneath a big shade tree I collapsed. Fading in and out of consciousness, I remember my brother saying, "What's wrong? Come on get up." He then carried me six or seven blocks to home. Francis followed, giving advice, even though she was the smallest of the three.

Wilberforce

"We were coming from that tent revival when I told Ms Adams she don't have to ride in the back seat of that streetcar. Know what she told me? 'I don't want no trouble with white folks,'" said Mabel. She always would start something. We rolled along State Route 42. Papa controlled the steering wheel of that car as if he were controlling the whole world by his actions, and to him maybe he was, for a great piece of his world was within that car. Ralph Jr. and Louis occupied the front seat beside him. The back seat held Mabel and Cecelia. That was most of the older children, except Lillian, the oldest, who we were all anxious to see on this day.

"Give her some gas, Papa, see what she'll do, we're in the country now. Let her go, make some dust fly." Mabel said.

"Nooo," Papa said. "I'm not gonna do that. We're gonna be just fine. She might top fifty, but we're not going to go that fast. The law says thirty, anyway." The Pierce Arrow rolled jauntily along, glistening in the full sun. We rolled along with the low hum of the motor and the pitty-pat of the rubber tires against the pavement, windows open to catch the breeze. Papa sat stiffly erect behind the wheel, as if driving his employers. His hands were gloved, though unnecessarily. He cornered in an assured, safe, and caring way. Papa was a chauffeur by occupation and caring was his mandate. With confidence, he carried out his mission to visit his eldest daughter at Wilberforce University, to pay fees, and deliver a love package from her mother. He would in any way possible help any student a roommate or the school itself by delivering a message or package.

On our way we saw cows and other farm animals. We saw recently-harvested fields beneath billowing clouds. Barns unpainted yet plastered with chewing tobacco signs. We saw a barefoot girl pull a letter from her mailbox, then leap into the air in glee, clutching the letter in her hand. Was it a letter from a sweetheart or acceptance to the college of her choice? The mangy dog following her seemed to accept it. As she ran toward a simple frame house, we laughed while wishing to know the true story. We heard the clang clang as the railroad crossing arm swung down across the roadway. While waiting, and with quick, deliberate moves, Papa clipped the end of a cigar and lit its tip. The aroma soon floated throughout the limousine. To the occupants of the car, this was what Papa did, a part of who Papa was. Again, he began to fuel the motor with his foot. We saw crows gleaning those recently harvested cornfields. We watched other birds change their flight patterns with acrobatic formation. The mood was one of joy and pleasure, a time to comfort one another in conversation.

Ralph Jr. related how Coach Simms had such great expectations of him. It was based on race, most likely, thinking Ralph's foot speed would add to his team. Mr. Miller was real funny. When walking into his classroom you never knew what to expect. He would walk into the room saying phrases like, "What's this world coming to? Girls walking around showing their bare knees. They roll their socks down and everyone has got the same hairstyle, all wanting to be Greta Garbo. The boys with their open collars don't know if they want to be cowboys, Little Abner, or Romeo." Then he would say, "Well, I guess it's like the old lady who kissed the cow said, 'Everybody to their own taste.'" He would pause while everybody laughed. His reason for pausing was intended to give time for his message to be digested, not for laughter. Then he would continue, "This world is in a terrible shape and you are the ones who will have to fix it. How are you going to do anything? You better hit the books. You kids better stop so much sitting in front of that talking box. You better hit the books. Knowledge is what got this great nation of ours to where it is today and you better know that. These new soap operas, yes that's all they are. Buck Jones and Wild Bill Hickok are entertaining, but let's just get into the lesson."

Ralph Jr. again said he remembered at fourth bell, entering Mr. Miller's classroom to see "J-E-E-T - - - J-E-T," written in big, bold letters on the chalk board. He wanted to know what it meant. No one gave an answer. He paused and again pointed and wanted to know.

"What does this mean? It was said by a ninth or tenth grader, your fellow students. Look at that again," said Mr. Miller as he pointed to the words on the chalkboard. He crossed his arms and rubbed his right hand across his chin. Still there was no answer. "The kid was serious," he went on, "and his friend knew what he was saying. 'Did you eat yet?' That's what he was saying. Now you can't make it in this world with that kind of talk. You all need to get yourselves together, this learning is serious." Then he went to his prepared lesson.

From the back seat, Cecelia spoke up, relating an occasion when Mr. Miller came into class on a day he was to assign the chapter to be covered in the next day's test. Instead he went into a long explanation of the prison at Alcatraz. How it was nobody could or would ever escape? Not only was the prison supposedly escape-proof, but the island itself was so positioned that anyone attempting to escape would certainly drown because of the current between the island and the shore. He said it was something everyone should know. He was unpredictable. You got more than just the book lessons in his class. But he was a fair grader, and I liked that.

This happened in the year 1932. Franklin Roosevelt was campaigning for the presidency and would soon be elected, inspiring hope of financial recovery. Within the nation, a national tax went into effect of one cent per gallon atop its regular prices of ten cents. Car sales plummeted along with loss of jobs. General motors went to a five-day work week. Federal troops forcibly dispersed the so-called Bonus Army of World War I. Veterans gathered in Washington D.C. to demand money they were not to receive until 1945. In Cincinnati, an integrated school system existed with Harriet Beecher Stowe downtown and Douglas, in Walnut Hills, serving a majority of its African American children. The city's Negro councilman, its newspaper publisher, its ministerial alliance, and business leaders fought hard to keep those schools on equal level. Small conclaves of African Americans lived in nearly every community, stretching far beyond the city. They went to integrated schools, and in most cases made up less than five percent. A top student of African descent with prominent parents or whose parents were educators went to Walnut Hills, and sat alongside the city's wealthy. We referred to them as classmates of the Burgers and Hudepohls, referring to the brewing company. This was the norm, yet the climate at the integrated schools differed from those nearly all African American schools.

On the entertainment front, great things were being accomplished by Negroes who fought against every effort to stifle their acceptance. The recording industry purposefully limited any progress. Louis Armstrong constantly held the top of the charts in popular music, singing songs that expressed life's burdens bared by all during this depression. Songs like, "Brother, Can You Spare a Dime?" "Cabin for Sale," and "Gone Fishing" were hits.

Wiley Post and Amelia Earhart were breaking records in flight. Bishop Sheen and Father Caughlin were preaching to the nation daily on radio. There was Jack Benny and Bob Hope, top comedians on radio, along with Bob Hope's Eddie Rochester Anderson, a Negro sidekick. They were all great (in fact the times were great), because the depression brought a unity of purpose. All wanted to survive and there was hope.

There was much radio news of crime and figures like Al Capone being captured and imprisoned. The body of the kidnapped son of Charles and Anne Lindberg was found in a wooded area of Hopewell, New Jersey. Just the evening before, the news was that some of the ransom money had been passed at a toll bridge in New Jersey. It was Papa speaking, "That Lindberg child killer needs to be burned. He's a snake of the worst kind. It's hard to imagine anyone so heartless. Coming from Germany and committing a crime like that. They will catch him, I know. Lindbergh was smart enough to write down serial numbers of that ransom money. That dirty crook will get what he deserves, he'll burn I'm sure."

"Yes," and "Me too," echoed the others.

Suddenly there came a loud "Pow!" It was a sound quickly recognized by Papa, but the first time heard by the others. It was, of course, recognized by all when the right front side of the car began to bump, bump, bump, causing Papa to grip the steering wheel, forcing the car to the side of the road.

"Stay put," were Papa's words. "I'll take care of this." We were little more than two hundred feet from where there came the sound of music. We heard, "Around her neck she wears a yellow ribbon. She wears it for a lover who is far, far away." We imitated and exaggerated the hillbilly sounds we heard coming from this highway farmhouse-turned-roadhouse. In less time than expected, Papa, with his years of experience, quickly changed the tire.

"That's that," he said. He pulled a large handkerchief from his back pocket, wiped sweat first from his brow, neck, and huge arms, then wiped the sweatband of his wide-brimmed Panama hat. This hat he would soon put away into the same hatbox, for many years of use. Then he would place it atop their chifforobe in the bedroom for another winter. While pulling on his thin leather gloves, he glanced at his watch, pronouncing that we could be there by eleven with some luck. Papa squared himself behind the wheel, again sitting erect, then reached out to release the handbrake while glancing around at his passengers. Only later would he slump into his more comfortable position behind that large wheel. Looking onto the front porch of the roadhouse I saw a plump, red-faced farm boy. He was barefoot and tussle-haired, in bib overalls and downing a bottle of soda.

"Wow," I said, "I can't do that, can't afford it."

"Well, you can't do what he's doing and he can't do what you are doing. Riding in a chauffeur-driven limousine," said Cecelia. Papa's employers, Julia and Sara Dernham, had given Papa permission to use their car for the purpose of driving his family to Wilberforce. This car, made in England, was the same limousine used by former president Calvin Coolidge. It brought stares with its show of elegance.

At times Papa fell silent; sometimes he was into the conversation. He believed it was his duty as a father to direct their lives, to protect them and secure a future for them. Yet he realized his workload kept him from being the influence he would like. In this case, he was more of an influence than he suspected. "You go to a good school," he began. "Learn as much as you can. Sometimes, to be equally good is not enough, you need to be better. Things are getting better, better jobs are still coming up. You have got to be prepared and ready. Then you must live within your means. Save some for a rainy day. Now when I was coming up, my Aunt Pearl or my grandma would fix my school lunch, sometimes just a biscuit or two in a lunch pail. The biscuit was bacon greased, centered with some of that thick sorghum molasses. That was it. Those sticky hands from the lunch would nearly make that reader impossible to read after a while. We would memorize. We came up hard. There were some good times. Prepare yourself. Now take Procter and Gamble. As big as they are, they don't hire Negroes. They've got this big employment office but don't even give you an application. They just say, 'We're not hiring.' Now everybody needs work, you gotta have a job. How can we buy what they are making? There should be a law against what they are doing. The government should step in." Papa had a passion for justice.

We were in Amish country. We saw much larger farms operated by several families. Papa explained they are a religious order. "They make furniture like the porch chairs at the Dernham house. They sell items such as baked goods, brooms, honey, and much more. I don't think we have seen the last of what they are doing. They don't believe in some of our modern ways, like automobiles. See those wagons?" Then, moving alongside a standing horse-drawn wagon, we could more closely see their dark clothing, long hair and beards, contrasted by such bright pink skin.

"There goes your last chance, Mabel. You'd better grab onto one of those," came a voice from the back seat.

"No I'll pour my own misery. Just wait, you're going to get a last chance to marry and it's going to be a real zoo, Suzie."

"Get off that subject," said another voice.

Papa cut into the conversation saying, "We need to find a place to stop and eat these vittles mom packed for us, we are losing time. The train, the flat tire, and these horse-drawn wagons have cut into our time."

A roadside rest area at this time was a shade tree in a location safe enough to drive off the road. Hopefully the grass would be short and if there was not a park bench, there would be a tree stump, a log, or an abandoned object suitable for sitting. Wasting no time, Papa pulled off the road, choosing a spot himself. The girls sat on the car's running board. The boys sat on an abandoned wood box while papa sat on a large tree stump. We each grabbed a sandwich from that shoebox inside the picnic basket.

The children engaged in a hush—hush conversation while eating until Papa's voice came into play with, "What's that?" he asked.

"Oh, we were wondering when will we be there?"

"We will be there certainly by noon or half past, for sure. On our way back, we've got to stop by the Ogletree's, and we are going to stop at Fiedelday Farms. That's where we get honey, poultry, and squab, when they have it."

"What's squab?" they wanted to know.

Papa laughed and explained, "A squab is a fledging pigeon. You can ask Louis about that. He has tasted Marie the cook's squab on toast."

"It's good," is all I would say.

Again, while engaged in conversation, I reached into the lunch basket for another piece of chicken.

I was shocked with, "What are you doing? Get your dirty hands out. You know you had yours.

"I thought," I said.

"Oh no? You thought like Litt."

"Who's Litt'?'

"Litt thought he farted but he shit." They all laughed while knowing Papa missed the conversation in his thought process. Soon again we were aboard the limousine. Papa looked around all were in their former positions. He again pulled on his gloves while checking the open highway. A short silence came over us while Papa steered the limousine onto the gravel-packed country road.

Cecelia asked Papa. "What do you think, Papa, about that thing last year when we all protested at the new Sharon Woods Park?"

"Well," said Papa. "It was the right thing at the right time for sure. I'm so proud of all who took part and especially you, my girl," he said, referring to Cecelia. "That new park was built by the state with tax dollars. That means we all paid for it. It's not just for them. They so unjustly want to stop our progress; they wanted us to allow them sole use of that brand-new park. I'm so glad for the protest. That's the greatest example of what we should be doing that I have seen anywhere. While knowing a cross had been burned at that park, indicating for us to stay away, they still went in. Allen Temple, Mt. Zion, Calvary, Southern Baptist, and others joined to move in early with trucks and busses to take the park for the day. I was so proud. Yes, it was so good to see the tables turned on them peckerwoods. I'm sure they never suspected that. If Jesus walked today on this earth, he would surely be on our side. The fair, the humble, and the just. Imagine them taking the cross, the sign of Christ himself, and using that to show bigotry and shameful hatred. That's an inspiring story. A great step forward was taken. Things are opening up. We must keep the faith," Papa said.

We reached the outskirts of Zenia, the school's surroundings. "What shabby town is this?" one questioned.

Again it was Papa who spoke, "This is Zenia. Those who live here mostly are faculty and workers at the school. They sacrifice to be a part of progress for our people. They don't make what they should, even though they have their degrees. Some even take students into their homes to help. They stretch dimes into dollars. They're doing good for colored. We should all be proud of what they do."

Suddenly there she stood before us—Wilberforce University. This group of rectangular buildings stood fronting a wide field of fifty-four acres. It was nothing impressive, except for what it stood for. This represented progress for the race, certainly. As history goes, these acres were first a health resort. Then they were bought for thirteen thousand dollars by the Methodist Episcopal Church Conference for the benefit of Negroes in 1850. Then it was renamed after William Wilberforce, the great leader for the abolition of slavery in England. The school failed financially in 1862. Then was bought, by the African American Episcopal Church (A.M.E.).

The school became known for the leaders it produced, especially in music and the ministry. Years later, in 1974, tornadoes destroyed most of its buildings. Now state-supported, she is mostly hope and history.

That big elegant limousine pulled onto the lawn and right up to and within twenty feet of the main building, where no occupant could miss its presence. This was another thing Papa did. He parked with an attitude. Before the Dernhams, his present employers, Papa had chauffeured for several prominent families in business and industry, the last of whom were judges. Rank has its privileges. He used this attitude, but the mere presence of the law brought respect. His statement was made.

My thoughts went quickly to my sister Lillian, who must have been a teacher's dream. She loved a challenge, mental or physical. Having been captain of the girls' basketball team at Norwood High, she showed her aggressiveness. She excelled in literature, wrote poetry, and was at the top of her class in math. She was kind and patient with children. A commendable quality for the eldest child in a large family. She always was the funniest. I was anxious to see her. She finally came from the girl's dorm building.

She hurriedly walked to the administration building where Papa also went, as if having been just called to meet him. Not recognizing the car, or thinking Papa was alone, she passed her siblings, who laughed at her long legs and lumbering gate. The girls were allowed to go to the dorm while the boys waited in the car. They watched the girls and the dorm intently. The girls turned up the radio and did hair maintenance while making dance moves outside. They gazed with curiosity at the limousine. Some, noticing occupants inside, waved with fingers only then backed off. One, having no shame in her game, came close enough to attempt playful flirtations. At eight and ten, we were still Mama's boys, and became silently bewildered.

"They must have fun at college," I told Ralph. His heavier voice was affirmative along with a reverent expression. *How fortunate to have a lead who is reverent, dedicated, and self-assured*, I thought.

We looked up to see Lillian hurriedly walking towards the Pierce Arrow, confidently ahead of everyone else. "Hi love," she said as she slapped Ralph Jr. on the shoulder. "Are you still beating Papa at checkers?"

Ralph Jr. said nothing, just gave a thumb up and a great smile.

She then turned to me with, "Hi baby brother. Who's doing your homework now?" Without an answer she went on, "Are you still carrying that one book tucked into your belt? Why do you do that anyway?"

"Cause I might have to fight," I answered.

"You're too old for that, you better get it together before it gets too late. Just bringing home that speller is not enough. Fifth grade is going to be much harder and Ms. Davis, the principal, won't like that. She's got a mean paddle. You'd better stay out of trouble."

Papa's long legs and big arms appeared, walking like a winner toward the car. Each occupant sat in their original position, ready for the trip home. I slid from behind the steering wheel. Papa seemed to hesitate, as if not too happy to leave, while putting the gloves and Panama hat on again.

"Tell Mama many thanks for the box and the food. I won't be home for Thanksgiving, but Christmas for sure." Lillian blew kisses, then stood still watching, with her hands on her hips. She looked like Grandma Williams, tall, erect, and with a determined look on her face.

Now squarely behind the wheel, Papa reached out and released the handbrake. He gave the car a good dose of gas with his foot and we were off again, leaving a trail of dust bigger than the one when we arrived. "We must stop at the Ogletree's and the Wilmer's on behalf of them and their children, we all must do our part, it's progress. It's share and share alike. Sometimes it's survival, but we must aid and support each other in these times. We need leaders and they must come from the educated."

"Yeah," I said. "Like Grandma Williams said when me and Leslie Jr. were fighting. Well, not really fighting over anything. She said, 'Boy, that ain't no matter, you got no cause to fight, that's your cousin, boy. We Negros have got to stand together. Equal justice, follow your leaders.'" She was half Indian. What did she know about this? What was her concern? Did not justice deal unfairly with both races? Somewhat disappointed by the silence of my elders, I was still apprehensive.

At one point Papa seemingly wanted to stop at one of those roadside stores, then changed his mind against it. A colored family driving a limousine would likely be viewed with suspicion. Who in the world are they? This was the early thirties. The depression, the lack of jobs, lynching, and many other atrocities were being inflicted on Negroes, though mostly in the South at this time.

Again, coming from the back seat, "I wish we could have heard that Wilberforce Choir. They say they are the lick, they are really smooth and have lungs to their toes. I hear so much about them. Mama said they sing like olden days. Coming from pain and suffering. Then with such an uplifting at the end. When she said that, it messed me up, because Mama has seen a lot. Mr. Penn, the Sunday school teacher, said, 'God made the family so we could learn to live together.' He is so right. Then God made our family big."

While the sun beat down on that big, glistening body of chrome glass and steel, Papa went silently into his work. Papa taught and we believed we were destined for better. Everyone now seemed to have a radio at home. First it was just a few and they seemingly had something to say. The news, Kate Smith, Paul Whiteman, then Bing Crosby, rarely did they mention the Mills Brothers, as good as they are and being from Ohio. They listened to the likes of Father Kaupland and Bishop Sheen, who liked to influence opinions on all issues, including politics. We heard the Olympics, the Reds, yet nothing of our Negro League team, the Cincinnati Browns. At school, they declared everything they heard on the radio was gospel. "I heard it on the radio," they would say. That makes it so? "It sure does," answered all.

I felt inclined to speak and break a somber mood by saying I had been touched by a teacher at the white church next to Allison Street school, in their Bible school class.

"She was just singling you out, boy. That's what they do. She did it while they sang, 'Red and Yellow, Black and White,' didn't she?"

"Now, Mabel, don't break his spirit," said Cecelia. "He don't need that."

The scenery became familiar, then came that sign, nearly hidden by tall grass and an array of overgrown fall flowers, hollyhocks, sunflowers, daisies, and others. "Fiedelday Farms," it said. This was a well-organized operation. Run by a large family who seemed to know how to please. Papa drove down to an area where each visitor or customer would be served. We were greeted like royalty, even when known not to be the expected occupants of the limousine. Rex, the large dog of undetermined breed, greeted all in his gentle manner, then followed Pat and Cynthia, who were the servers. After our greeting, we observed the vastness of the farm. We could see beehives over the hill and tractors in the distance, laying a trail of smoke as they went. Rex took his pats on the head in a pleasant manner and then retreated to the large porch. As he did, Papa recognized the one sister with osteoporosis.

He loudly said, "Hi Liz!" But Liz did not answer. She sat on a rocker, head nearly between her knees.

Said Cynthia, "She hasn't been too well lately. She has had it rough since the winter, but hopefully she'll get better. At least she is not in great pain now." Those Dernham sisters were not along today, this would be Papa's buy. He was given the biggest portion for his money and more. The Fiedeldays would be compensated as Papa would be alone on many occasions when buying for the sisters and money would be no object.

"Ralph, try to bring the sisters when you come. Tell them we missed them. Goodbye girls and boys," said Cynthia.

Along the road back to the highway, the fall flowers were beautiful. Ralph Jr. asked to stop for a few but we were too short of time, Papa said. We stopped at the Ogletree home in Blue Ash. Theirs was a country setting, with vegetable gardens, fruit trees, and chickens. In repayment for carrying messages for them, the Ogletrees gave Papa some homegrown apples and grapes, for which he showed his appreciation. Then to the Simmons home, where we delivered their daughter's package of mostly written music and correspondence. Then Papa bore down on that much-familiar Route

42 with a group of tired and eager-to-return children. Papa allowed them to enter first, but they stood aside waiting for Mom and Papa to unite first. They would not embrace. They would, however, show affection by touching and smiling. Then brother went to Mama with his inability to get those flowers he so much wanted to get for her, but for lack of time he could not. Mama accepted his words with passion. She cupped his head in her hands. At ten he was nearly as tall as she.

She touched her forehead to his, "That's alright, that's alright, my son, you are all I want you to be and you are blessed."

EASTER 1933

Christmas has come and gone. It has been three months now. We anxiously look forward to Easter. Biblically, it is hard to say which one is more important. It takes both to explain the roots of our faith. At Sunday school, there is always class participation. I stepped upon the stage; my heart went pitter-pat. I heard somebody say, "Whose cute little boy is that?"

The memory could last forever; standing before your peers and parents as pretty as they could make you be for that hour. Easter Sunday was special. Its place in the heart and mind of children could never be duplicated.

Mr. Mendle, who Papa drove to and from work, operated a men's clothing store in Northside and always attempted to sell Papa items in his store to reduce his bill for Papa's services. The week before Easter, Papa refused to buy anything, as he needed the money for car expenses and the mortgage payment. Right away, we thought his Easter Sunday would be different.

I entered the church's front door and heard a loud sound as the heavy door slammed shut with the announcement of my presence. The vestibule so well-lit it made me look as if I were on stage, before my friends who were waiting to see how well I looked in my new Easter suit. At least that is what I thought. They stood in unbelieving awe at me. I was dressed in the exact same gray suit my brother had worn the Sunday before. Their stares without comment crushed me. I followed along thinking, *do they not know or have they forgotten that we're in a depression?*

The Lackeys

I met Gene McDonald at the corner of Hopkins and Webster Street, where he lived. When we saw no activity at the ballpark across the street, we decided to go to the end of Webster Street where the Schmoody family had a Shetland pony. We were not permitted to ride him, but we could pet him and maybe find something to feed him. We found the pony in his stall and apparently no one was home. We returned to the corner of Webster at Hopkins where we lingered in conversation just by the street sign.

Suddenly, a Norwood police car turned into Webster, a dead-end street. They turned the car around in front of Sam Lackey's house, and returned to stop directly beside us, where there was a sidewalk without a curb. The officer on the passenger side asked what we had in our pockets, suspecting we had rocks or something. He asked why we went to that house, pointing to Sam Lackeys' house. In unison, we answered the same, "We were at the Schmoody's down there," pointing.

"Where do you two live?" he asked.

"I live right here, this corner house," answered Gene.

"Then why don't you two just go home and not bother anyone again?"

We heard the driver then say, "It's just like I said. The old guy on the porch is daft. He likes to start trouble. I knew the story as soon as I got here. He's done this before. I don't side with the colored, but our job is to protect and they are both citizens."

That man referred to as the daft one was Sam Lackey. Sam was the head of the household, and he had a wife and seven children, three of whom were born deaf. They attended St. Rita's school for the deaf. Sam ordered his children to not associate with colored people, which they followed when on Webster Street. The deaf seemed to prefer to be with colored, especially when playmates were few. Sam and his wife, who was rarely seen, never ventured beyond their front porch. The two ignored the facts that their children played with all participants when at the park on a daily basis. Sam Lackey, however, would call the police with seemingly no other reason than to intimidate. Though he knew who you were, he would call the police on you simply for walking past his house. We wondered how he could afford the expense of a phone. He had no car and seemed to be unemployed. This embedded hatred embodied him. From the rear of 1709 Hopkins we were less than a stone's throw from Sam's rear yard. Sam's brother, John Lackey, lived just two houses above 1709. The house was frame as well as all the others in its construction, but it differed in every other way. The hillside had no sidewalk or any kind of pavement. There were only weeds where grass should have been. Heavy rains washed mud onto the sidewalk. Although they had no car or telephone, oil cans, tires, and other car parts lay on the hillside. They kept chickens in their backyard and were overly protective of them and hinted others were attempting thievery, like others could not do the same if they wished.

John Lackey had a wife, also seldom seen outside the house along with their children Carl, Bill, and Hazel, the youngest. John could step outside his back door and call Sam's house for one of his children in a loud enough voice to be heard. If he did not get an early response, he would come down the hill, provoked, walking with a cane supporting an obviously once-broken leg. He had green eyes just like his daughter, Hazel. On one side of a balding head his hair stood above his right ear and refused to stay put, no matter how often he brushed it. His face was extremely wrinkled. Not only was he red-necked, his face was nearly as red, with a beak-type nose that was the only part of his upper body not wrinkled. John wore ill-fitting dress pants with a tab collar shirt, sleeves rolled up, and went shoeless on summer days. He was a frightening sight as he peered down on an unsuspecting child with his perpetual frown.

When John reached Bill or Hazel at the ballpark at Sam's or on the way, he would point his walking cane at them until they came to him. He then would raise his cane as if to strike them, though he could barely stand seconds without the cane. When they seemed not to fear these antics, he then pointed the cane to his house saying, "Go." When he did this at the ballpark, some snickered and others just shook their heads.

John was a product of the past, before the automobile. He had an older son who came from Kentucky on occasion to visit, driving a Tin Lizzie. John would jump in with cane and barefooted. He then would position himself as close to the door as possible, his shoulder and arm extended beyond the window opening, his hand on the frame, and his elbow pointing to the ground. He then leaned forward as if to anticipate a crash.

John might have gained sympathy or been considered a clown for his ways had he not been so vile. John was the oldest of the Lackey clan, and played his role as the dominant one. "Goddamn" and "by God" were his favorite words. John was likely more than fifteen years older than Papa. On their first meeting, Papa spoke to John, who ignored Papa, and that was it. Papa classed John as a white southerner of the hated past and not to be trusted.

"His vulgarity is his bluff. He's a coward who will prey on any weaker person. Look him in the eye and show no fear," Papa said.

WHERE ARE WE?

At Allison Street School, in connection with the First National Bank of Norwood, we participated in a program that was intended to teach children the art of saving. This went well with the thriftiness of the majority of the German Catholic citizens. Each child would have his or her own savings account with an official booklet to enter each deposit and totals. Papa gave each child twenty-five cents weekly, then at the end of the school year when he decided to order coal for the winter, he withdrew from all accounts. This was to pay for the winter's supply of coal. When the coal arrived, we would be prepared. We dressed for the occasion and we tried with great effort to finish the job before Papa returned from work, although we never did. We all participated. Papa alone at this time could handle a wheelbarrow. The boys carried the bushel and half bushel baskets. The girls carried the smaller baskets down to the smallest peach and grape baskets. With great effort, a sizable amount was already stored when Papa came. When all was stored away and after washing up, Mama would have a dinner of plenty. It was a dinner that would fill every stomach and every heart to its fullest. It was a Sunday like dinner minus the pan rolls and chicken. This total participation by all united the family in just the way Mama and Papa wanted. Along with the unity and appreciation of family, there was love.

This was the time Papa had it out with Julia and Sarah, his employers, and had turned to the WPA. The WPA (Works Progress Administration) was one of the many programs initiated by our new president, Franklin D. Roosevelt, to alleviate joblessness. It employed the unemployed to do government work building and repairing the nation's roads, bridges, and structures. Louis had a joke he wanted to tell at the dinner table, though he was nervous as the joke was on Papa.

Finally, he spoke up, saying, "Coming home today there was a *Cincinnati Enquirer* reporter who stopped at this WPA job site. He got out of his automobile with a clipboard and pencil. He saw a man on the job who also had a clipboard. 'Are you in charge here?' he asked the man.

'Yes,' said the man with the clipboard. 'I'm in charge here.'

'Well, first of all, may I ask how many men do you have working here?'

'Well' replied the boss 'at least half of 'em.'" Louis was relieved when Papa laughed, as Papa was the butt of the joke.

We all retreated upstairs to the living room. We listened to the radio with new stories of others, struggling farmers, low-paid un-unionized textile workers, and Appalachian coal miners, all struggling to unionize for better working conditions and a better life. We wondered who was better off, them or us. We heard about a revolution in Spain and saw an occasional picture in the news of how an airplane with bombs could destroy so much of a city. We wondered even more when we saw the *Chicago Defender* or the *Pittsburgh Courier* with pictures of lynching in the South. We painfully grieved and began to know our true situation more clearly and realized we had nothing to rejoice.

As children, we saw wealth close up. We saw poor more closely. We sometimes pondered the situation when we had a new car and our friends at church did not, nor did most neighbors or schoolmates who were white. When Papa was on call, a telephone was a must, so we had one when others did not. Were we rich or poor? We knew Mama would laugh at such a question. We knew as well what she would say. "You are not rich, you are blessed."

Sundays

Sundays are a dream from morning to the very end of the day when you lay your head on your pillow. We don't eat breakfast; we all are just getting ourselves together at the same time. We all laugh, help, and tease each other. Mama won't allow any fussing or unkind words. The older ones help and direct the younger ones. If they tell you to button your coat, you button it. If they want to button your coat for you, you let them.

When you reach church there are smiles, handshakes, and flattering compliments. You'll have a friend to talk to after Sunday school whose parents are just like yours with encouraging expressions of love. After Sunday school, your teacher says thanks for coming and then shows her appreciation, sometimes with a hug. If you ran an errand during the week and still have your nickel, this is the best time to spend it. You can go to the sweet shop or the corner drugstore where you can get a great big Powerhouse candy bar with the silver wrapper, eat some, then hide the rest in your pocket for later. In church, you get a message that's uplifting and points your way to a promising future. Joy seems to be everywhere.

Then when Papa comes, we go home to the hot and yummy dinner Mama has prepared. They make you eat with both hands until you can eat no more. Then the most special time of the day comes. Papa gets out the car again. We are going to Woodlawn to visit Grandpa and Grandma Williams. We will visit the Waller cousins while we are there. The Ford, Tin Lizzie as they are called, is quickly filled. I got there first but got pushed aside and am invited to sit between the legs of sister Cecelia. But I don't care.

As we pass through Wyoming with its homes showing wealth, Papa straddles the outside streetcar tracks for a safer, smoother ride. Papa shows his pride, head held high and erect, hat tilted to the side. Mama sings a refrain ending, "Lord, plant my feet on higher ground." The older girls meekly join in. No one could be happier. This is the time of the Rockefellers, the Kennedys, and Henry Ford. We grow up knowing each individual is important. The most important thing we shared was unconditional love. A love that depends on nothing at all, except that you are family.

Papa and Uncle Leslie Waller Sr.

This picture shows Papa on the right, standing at six feet two and well over two hundred fifty pounds. Notice his huge hands and feet, although the feet don't show so well. At times, Papa showed an air of superiority, partly because of his size, but more for the things he had accomplished, and his large family, which eventually stretched to ten. He loved automobiles and the mechanics involved. He played what was considered Negro Minor League baseball at an early age. As a switch-hitting first baseman, he had unusual home run power enabled by his keen eyes and massive arms and shoulders.

On the left is Leslie Waller Sr., a man of very visible American Indian heritage, shown in his high cheekbones and nearly straight, black hair; a man barely half the size of Papa. Uncle Less, as he was affectionately called, was an honorably served and decorated veteran of World War I. Having been one of those who were gassed by that dreaded mustard gas so dastardly and desperately used by the Germans, he was compelled to a life supported only by government pension. Yet from this frail body he continually showed his spiritual faith, his faith in his country, and great love for his fellow man. We all are better because of this great man who was not always present at family gatherings, due to his physical condition. Family reunions were not the same when he was not around. Uncle Leslie was husband to Mama's beloved and closet sister and really greatest friend. When he passed, much of the family togetherness came to an end. Then the bottom fell out of everything when Aunt Marie passed. Aunt Marie was the beautiful sister and faithful companion of Mama. The loss of the two so shortly after the death of Grandpa and Grandma Williams was a blow that changed Mama forever.

Uncle Leslie Waller Sr. on the left and Papa on the right.

North Carolina 1935

When lingering at the dinner table, Papa abruptly spoke out. "I'm going to North Carolina." This somewhat sudden statement would draw little questioning. Papa's words were final. The only question would be when.

"I knew it," said Mama. Mama was completely comfortable with Papa visiting his family. She would see his restlessness, having not seen most of his family for more than five years. Only days before he had negotiated a mortgage loan to buy a new car. That's how Mama knew. The last time he went to North Carolina was right after buying that 1929 Ford he had just used in bargaining for this new 1935 Ford. Papa made all arrangements, the time, and who he would take along. He made no announcements, just went about preparation daily.

If asked when or what time, his answer would be direct, only if it was final in his mind. Otherwise, he said, "I'm not so sure about that yet." Some siblings were painfully awaiting his decision as to who would go along. Who would not go along? "I think it's about time for the boys," Papa said finally, "they should be old enough." There was little rejoicing; his plans would not be changed. The boys, one fourteen the other nearly twelve, knew little of what to expect. They had heard mostly negatives from the older girls who had been there. Secretly, Papa had long held a desire to give his boys the experiences he had as a child, good and bad, mainly the hardships that molded him. This was the depression, however. There were hardships everywhere. Comparatively, his childhood experiences were not harder, just different. Beans or greens without a piece of bacon in Cincinnati would be the same in North Carolina.

"I packed a pretty good lunch here for you and the boys. There's, something special there too," said Mama. Then with that deep feeling of being torn from the family, we gave our goodbye's reluctantly. There was only wonderment. The excitement would come later. We crossed the bridge to Kentucky, the first time for the boys, who had only viewed the bridge and Kentucky side from Eden Park and the park at Fern Bank. We gazed at everything along Route 25 South. Papa carefully maneuvered the car up and down the hills and around the many curves that became more severe as we ventured south. He relaxed when reaching a mile or so of straight road. We asked how much farther we had to go, and he just laughed. We saw horse farms and rolling hills. We crossed streams and rivers. We crossed train tracks and heard the sounds of fast-moving trains as they crossed the highway and faded into the distance, constantly belching smoke. We saw men walking the narrow highway single file, carrying lunch pails in one hand and hard hats in the other. Papa identified them as coal miners. We reached the area of a park high in the mountainous region called the Cumberland Gap, a natural passageway through the mountains of Tennessee. Here, three states could be, seen from this mountaintop park. We saw a background of blue mountains, with wisps of milky clouds that seemed to float along at intermittent levels. There were few vacationers at the large overlook where we stopped. We ate our biscuit sandwiches standing by a bench without a table. A large jar of lemonade was Mama's surprise. This would be our last stop except for gas. We saw some whites living an existence in squalor along hillside homes approachable only by foot, and they all seemed to be barefoot. "Barefoot heaven," was Papa's remark.

As we rolled along in this new, car Papa related a story of the Civil War. An escaped slave who joined the Union Army was positioned to return to his former master's plantation. He confronted his former master with these words, "Bottom rails on top now, mossa." It was not like that anymore, but things were changing. Even a child could recognize the resentment seen on the faces of many southern whites when passing through small towns. The scenery was nevertheless beautiful as we watched a different life unfold before us.

We pulled into a gas station near Knoxville, Tennessee. The station had an old vacuum hand pump gasoline dispenser. The pump would fill a cylindrical glass container, with markings at its top indicating gallons. Papa wanted five gallons, so the attendant pumped gas to just above the five-gallon mark. He then inserted the hose and the gas flowed. When the indicator showed the gas at its original level, the attendant stopped the flow. Papa stood aside with change in hand waiting for the final tally. Papa told the man he questioned his measurement and that his prices were outrageous. "You're getting city-like prices here in Tennessee." The man ignored Papa, which really angered him more. We knew Papa wanted to say more. Down the road apiece, it came out. "Those crooks, they are just suckers who want to get all the money they can from folks like us who work hard every day. Be a little crooked and not get caught, that's their way."

At one point Papa passed off some inquisitive southerners by stating he was a chauffeur, knowing they could not handle seeing a Negro driving a new car through their domain. We then saw the "Now Entering North Carolina" sign. We cheered, thinking we would be at our destination. Papa laughed. We reached the mountainous part of North Carolina. "That beautiful city of Ashville is just ahead," Papa said. We reached more closely-built houses, then hillsides much like our Mt. Adams. Now there appeared a distant lake, surrounded by hotels and massive homes of the rich. The lake mirrored the many lights, and it looked like a massive diamond ring surrounded the lake. With the dark, nearly indigo sky, the sight was stupendous. We stopped and parked on a steep hillside, then went to a home where we were greeted by a lady known only by Papa. The lady welcomed us all, she showed pictures of her two children who were away in college. We spent the night in Ashville, North Carolina.

Arising at an early hour, we drove on the thirty-five miles of narrow and sometimes unpaved roadway. Some places the road was under repair. Some places there was storm debris or even washed-out sections. Papa said some of the farmers felt they still had the right of way or had rights others did not have, so they blocked the road passing through their land with their equipment. Again, Papa abruptly pulled off the road. This time, we were in an area of small farms, much like Grandpa's farm in Woodlawn. He pulled onto the front yard of one farmhouse directly in front of the door. Not wanting to annoy anyone by blowing the horn, he looked around. Clearly someone was home. He stepped from the car, still looking around, hesitant to go to the door as we intended to get to the homestead by noon.

Suddenly, he was recognized by a woman who was hanging clothes on a line beside the house. She came quickly to the car, with clothespins in hand, calling out, "Ralph! It's you! I didn't recognize the car. Oh, how are you? It's been a long time." She went on saying she had eight children now. "Eight," she repeated.

"Well, I've got ten now myself," said Papa.

"You must have a lovely wife," she said.

"Oh, for sure," said Papa.

"What would you and I have done?"

"Oh, my," she said. They both laughed heartily with the brightest of smiles. Papa questioned the lady about some of their past acquaintances, then while still talking, he got back behind the wheel. When he started the car, she backed away with the big smile and a wave. Eyes looking and ears fixed, we wondered about the past, their past. Obviously, Papa was enjoying some fond memories. Back on the road, again Papa fell silent while gazing across the hood of the car and beyond, as if he was seeing more than the scenery before us.

"Yeah, Dottie was one of the very few young ladies around who was not my kin. The Flaxs, the McIntyres, the Whitmores, and even others are kinfolks. Whether it was Brackeytown, Rutherfordton, Forest City, or Spindale, our relations were everywhere. Imagine walking miles to a town, expecting to find a gathering where you can have the pleasure of young ladies to socialize with and have fun, then they are cousins. That is why so many of us ventured so far," he said. After another silence, he continued. "I love these hills, I love my people," he said. "There are some who were raised up here as I was, and they have never been farther than Charlotte, just up the road. Up and down these hills is all they know. A broader life is better. This is where your Aunt Lillie lives," Papa said. Referring to his younger sister, Ralph Jr. and I cheered as we passed the big sign reading "Now Entering North Carolina, Rutherfordton, the County Seat." The little town with such a big name was somewhat as expected. It was small, farm-like, with homes on smaller lots. Most raised chickens and some fattened hogs in small pens. After meeting our cousins, then unloading our small bags of belongings, Papa pulled the car behind the house as close to the kitchen door as possible. This was to avoid the curiosity of neighbors. We boys slept in the car, where the many sounds, many unidentifiable, lulled us finally to sleep. Morning came quickly with our newfound little cousins, Mathew and Ralph, (named after Papa) pounding flat-handed on the car windows. Then, after a hearty breakfast, including a big skillet of fresh eggs like never seen at our house, we were sent to the store. We passed the largest building seen so far in this state. This being the county seat, this building stood out by its structure, its well-manicured lawn, and fresh paint. We passed a large, red-brick building, formerly some kind of mill, now used as a jail. Steel bars were secured across open windows. The inmates reached out, attempting to draw us closer.

Mathew spoke out saying, "Pay no attention to them." This was an everyday occurrence to the cousins, but a shocking experience for Ralph and me. Entering the one step above the sidewalk store, a large, likely mixed German shepherd dog lay before the counter, seemingly having no animosity for the cat that strolled before him.

The short, bespectacled, nearly bald clerk stood at a table behind the counter. He scooped sugar from a large burlap bag, then filled and weighed smaller one-pound bags. After several of these operations, he turned toward the patiently waiting boys. "What y'all want?"

Again, we passed the jail. I looked more closely at the pitiful faces this time. They seemed to be less bothered by the confinement than I would have been. What crime had they committed? Had they been walking the street instead of reaching from a jail cell window I would have been even more compassionate. It's the way I was taught. The little post office had no mail for the boys. We returned to the house. Mathew rolled out an old automobile tire, which we played with, then took turns climbing inside the tire then being rolled by a cousin. Papa then came up with a ball and glove, which we tossed on the front yard. Now having talked with his relations in Rutherfordton, Papa was ready to go to the homestead, where he was raised. Papa pulled the car off Route 221 onto a less-traveled highway, a dirt- and gravel-packed road. Suddenly, trees were closer to the road. We passed two houses only in nearly two miles. Papa named the past residents of those houses as he remembered them—the McGuffeys, Job and Missie Banks, school teachers. The sights and memories of his past brightened and intensified the smile on his face. We were suddenly on the homestead itself, accessible only by this narrow, one-lane drive. We straddled puddles of mud, increasing in size as we went. When we arrived at a puddle that seemed impossible to negotiate, we got out of the car. Looking back, we could see from whence we had come. However, the road ahead curved and was completely invisible from our location. His big smile gone now, Papa was clearly puzzled. To back out from this point would be impossible.

"I'll not leave my new car anywhere unattended," he said. "I'm blocking access to the homestead. I don't want to do that." When we attempted to leave the car to join him, he refused. "Stay put," he said. We stood on the opposite side of the car while he pondered. Suddenly, we heard sounds of someone walking and nearly at the same time appeared Taft Forney, the son of Papa's favorite Aunt Pearl. They embraced while we watched and listened.

"Hood, my brother, is on his way," said Taft. "Don't panic, Ralph. You can make it there. We had a big storm last night. It washed out some spots in the road, but we can get up to the house for sure. Don't worry about your new car, it will be safe. It's a beauty, Ralph." Then Hood arrived. They both pushed the car through mud puddles. They filled openings too deep to cross with rocks, enabling the car to reach higher ground as we slowly climbed the distance of more than two miles to the mountaintop homestead.

On arrival at the homestead, we found only adults. Then in the time it takes to fix a quick meal, we had one. The food hot, heavy, and delicious, yet we were told tomorrow's dinner would be better. We followed Papa and his cousins around the farm while he was being shown new additions and improvements. Again inside, we listened to stories of the past with sleepy eyes, until we were directed to our sleeping quarters for the night. The sleeping place was a loft, on the back side of the large, one-room log cabin. We climbed into the small bed onto mattresses, handmade and stuffed with straw. The adults lingered at the big, unlit fireplace, reliving the past. This was surely one of the experiences Papa wanted his boys to have.

Suddenly, we awoke in unison, not knowing what aroused us. Just as Papa said many times before, the smells of breakfast reached the loft sleepers first. Oh, what tantalizing smells they were. "Ralph, tell your boys they can come down when they are ready," said Aunt Pearl. Papa directed us to an outside wooden stand where we washed in a wash pan with water drawn from a well. Papa made us feel even more welcome, in fact we felt a connection to this place. The breakfast was immense. Chicken was added to the biscuits, grits, gravy, and eggs. Without any type of cold storage, the bacon was salt cured or smoked, thus chicken was added as a fresh meat. Rather than milk, we had fresh fruit or melon. There was plenty. In these days of depression, few people ate this hearty at breakfast. For city folks, chicken was reserved for Sunday.

Loby appeared in front of the doorway just as we finished breakfast. I observed that tall figure, somewhat like me and just as much like Papa. Long arms, big hands, tracking eyes, short hair. Loby came to meet his cousins from far away. Seeing his caring desire to please and act as a chaperone, I happily stepped forward to accept his offer. While we stood there, Aunt Pearl gave Loby a biscuit with bacon, which he returned to the table with to drip some sorghum syrup into the mix. This syrup, mistakenly referred to as molasses, was made right there. Not from sugar cane but from a tall, grass-like plant brought from Africa. "Y'all make the best right here," said Loby. "They are so clear, you can hold them up to the light and see nothing but pure syrup, I swanee." Swanee meant "I swear."

I wanted to see more, and know more of this new horizon, to learn about my family's past as we traveled the paths. The thoughts ran deep as we traveled the well-worn paths. Rock piles designated boundaries. Ancient pieces of farm equipment were left standing. *How long have my people been here, what happened, or what might have happened here? Was it like* Uncle Tom's Cabin? *Were they beaten like in the story?*

Papa said in the past North Carolina was not as bad as some other states, but he did not explain the reason. We crossed hills and we crossed streams. We passed through fields of corn where the corn was much taller than we were, yet Loby came out at just the point he planned. He knew at all times whose land we were on. He knew who grew the best tomatoes and melons. The best fishing places. He knew who would or who would not complain if we were to sample some of their crops. I knew when we stopped and Loby pulled a large, ripe watermelon from its vine that he must have done this many times before. There stood a large shade tree perfect for the occasion. We ate the watermelon, filling our stomachs and quenching our thirst on this hot July day. "What's next, Loby?" I asked

"Uncle Joe's, right over yonder a little ways," he answered, motioning with a sweep of the hand. At the moment he sounded like Papa, as well as most of his family.

"We have so many people here," I said.

"Now you see why so many have gone away," he said. He mentioned some surnames, many of which I had heard before.

At this stage in life, having attended Norwood High, more than a mile away from home, then setting pins at the bowling alley, I was physically prepared for all the walking. With a dogged determination and childhood wanderlust, I followed Loby. We passed that sawmill Papa talked about many times, now a small, worn-down frame building surrounded on three sides with piles of sawdust. This rotting mass included pine needles making for a rich and fertile soil. Now it flourished with dahlias, amaryllis, and Boston fern, beautifully and abundantly arrayed across its bank.

We suddenly burst onto a somewhat paved road one city block away from the one stop sign that seemingly marked the center of Union Mills, North Carolina. We were just between the little store and the mini post office and beyond the train station. Well, the train station was just an office with an extended roof for shelter. There was only a wood platform from which to board the train. During daytime hours you could walk in the street, the cars came so seldom. The cars would likely speed through this town's one stop signs town at almost thirty miles per hour, except for the road's bad conditions.

At the store, Loby asked me to wait outside. He took my dime for a strawberry soda. He returned with a large bag, and we then retreated to the back of the store. Loby pulled out and opened a can of sardines then placed it on a large wood box. He opened a box of soda crackers, pulled half the crackers from the box, and laid them on his lap. He handed me the other half. Then with his knife he opened a can of pork and beans, which he dumped into the empty wax papered cracker box. We then proceeded to finger the sardines one by one from hand to mouth. We scooped the beans onto the soda crackers and into our mouths. When finished eating and while drinking the soda, Loby pronounced, "I'll take these bottles back to the store and then we will go to the church."

The A.M.E church was the only church on this main road and the only building other than the train station post office and small store. Loby asked if I had been to church. I had never imagined a church so small. "Yes, but not like this," I answered. There were only five in the congregation, who momentarily stopped the service when we entered. We sat in the last pews watching what followed the short but fire-filled preaching. The minister led the tiny group in song without any type of music. The minister then called those who were not yet members to come forward. Two young boys, appearing to be young teenagers, came before the altar. They were then surrounded by the other three teens, or young adults, along with the preacher and his wife. The group started chanting, not in unison, but with individual urging to accept the Holy Spirit. Accept the Lord. Get saved. Feel the spirit. Accept it. Rise when you feel the spirit. "Rise," they said, "for you are surely saved."

When Loby said, "Let's go," I followed, yet attempted to watch as long as I could. "I wanted to spare you of this," he said. "They will keep up the urging until you declare you have seen the Holy Ghost. If you don't, then you are a complete sinner to them. It's that new preacher Reverend Simpkins who started all this."

We then followed the road back to the store and post office, at which point Loby turned into a large cornfield. When exiting the cornfield we continued to a small farmhouse where flickering lights could be seen within, though it was not yet dark. Clearly we could see there was a party going on inside. Surprisingly, there was live music, though with only one musician, whereby the small group of partygoers had long tired of the monotony. We walked onto the front porch. One of the families came out and invited us in. Loby asked for a friend by name, who came out, inviting us once again. Loby, declined again, saying, "This is my cousin from Cincinnati, I think not." He introduced me to two of the girls, after which we left. We again entered a corn field from which we exited by the creek near his home.

The house was a perfect retreat standing quiet and serene above the slope to a fast-moving creek. A bridge crossing the creek made this a scene to be remembered. We entered, and were met by Lois, Loby's older sister, who acted motherly. I was led to the room where I was to sleep. They explained the straw-filled mattress, which was to them something good. They lit a lantern then Lois said, "Don't pay any attention to Loby. He is trying to frighten you by telling you some wild stories of what could happen here at night." The thought could not restrain me, as I was extremely tired and emotionally drained. Sleep came quickly lasting until morning.

Again, it was Loby with a simple. "Come on Louis," he said. As quickly as possible, I prepared myself to follow. He carried one towel and one bar of soap and we went to the creek a stone's throw from the house. I was surprised to see the creek had a pool of water and a huge rock forming a perfect place to bathe. I watched Loby disrobe, wet and soap down his naked body, then dive into the pool. He urged me to do the same. I was at first reluctant, but this was the only alternative. There were no bathtubs, only those galvanized tubs we used at home before the new bathroom was installed. The same as what Loby's family used in their short winters.

"Okay, get me a towel," I said. I knew he had expected me to use his, but I stood fast. He got the towel and I bathed.

"Now, don't that feel good?" he said. "I know ya'll don't have to bathe outside, but it's fun."

Lois placed before each of us a piece of chicken, a fried egg, and two biscuits. She explained that the chicken was because I was company. "It's not an everyday thing," she said. Following breakfast, Loby again led the way to the mountaintop where the large family of foreigners originated. We met papa and Ralph Jr., who informed us this would be our last day in North Carolina. Tomorrow we would be leaving. Papa would pick us up at Loby's house, and we were to be ready when he got there. Loby led me to a cave dug between and beneath a large stone formation at the mountain's peak. He showed how cool this underground storage space, the size of a small kitchen, could be in July. It could store fruits, vegetables, canned foods, and some cured meats. Our ancestors must have used this method of preserving food, far in the past. We observed the homestead's structures, a log cabin dating far past emancipation. Loby pointed out the huge grinder once used to produce the sorghum molasses, and the old stoves where the juices of these tall grasses were broiled into syrup then into sugar. Papa loved this very thick and extremely sweet, distinctive taste.

When thoughts of the distant past come into mind and you look around at a land that has stood for ages, there comes a feeling that overtakes the body. A feeling that you have been here before. You are an extension of something in the past. So many of the things that happened right where we stand are reflected in us. I looked at my cousin Loby as he walked away. In his walk and his talk he was more like Papa than I. His voice was a take-off of Papa, maybe like Papa was when he first arrived in Cincinnati from North Carolina. I saw the past and the future—or what I thought was the future. What usually bothered me when dealing with others never bothered me with Loby, he was so openly honest and sincere. I felt a closeness never before experienced with any of my few friends.

We arrived back at Loby's house in the valley by the creek. I liked the retreat look about the location with its bridge. Papa said he could not live there after being raised on the mountain where he could see forever. Loby's daddy, Uncle Harvey, was a hard worker and a good provider. Theirs was not a farm, they just had some chickens and a hog or two. Lois, the oldest girl, was in charge. Justion and Lottie the other siblings were not at home at this time. This was the hard times of the depression, where many survived on more meager means, yet a good feeling existed in this family. As we arrived, there appeared two young ladies talking to Lois on the porch. Then Lois retreated in to the kitchen as we came near. Loby seemed somewhat surprised to see them, but went directly into a congenial conversation with the two. Being an extremely shy youth I wish somehow this would have never happened. I was invited to sit beside the one introduced as Daisy McIntyre. I listened without remark as the conversation centered around the three of them. Then, as expected, the conversation changed, much to my regret. Daisy struck me with questions. I answered them with the least possible words.

She went on, asking, "What is it like where you come from? How would you like living here? When will you be back?" I answered all her questions. A car came to pick up the girls. I promised I would indeed write. As I could not say when we would return, I felt my resistance to a girl's presence slipping away. Suddenly I saw girls in a somewhat different way. It was not like my big sister or even Mama. I was infatuated to the highest degree. I did not know what happened and did not care. My resistance to any boy-girl association had been breached. Oh, what a reckoning. I watched with sorrow as they went to the car, vowing to certainly write, as promised.

Morning came and so did Papa. All the extra space in the car was occupied with containers of all fashion filled with his favorite sorghums as well as many other products of his North Carolina homestead. We boarded the car in a somber mood. A car pulled alongside, occupied by the girls with Daisy in the back, waving. I waved back with a sinking feeling. What could I do in appreciation, or to show remorse for my crude actions? At the next highway intersection, they were suddenly gone. A gloom overtook the car and lasted as long as the mountainous scenery. Then the loss of friends lingered as a part of the past. Never would our hearts be the same, but forever would be the memories.

When we got home, I knew something was different. My big sister Lil was home. I missed her. I was always glad to see her. She was so different since she came from Wilberforce University. She spoke with authority. "I am three times seven and that makes twenty-one," she would say. She dressed differently, with her hair short and always something clamped or stuck in it. There were no more knees showing and no more tight belts. In just one year, she had changed so much. She said she came to help Mama out, but they just talked, talked, and talked about the Bible and the church. After visiting several churches, she was now baptized. She learned parliamentary procedure. She was now organizing women's groups to support her church and broaden its community base, at least that is the way we heard it at home.

While away at school, she also developed a taste for steak, which was unheard of at 1709. She also learned how to cook steak. She laid it out on its wrapper. She sprinkled salt and pepper then she cut up a small onion, squinting her face as she chopped it. "Oh this onion is so hot it almost makes me cry, but that's what makes it good," she said. I watched as she made a roux, placed the steak in the skillet and lightly basting its top. She was a terribly sweet, kind, and loving sister, yet she came to the house with only one T-bone. Which she intended to finish off before school was out. I knew what she would say when someone came up. "You already ate."

I finally decided I would ask her. She would tell me and not comment critically or blab to the other family members. She would be gone. Yes, the time was right. The aroma of steak and onions filled the kitchen and spilled throughout the house. I heard the door shut as she came from the furnace room where she and mama were washing clothes and talking church. I was sitting at the big table closer to the stove, pencil and paper in hand. She lifted the lid from the skillet and remarked "Oh yeah, oh yeah." So near to her desired medium rare was her steak that she could not chance leaving the kitchen.

She sat down beside me and I finally asked, "How do you spell McIntyre?"

"What's the first name?" she replied.

"Daisy," I answered.

"That's a girl and you're twelve," said Lil.

"I'll be thirteen my birthday," I told her.

She said, "Oh she's one of those McIntyre's in North Carolina. Don't you know she's your kin folk? You don't cross that line."

DAAWG

Walking along Montgomery Road on his way from Fenton's Dry Cleaners, carrying his suit—the only that fit his long legs and arms—Louis collected his thoughts. It was Saturday, school was out for summer, tomorrow would be Sunday, which meant church and Sunday school. Nothing different from last Sunday. After church and dinner, a trip to Woodlawn to visit Grandpa and Grandma Williams. If not that, then a walk to the movie theater. Last summer he had gone to North Carolina with Papa and his brother, Ralph Jr., for his most memorable summer ever. The summer before was a good one, ending with Lacy leaving. He looked forward to his summers, as each one seemed to change things. There were boring times. There were great fun times when his family and the Waller cousins gathered on Grandpa's farm. As he grew older he was trusted more and ventured farther away from home. He wondered how this summer would be different.

Crossing Khan Street at the top of Hopkins Street Hill, he saw a familiar teenager approaching the same corner. Louis remembered having met this person when he and Lacy were at the ball field. He was a country-time white boy. His manner of walking gave him away. Remembering how this kid came upon the name of Daawg caused Louis to smile. Louis did not remember his real name, but he remembered there was something about Daawg that he and Lacy did not like. His name was Eric Hinney who had a habit of constantly prefacing everything with "Daawg."

"Daawg, let's stop sitting on the porch. Daawg, can't we play baseball? Daawg, nobody's got a baseball. Daawg, it's going to rain. Daaw—that's my mama calling me. Daawg!" Daawg was coming from the direction of Printess Street at the end of Kahn, where he lived. Two large multiple family buildings facing the railroad tracks were inhabited by migrating people from Kentucky and father south. People like Daawg. Not a neighborhood preferred by many, being overcrowded by people of Daawg's type. Printess Street was not in the path to anywhere Louis needed to go.

As they approached each other eyeball to eyeball, Louis could see the same old country look he didn't like. He would be just as comfortable if Daawg did not speak. They didn't need to be friends. Daawg wanted people to look up to him. *He should look up to me*, thought Louis as he walked with his newly-pressed suit slung over his shoulder, dressed for the trip to downtown Norwood. "Howdy" said Daawg, with a suspicious look on his face. At least suspicious to Louis's thinking, speaking from the side of your mouth.

You wouldn't have spoken to me if you met me twenty minutes ago downtown, thought Louis. "Hi, Daawg," said Louis, looking into Daawg's eyes to catch his reaction. The name Daawg sounded too much like dog, and as expected the reaction was negative. It was okay for his friends to call him Daawg, but something about this Negro boy calling him Daawg was upsetting. Daawg's complexion changed with each expression. Louis was intimidating to Daawg; that was clear.

Whenever in this situation, Louis would look the person up and down, observing him physically, his size, weight, and height, looking in his eyes to determine his aggressiveness. Daawg was a hefty white boy, but he was no rock. A fight with Daawg would be a tough one. "Y'all live down Hopkins?" asked Daawg.

"Yes," answered Louis. Then, feeling this conversation with Daawg would eventually lead to something Louis was passionate about, resulting in a fit of anger, he threw his dry cleaning over the other shoulder and went into the direction of his home.

"That new Sunday pass is a humdinger," said Lill, Louis's big sister.

"It's a humdinger and a whoop-de-doo, Big Sis," he replied. "Last week I went all over downtown Lockland, all the way out Vine Street. That long, long ride. That Madisonville and Oakley cools you at night. But what about that incline, how it chugs its way up and then a big clang when it reaches the top and comes to a sudden stop? You can see all downtown, the river, bridges, and Kentucky. Ride all you want, too, on a twenty-cent pass. Today I'm going to the zoo then ride some more."

It was the summer of 1936. Louis would be sixteen in a few weeks. President Roosevelt's reform program had given the nation a feeling of hope and some anxiety, but the greatest event of the year was Jesse Owens winning four gold medals in the Olympics. A Negro. Louis enjoyed new liberties that summer. On a few occasions he traveled with a Sunday school friend, Leonard, and sometimes with his friend Julius. Mostly, though, he went alone for its daring and just to make all decisions; thereby gaining more time to enjoy those precious Sunday afternoons.

Arriving at the zoo in early afternoon he found an immense crowd. It was Food Show Day. Booths lined the walkway on both sides. Food samples of all sorts were given away, thus Food Show Day as it was called. Louis stopped when he noticed something was missing. The large football-field-sized area stretching from the gate to the reptile building was bare. The huge wigwams were gone. He remembered just last year they were there, and now were gone. Partially blocking the emptiness were the canvas-topped booths. Indians once lived in this high-fenced campground, and there was display of how they and their ancestors lived. Everyone knew Indians hunted, fished, and planted food. They could do neither on the zoo grounds. He remembered his last visit and how he had seen young Indians who had suspiciously strong Caucasian features. Then even younger ones who wore gunnysack handmade shorts. What is this about man being made in the image of God? How can a man be on display unless one puts himself before and counts himself greater than the other?

Following along the trail were demonstrators hawking all sorts of gadgets, egg beaters, rug beaters, potatoes peelers, and fixes for anything broken. They made the difficult seem easy. They had medications to gain or lose weight, end fatigue, or grow hair. As they hawked their wares, they guaranteed everything. All items guaranteed needed at least a three-day trial, in which time all merchants would be long gone. Now in sight was the greatest attraction the zoo ever had, Suzie—the first and only trained gorilla ever in captivity. Three years ago, Louis remembered Suzie sat in a cage tied upon a flatbed trailer, chewing what looked to be bamboo or sugar cane. Last year the rebuilt monkey house showed Suzie's new quarters, a heavy iron-barred cage surrounded by glass where she did her thing. Her trainer was Jim Mussman, an extremely accomplished trainer with years of dedication to his work with animals. After Jim placed a large bib around her neck, Suzie would sit and eat from a plate. After eating, she would appear to make Jim the butt of her joke by turning to the crowd and showing her teeth in a laughing gesture. The crowd loved it. Louis's joy was tempered, however, by an article he recalled in *National Geographic* magazine. The article dealt with the capture of these beautiful and exotic animals. Their captors, wanting only the babies, killed the parents and sometimes an entire family to safely take the baby. Then, without provocation or warning, Suzie turned on Jim Mussman, seriously injuring him. This often happened when animals taken from the wild reached their teens.

Louis stood watching Suzie as he battled with his thoughts. He saw an animal taken from the wild, her parents, and her natural environment, to be caged the rest of her natural life for the entertainment of people, because she is so much like them. Louis then turned a very short distance to watch the huge display called Monkey Island. On an island made possible by a moat, this one species of monkeys went about their lives, doing all things possible without shame before their audience. Louis laughed as he remembered words written from talks by that great author and story teller Samuel Clemens, when he said, "God made man because he was disappointed with the monkey."

Louis turned again towards the zoo entrance, where the lines of food stands with the free samples began. Having only enough money to buy either a pop or a candy bar, he wanted to make a meal from the samples. At his first stop he noticed the foods he desired were advertised and displayed, but in much smaller portions than the year before. After one round of samples he was not nearly satisfied, so he went for another round then called the game. He rode the street cars a while before going home and get the most from that twenty-cent Sunday pass.

Louis had a new friend, Gene McDonald, who moved into the corner house downhill from 1709. Gene was only eleven years old, with a younger brother, Donald. Having gained the confidence of Gene's parents, Gene was allowed to venture away from home and into the wooded areas of the neighborhood. In this neighborhood, mixed but predominantly white, playmates were few. Though only eleven years of age, Gene was quite physical and daring, something Louis liked to see in a friend.

One Saturday in the summer, Louis and Gene traveled through the woods. Louis was quite familiar with the surroundings, and he explained everything to Gene. Down the bridle path, across the marshy field through the thick bushes, then ascending the hill beyond, they reached a place Louis was anxious to show Gene. Years ago, a very large tree had fallen across a small creek. Along with most boys in the neighborhood, Louis had crossed it many times. In a surprise move, Gene suddenly ran across. At one point he slipped, did a dance-like step, caught his balance, and quickly stood on the other side. Louis, following Gene, ran across, unintentionally slipping in the same location as Gene. He did the same steps as Gene, and landed just as he did. They laughed loudly at their acrobatics.

Across the railroad tracks from where Daawg lived on Printess Street, people had fashioned a park. They had made swings using ropes, chains, and old fire hoses hung from large trees. Kids played with hoops and old automobile tires. They jumped rope. They sat on hard-packed dirt playing jacks, jack straw, mumblety-peg, and tic-tac-toe by drawing in the dirt. The so-called park made by people on the street was meant for them alone, so Louis and his friend kept nearer their own ball park and the areas closer to home.

Louis and Gene were now within a stone's throw from this makeshift park. They could hear the laughter. Gene was excited and anxious to move closer. Louis was not, yet he did not want to spoil the day for Gene, so on they went climbing the hill toward the park. Suddenly they heard a long and vicious scream, followed by a second of silence. Then, as if everyone at the park was hollering at each other, their voices blended into something inaudible. Quite puzzled by the sounds they heard, Louis and Gene raced to the top of the hill and just beyond the trees to a spot where they could see what was happening. The makeshift park had suddenly become bare. The children had all retreated to the apartments where they lived and were standing in front. In the middle of Printess Street, walking as fast as she was able toward her home, was Dorothy Elcho. She was clutching her ripped up blouse to her chest. Her long hair was pulled from the ring that had bound it on one side. She wore knee pants, appeared very upset, and was crying.

"Daawg done it," said one.

"It were Daawg," said another.

"Yeah, it were Daawg," they answered to the questioning parents.

"Who's Daawg?" questioned Gene.

"That's him, Gene, the one walking like this," said Louis, demonstrating. "He pumps his body forward, then straightens up, then hits the ground hard with his feet like he's stomping clods of dirt in a cornfield. Look, he's going straight to his parents so he can tell them first and they gonna defend him in his lie. That's just what a punk would do," said Louis.

Dorothy Elcho was a beautiful girl of Italian immigrants. Olive-complexioned with picture-perfect, long, curly black hair, she was either adored or envied by all who met her. She was thirteen. Her parents, seemingly because of their landscape business or a desire for unity within the community, were outwardly friendly to all. Dorothy had no problems at school with the teacher or students. Only those on Printess Street who envied her left her to be abused, mostly verbally by her peers. She became somewhat isolated, being the oldest child with the responsibility of the trips to the store. By far the shortest route to the store on Hopkins was out her back gate, across Printess Street at Kahn. Her problem was only that Printess Street crowd of hillbillies, as they were called. Louis, however, refrained himself from the use of this language, as he in turn rebelled violently when called nigger.

Weeks later Louis and Gene walked to the low wall in front of the garage and sat. Suddenly, they heard sounds of excitement along with wheels churning and feet dragging the pavement. They turned and stood on the sidewalk to see two wagons racing down the sidewalk. The one in front was what was called a jitney or go-cart. It was a bootleg, a makeshift vehicle put together by any means. Following was a steel wagon, a store-bought job, steered by a kid of about nine or ten. Louis and Gene recognized that hunched over figure in the lead ride. Daawg! They wondered what had happened to him since that day at the makeshift park. Would he say anything about it without being asked? Probably not. They sat on the wall waiting for the two to return from the end of the ride. They returned, Daawg and his younger friend, talking to each other without a sign of recognition of Louis and Gene.

Being somewhat offended when Daawg passed in front of his own home and ignored him, Louis had other thoughts. "Wait a minute Gene, wait right there," said Louis. He ran into the house and to the door leading into the basement, reached inside, and pulled out one of Mama's shopping bags, then returned to the sidewalk. He went behind the garage and got one of the large concrete blocks Papa used when working on cars. He placed the concrete block inside the bag and put the bag in the middle of the sidewalk, in a way that the bag would appear empty. He looked up the street to see if he had been noticed and if they would take another ride down the hill. Yes, they would, and he fidgeted while waiting.

Daawg was in the lead again as he came through at top speed and struck the bag, thinking it was empty. Sliding off his ride, uninjured, he turned to Louis, charging him with the words, "You did that." Louis did not hesitate. He charged back. They fought furiously the way children fight, throwing rights and lefts, left followed always by rights, no variations. They pushed and shoved. Louis heard ringing in his ear. His nose always bled, so he fought on with a fearless attack. Daawg backed away, putting his hand to his mouth to check the bleeding. Showing signs of not wanting to fight any longer, Daawg looked up from his bloody hand and said,

"Damn you, nigger, damn you." Louis was now angrier than before and wanted to inflict some serious pain on Daawg.

He charged Daawg again in fury, again with lefts and rights to an already defeated enemy. He pounded Daawg, saying, "You want some, nigger, I'll give you some, nigger!"

Daawg backed off and covered his mouth with a bloody hand while his ten-year-old friend screamed, "Stop, stop, please stop!" Partly in defense of his friend, Daawg grabbed his ride and started dragging it back up the hill while Louis watched.

Daawg again tested his lip with his hand, then looked back while continuing on his way, saying, "Damn you, damn you."

Louis raised his arm, waved his hand as if to say good-bye. "Go home, dog, go home," he said.

January 1937

As soon as dinner was finished, Papa would look at his watch, then he timed his exit from the kitchen to the living room perfectly. He would turn on our radio in perfect time to get the seven o'clock evening news. We all sat around the radio listening. We heard no news of our local leaders, city councilman, entertainers like the Mills Brothers, or any national news from the aftermath of the 1936 Olympics. Nothing of the annexation of Ethiopia by Italy or the fighting back. The news of Amelia Earhart topped the news—she was missing somewhere in the Pacific Ocean. The news ended with the announcement that the Ohio River was at a flood stage. W.C. Devereaux, the city meteorologist, predicted the warm temperatures would be reduced to freezing, ending the flooding. This weather report came nightly without much concern. Still, in the depression we could not reconcile another disaster. We were bombarded with the threat of flooding in our city. How would a flood of the city affect us? The threat continued with each newscast. Then we heard the East End was hardest hit, with gas service cut off to many homes. Shallow water covered many streets in the Mill Creek Valley, hampering traffic days. In following newscasts, the news of the flood became first rather than last, as conditions worsened. Suddenly there were evacuations of homes, forcing many to leave. We listened as we were told of rats forced out by the flooding, and people being rescued from the second floor and sometimes the roofs of homes. Aerial photographs of the city's neighborhoods now under water filled the newspapers. The little Miami River along with the Mill Creek flooded their banks, forcing evacuations. W.C. Devereau continued to predict a crest, yet the rain and warm temperature continued. The flow from the mountainous Rockies around Pittsburgh and the Allegheny and Monongahela Rivers continued.

The flooding continued its devastation, now washing away homes, heavily damaging and destroying California homes in all of what is now Queensgate, Linwood, and the East End. Along the Little Miami in Kentucky, Newport, Covington, Ludlow, Bellevue, and Dayton were hard hit and now without water and electricity. We continued school in Norwood daily, then listened to the news each night of the worsening condition of nearly forty percent of our neighboring communities who were now living two and often three families in two rooms. We lived in Norwood, a city whose water came from four artesian wells. Grandpa Williams and our cousins, the Walkers, in Woodlawn are safe. Aunt Hattie in Avondale is safe. Big sister Lillian is on Sixth Street Hill where much is visible yet she was protected. Grandpa Gardner, with Irene and Melvin, along with Fannie, Mama's youngest sister, lived in the West End. They have no telephone and have no cars. We did not hear from them, so we all pray. The river, along with its tributaries, continues to rise. Cincinnati's two water treatment plants, both necessarily by the river, are suddenly under water for more than two weeks. There would be no water for the city residents. Residents were told to fill their bathtubs.

There was a knock at the kitchen door. Papa answered, seeing a tall, dark figure dressed in a chauffeur's uniform with a cap and gloves. The man introduced himself as Arthur Goodin. He pretended to know Papa, whom he called Ralph. Arthur wanted water for his employers, whom Papa seemed to recognize by name yet he did not really know. We could easily tell that. Papa was a chauffeur himself, but he did not like and in fact refused to wear a uniform. Arthur quickly switched his persona to a plea for some water for his seemingly beloved employers. He reached into his pocket and came up with some quarters, which Papa accepted. Arthur then went to his limousine at the curb, returning with a large glass twenty-gallon jug. He filled the jug, took it to the car, and returned with another. Arthur filled the second jug, thanked Papa and said, "I'll see you when this runs out." It must have run out before the night, because Arthur was back the next morning with more empty jugs. He brought a helper along. He then came the third day with another chauffeur and the three of them carried six or seven jugs of water. Now, because Norwood was endeavoring to help as much as possible in this disastrous flood, our water pressure was much lower than normal. Arthur was now interfering by coming while Mama was cooking. He came when dishes were being washed. There was but one faucet at 1709. The kitchen had a dining room table to accommodate a family of ten. We used an additional small table for the youngest, making for cramped conditions. Arthur and his helper would come often at precisely the wrong time. They squeezed between the tables with those large jugs. They held the door for one another when carrying these jugs. It was January, and the kitchen would quickly lose its heat and we caught chills. They acted as if their job of supplying water for their employers was all-important. Then Papa suspected he was being used. They were taking water to more than their employers. Papa's benevolence had its limit.

Sunday came. It was called black Sunday, because it was the worst day of the flood. Now without water, the city was without electricity. Papa loaded all into the car to ride through the devastated areas of the city. This event was historic. Never again would this be seen. We returned with a realization of having been spared. We were blessed. The news was now that the river had reached its crest. It would take twelve days before the river would be back to sixty feet, still above flood stage. Monday, however, Arthur returned for water. We were again at dinner. Papa's back was at the door and stood the brunt of the cold air as they went in and out. They seemed to take so much time. We watched the expression on Papa's face as he only grunted. Arthur attempted to bring humor. Papa was clearly disturbed. While squeezing between the tables where we all pulled ourselves closer to the table to accommodate him, Arthur's helper said, "Oops." This disrespect and lack of appreciation was more than this protective Papa could take. He thought they should have been more polite. Papa stepped outside in the cold January air to tell Arthur where he could go and he could get his water there. We laughed. We did not think Arthur would get any water where Papa told him to go.

Spring of 1938

When I was just a kid from the country I sometimes went into Bucktown just to see what went on there. There was this big buck of a Negro who stood much more than my six two. They called him Big Bubba.

Now Bucktown, as one would expect, was a haven for recently-arriving Negroes from the south. It was the location of many landings by slaves in the distant past. They lived or existed in those wooded unpainted row houses without plumbing or electricity. Having few skills other than farming or picking cotton, they waited and hoped to be picked up for any type of job or service work, while surviving by grit, wit, and wisdom. On Sunday they had church from the small front rooms or porches and the crowds filled the sidewalks and spilled sometimes into the street. In summer months they had church by the riverside where they prayed and praised the Lord with singing and had baptisms

On Saturdays, though, it was different. Out came the made-up guitars and banjos, which originated from the motherland of Africa. They had drums of many descriptions and sometimes a piano so beat up it was missing keys, but they played, danced, and hollered the blues in a chanting rhythm. The whole street was filled with the revelry. There were some who existed for this time of excitement, and there were those who profited by selling food and especially whiskey. Suddenly, sometimes after midnight, without provocation or warrant came a contingent of white police officers with billy clubs. In their mind, the assignment was to put those Negroes in their place, to quiet them down. "What's all this ranting and raving about?" they said. The real motive was fear. They feared rebellion. With all the mistrust and misunderstanding they stood at Broadway and Second Street in full force, ready to clear the street and bring the neighborhood to silence. Then along came Big Bubba, who stood face to face before the oncoming police and challenged their very reason for being there. Big Bubba took the challenge for the neighborhood. He took their beating and suffered, and was cuffed and led off to jail. He had protected the neighborhood on his own. By the time Big Bubba was locked up, and the police returned, the neighborhood was quiet. Big Bubba was happy and proud when released, feeling he had done a big service to and for his people.

When the city wanted to test a Negro to take the job of policing Bucktown, I was urged to apply because of my age, size, and demeanor. I could not handle that job. "I believe in law and order, but not beating of my own because of a lack of understanding," said Papa.

At that barbershop I had a different kind of experience. Mr. Sid Crew came into the shop for a shoe shine very late, in fact the last minutes before an early closing as the cloudy weather had caused business to be very slow. Mr. Crew was the man who has the builder's supply company across the street from the shop. He also owned the barber shop building—he was the landlord and had a garage for his trucks behind the shop. Mr. Crew was quiet and seemed to have a burdened mind.

Mr. Saunders, my boss and the shop owner, was reserved and wanted to ask questions. "What's the occasion, Sid, you're getting a shoe shine this late on a cloudy day"?

"Well," answered Mr. Crew, "I'm going to the Union Hall. They are telling me how to run my business."

"Is that a problem?" asked Mr. Saunders, the barber.

"Yes it is," answered Mr. Crew. "They are telling me who should and who should not drive these new concrete mixing trucks I'm getting. They want me to deny opportunities for those Negro employees."

Answered Clarence, "It's a deep concern they have, and maybe they have a need to protect their jobs and future." He said this after having heard conversations by his union member customers.

"No," said Sid Crew. "Listen, I started this business long ago. Those Negro boys were all that I had and we made this business what it is. You remember me telling how I came here with fifteen dollars, found this railroad side yard, and was told I had to have a business plan? The only thing I could do was builder's supply. I had no money for a bigger venture. So I bought it. Then for more than two years together, summer and winter, Jeff, Willie, and I heaved sand, gravel, lead, and clay pipe to make a go of this business. Now they want to tell me who I can hire or promote because of these new concrete mixer trucks. No, I'll fight to the last for justice! This country is in a struggle. It's 1938. Hitler in *Mein Kampf* has already said what he is going to do. We have to do what we have to and it will take us all. I'm a stubborn Brit, as you know Clarence. I must declare myself. I'm for the right and it's the best for all of us over time."

"I like Mr. Crew, Papa."

"Yes," answered Papa. "There are those whites who will deny you, and do all they can to keep you from any kind of success. You have to believe and keep pressing 'cause there is someone out there who understands and will give you the very chance you need to succeed."

Note

Compromise was reached with the union. Two Negroes were to drive the new concrete mixers at the increased level of pay. The third Willie was to stay on local flatbed delivery until other trucks were added to the fleet or a vacancy existed. Though Willie was not promoted before his retirement, it was a victory for Sid Crew. Willie himself was a community activist who quietly accepted his position.

Mr. Sid Crew was an immaculate dresser. He was perfectly groomed from head to toe, even well-manicured. If you did not like him for his looks, you had to admire him for his personality, for he was what he believed and he believed in justice for his fellow man, color un-accountable.

Mr. Clarence Saunders was also very immaculate dresser. Always in a color complementing his pink skin and gray hair, blues but mostly gray. Mr. Saunders, however, flowed with the current of public opinion. He was not strong on his convictions. Thus, when I left the shop to work in the bowling alley, I left with much appreciation for the experiences I had gained as well as some of the advice Mr. Saunders had attempted to pass on. However, I had little regret in leaving. I worked two weeks, without a change of mind as he had probably expected, which meant working two jobs two weeks, which I happily survived.

LATER IN 1938

We were in the home of Julia and Sarah Durham, those sisters for whom Papa has so long worked. Sarah had passed some five months before. Now Julia was gone. Her funeral was the next day. We, by request of the bank, were to stay at their home on nights for the days needed to appraise and make preparation for the auction.

I had already explored the house, pulled the tassel to summons the butler who had never existed. I explored the basement, finding many unexpected saved or preserved items, food preserved and wines packed in straw. In the library with its French provincial furniture were shelves of books I wanted to explore but time would not allow. I wondered what would happen to that Pierce Arrow automobile, who would enjoy it? Then I thought about the kitchen, where the cook, Marie, had allowed me to taste so many of her delicacies: German chocolate cake, chicken and rice, pumpernickel bread, and that most delightful of delicacies, squab on toast. That delicacy most people I know had never experienced or even knew what it really was. Marie the cook had been so gracious as to educate me on the finer foods and some drinks, like orange juice and apple cider. I explored the bedrooms with sorrow as I passed where Papa had sat beside Julia, who was the manager of all things, steadying her hand while she signed a check, which would be for the entire week's wages and expenses. I remembered how Papa would patiently wait for the two sisters to climb into the car, for a shopping trip to the country or just a joy ride. When his patience waned he would take Sarah like a doll and place her onto a back seat. I would look with astonishment, she would look back with an accepting smile like this was okay. On such trips Papa was always allowed to add on a chicken or even a turkey in timely fashion. I suddenly realized how much they had really meant to the family. Now I knew but what could I do in appreciation? I was there to protect property only until the auction. I hoped there was some benefit for them.

Note

Papa went on to the Delco plant in Norwood. Marie sent for her German high school sweetheart the year before. He worked as a mechanic then they were married and opened a bakery on Montana Avenue in Western Hills. I went to the Wright Aeronautical Plant in Lockland until drafted. After the war (WWII), I found the bakery was on Montana Avenue. It was fifteen years too late to meet the originals. Marie and Papa received an inheritance of one thousand dollars each, which now reached fifteen hundred dollars. This was due to one of the sisters who outlived Julia because of a drastic accident and had lived in an asylum. I will always remember that at age of fifteen I began to appreciate the good and feel the effects of the bad.

Ms. Epps

Bold and erect, she sat behind that big wooden desk. She graded papers, or whatever it is that teacher's do at the point in their day when the next class files into the room. Ms. Epps was a substitute teacher. On this day she was filling in for Ms. Goodman, who had been absent for several weeks. None of the students knew why she was gone. Ms. Epps was not liked by many. She showed open favoritism. There was no great anticipation for her presentations, as she embodied her family and herself into her history lessons.

She glorified the southern past. She was self-centered and ignored the somewhat subtle responses of the students. Ms. Epps traveled fifteen miles from Franklin, Kentucky daily to fill this vacancy. She felt this was a testimony as to how greatly she was needed, ignoring her own need to supplement her meager retirement income. She sat behind the desk, seldom ever moving throughout her presentation. She was old, obviously beyond all others at Allison Street Elementary. A small woman by weight and stature, she was not the formidable figure she wanted to project. Her hair was totally white, much like the wigs of George Washington or the ancient British Parliament. This was her front. She wanted to portray herself as a link to the past and more glorious days; but her past was more likely troubled. Thin and nearly lipless, her skin was wrinkled and her deep blue eyes seemed to reveal her real character. She was more likely to gain pity than the adoration she desired.

Still sitting behind the desk, she told the last student who entered to close the door. Then when all were seated, she scanned the room with her eagle eyes. Without any type of greeting, she went directly to her planned presentation. "I'm here through great difficulty today," she said. "Uh hum. This extreme cold weather we're having and the distance I must travel from Franklin, Kentucky has been extremely difficult. Today I want to reward you for being so attentive in class by reading you a story as it is so near Christmas. I'm going to read to you from a book that has been in my family for many, many years. The story dates back to antebellum years. To those who don't know, antebellum means before the conflict; the conflict meaning the Civil War. This was a great period in our country's history, when we grew from colonies to the great nation we are now."

Just listening to Ms. Epps I knew something was coming that I would not like. Then I remembered that sticks and stones can't break my bones. *Forget that*, I thought, *I'll just pretend to listen, yet show no emotions, joy, or sorrow as she reads.* Ms. Epps herself was in a position new to her. Cities in northern Kentucky close to Cincinnati, like Newport and Covington, had mixed classes. Ms. Epps, from Franklin, had no previous experience with colored people. Having just one colored class member, she would just ignore the situation and run rampant above and beyond his conscience. As she continued reading, she occasionally paused to gauge the class's reception of the story, as she well knew it was new to everyone. Soon she read a portion of the story about a nigger and his piece of chicken. Suddenly, I was outraged. She scanned the class again.

She paused and looked directly at me while the class stopped in response and turned to look at me. "If you don't like the story you can go out in the hall." I had never been so outraged before. I was stunned and did not know how to handle this. I simply continued to sit. Ms. Epps read another sentence or two then stopped again. "I said, if you don't like the story, you can go in the hall." I did. When I was in that cold hallway, I was outraged again when the thought came to me that she wanted me to leave before the story got more ridiculously racist and bigoted.

How could she do this? Why? I had done nothing. I should have said something. I didn't know what to say. She was so ugly. Everything about her was ugly. Her nose was like the stem on a Thanksgiving pumpkin. Cut off too short. Like God gave her the right to make her own, and greedily she got too much and had to cut some off. She was ugly. I hated her. I wish someone would confront me. I would beat their face in. A white one would be better. What of those who were my friends? Singled out and ridiculed before them. Again why? I stiffened my body, attempting to curb the pain and release some of the anger. I could do neither. Tears began to form uncontrollably. I did not want anyone to see me cry. Slowly, I began to walk the hall, collecting my thoughts. My brother was already in the locker when I arrived. One set of checkers and a board had been brought by the janitor. He knew the boys' and girls' locker rooms were the only warm rooms outside of the classrooms on such a cold day. My brother was sitting in front of the checkerboard and he was beating everyone. I knew he would. I watched as he motioned for each player to take the first move. Then he would beat them. No one beat him. I watched with pride. My brother played Papa and Papa was the best. Papa beat all extended family members and any challenger. He gave no one a chance to win. You must earn it. You had to beat him to win. My brother stayed with him game after game, relentlessly, until he found the answer. I'll never forget his smile the first time he beat Papa. They played each other on winter days like this one. They played, I watched. They never gave away their secrets and I never ever beat either of them.

I walked the length of the first-floor hallway and to the basement boys' room. I passed the principal's office. I observed Ms. Edwards on the phone, sitting behind her desk. Ms. Edwards was a large woman, likely more than two hundred pounds, and hair red as fire. What is it they say about red-haired women? Scornful! I don't know what it really means, but if you come by her you better be right. She would blister you with words or her paddle. Now I was once more by Ms. Epps's door. I thought I should have noticed the time on that big office clock. I must have had another half hour or more to stand in the cold hall. Then I remembered coming from this same room in early September. Ms. Goodman had sent the class to the gym for some demonstration. When we were leaving, something happened with the first two students leaving the classroom. They ran screaming down the hall past Ms. Edwards's office. The entire class followed, screaming. As they passed her office we heard nothing. She was probably on the phone. I started to run. Rushing to the hallway, Ms. Edwards observed the situation and summoned me to her office. "What is all this running and hollering?" she asked.

"I was running but I was not hollering," I said. Ms. Edwards knew I was one of the quiet ones and was not hollering as I stated.

"Well now, at least you are honest. I'll excuse you. I know some of these other hooligans are going to say it wasn't them. You are excused. You may leave."

Again I left my station outside Ms. Epps's door. Down the hallway and to the boys' bathroom, I went. When returning, I alerted Ms. Edwards in my passing and was called into her office.

"Why are you just loitering in the hallways? I saw you on two occasions passing my office and all in this third bell. Why are you not in your classroom?"

"She told me to leave," I said.

"What? I'll see about this." She told me to take a seat. She took papers from her desk, put them into a drawer, then shut the drawer. As soon as the end of class bell rang she motioned for me to come follow her. She went directly to Ms. Epps's room, where the class was filing out. We waited. With the room emptied, I went to get my books. I walked from the classroom hearing the blistering words of Ms. Edwards to Ms. Epps. "I'm in full charge here, your lesson material is given you and anything else you use must be approved by me. Do you understand Annie Epps?" I quickly turned to get a glimpse of Ms. Epps's face, but Ms. Edwards' body completely hid the little weasel. I strolled to my fourth-bell class, happy that Ms. Epps got what she deserved.

Sport

As a child I was known to be borderline sickly. We learned early that my stomach could not hold cow's milk. One Thanksgiving day I started vomiting at Aunt Marie' s house after eating a salad containing celery. After this I could not eat anything with celery, including most stuffing and dressing. My second grade teacher once bought milk and cookies for me. She stopped after observing my returning the partially-consumed bottles, which I could not drink, yet did not inform her. My sister Mabel's suitor and future husband who worked at Martha Washington, an ice cream and candy store, often would give me a small bag of delicious chocolates. I sometimes did not share them and would become sick. I became sick with stomach pains after eating green apples gathered in the wooded area nearby. I also suffered fallen arches, recovering only after wearing arch supports for several years.

On a beautiful, sunshiny day on my way from Allison Street School, I suddenly realized a stray puppy was walking alongside me. The poor thing was a curb setter, not trained in any way. Just a lost an uncared for and unwanted mongrel. During the depression, many pets were ejected from their homes because of a scarcity of food. Many who were unemployed were unable to accept another mouth to feed, so they simply abandoned their pets by any means possible. They dropped them off on some lonely highway, or by extreme neglect. The puppy continued walking alongside of me. When I stopped, he stopped. He came close, sad-eyed yet expressing friendliness by wagging his tail constantly. His thin body and unkempt appearance, with such a wire-like coat, made me hesitant to pet him. My feelings were for companionship, his was for survival. There was little chance I could burden my family with another mouth to feed, especially one that barks. I was backed into a corner.

No one would feel as I do. *This dog needs me*, I thought. *I'll feed him I'll find a way.* I knew he would have to stay outside—Papa's rules. I approached Mama and said, "Can I have something to feed this puppy? He seems so hungry."

"Son, this is no time to bring another mouth to feed. There is nothing here just now. Maybe after dinner there might be something. What's his name?"

I had not thought of a name this soon, but remembering some of Papa's stories, I said, "Sport." Mama didn't say anything else, she just went to her preparation of dinner. I now knew keeping Sport would be at my peril, and I began to question my own will to feed the mongrel from my own meager portions. After dinner, I gave Sport a mere pinch of food.

Still my thoughts were to take care of him. *I'll make him a pet to be proud of, that's what I'll do*, I thought. Mama said nothing that would indicate a commitment he would be fed. That's not like Mama. What's worse, Papa knowingly said nothing. My faith was waning. Why couldn't my Sport be comforted? He sniffed at my hands. Hunger was the cause. His last feeding must have been by hand. He sniffed continuously at the remnants of food stains on my unwashed hands. He licked my fingers. I pulled back my hand, fearing his next move would be to bite. I look again at this thin, big-footed animal who walked badly, asking for pity. He found it in me. He tweaked my sympathetic vein like nothing before. I was convinced I must take care of this homeless creature. He just had to make it through the night.

While sitting on the front steps, just Sport and I, my mind began to wonder. Where had he come from? Why did he leave? What might have been his fate had he not followed me? What if I could travel free like him?

When darkness approached, Mama came to the door to say, "It's time to come in." She held open the door, then closed it between Sport and me. Suddenly I realized my Sport was not only hungry, but he had not been given water. I went to the front window, looking out to see Sport.

"Oh, don't you worry about that thing, he's just a dog," said an older sister.

"Papa had a dog named Sport, and he was a champion hunting dog," I said. "Sport might save someone's life someday.

"He's still a dog and he's half past dead," she responded.

"Send him home," said another. I could not stand the laughter. I went to my room, badly hurt that I had convinced no one Sport was worthy.

On awakening, I rushed to the window to see if Sport was still at the bottom of the outside steps where I had last seen him, as I wasn't allowed outside before breakfast. I could see no Sport. After breakfast, I went outside, desperately in search of Sport, and was struck by the strangest phenomena. Somehow, a fine powdery dust had ever so lightly settled on all outside surfaces. This powdery substance was earth itself, and not visible across the lawn. The slightest breeze would move it into cracks in the sidewalk or take it airborne. The evening news would explain that this dusting came from those earlier mentioned disasters in the far west, particularly Oklahoma, where a drought left newly-plowed fields in ruin. Now a dust bowl was all that was left. The winds of change brought the dust, to be settled in its easterly path. We were in that path. The news continued related stories in the following days. John Steinbeck's novel, *Grapes of Wrath*, tells the miserable tale of a family already in poverty, who are flushed out of their homes during the Great Depression by a drought that turns their homeland into a wasteland. We were reminded that others have life as hard as did, if not worse.

I went to the window again, looking out for my Sport. My elder siblings again caught my emotions with remarks and questioning.

"What are you looking for, little brother?"

"He is gone, forget it."

"He is better off and so are you. Forget it let it be. Just let it be."

THE BAPTISMS

"No, we are not stopping at the Waller's," proclaimed Papa. "Every time when it's time to leave you guys are all scattered out at the Waller's, some at the farm and some on the road in between, it's too much back and forth."

"Okay, Papa, then just slow down when we get there," said one of the older ones. Everyone laughed, all knowing Papa would relent. He indeed would drop the older ones off if he didn't stop. We, however, must be mindful of what he said.

Soon there was a large gathering in front of the Waller home, two large families of cousins along with some neighborhood children who could not resist joining in. Being students of similar schools in Norwood and Wyoming, they had many a story to tell. The twins, Mary and Dorothy, told how they fooled the teachers who could not differentiate one from the other. Harriet told about walking to the store on Vine Street following an ad recently circulated in the neighborhood where silk stockings were ten cents at the dime store. When she got there, the stockings were ten cents per leg.

"That Ms. Palmer is foul," said one. "She knows I do all my work. I get grades as good as anybody in class and she gives me a lousy C. 'Oh the C is for colored sister.'" Another told of going on that pre-Christmas trip downtown that the many schools took. They would be taken by bus downtown to see the decorated windows at Shillito's and Mabley & Carew. The bus would drop the class off at one store then pick them up after they walked to the other. They told how another Negro would think they were lost, since they were the only Negro in the group. The Wallers would turn heads around in history class when telling how their father was a WWI pensioned veteran and their grandfather was in the Civil War. Many classmates simply wondered how this could have happened. They told of a Mr.

Martin and Ms. Stewart (school teachers) who showed affection for one another yet attempted to pretend innocence.

I told them about how the students of Mr. Humphries's homeroom stood at the classroom window one day watching Woodrow, the citywide drunk. He staggered along the school's iron picketed fence, struggling mightily to keep his feet. I felt sorry for him. I don't know why the others did not. Why were they not ashamed then, because Woodrow was white? Mr. Humphries, the teacher, interrupted by saying progress is what we need and drunken people can't do it. "Come class, let's get to the lesson," he said.

The group of kids talked about experiencing violent racial epithets without cause, and often pressed to a point of causing immediate retaliation. They felt their accomplishments ignored. Their papers unfairly graded. Through bigotry and hatred they had survived. When our children are not able to express their greatest potential in a competitive school, they are assumed to be inherently unequal. This is what our parents feared.

The sun shone bright and the temperature was high on this Sunday in August. Someone shouted. "They are baptizing in the creek! Right over there," they said, pointing toward the intersection.

I remembered a year ago this same thing happened and I was stopped with the words, "You are too little, you must stay here. You cannot go." This time I grabbed Cecelia and Ralph Jr.'s hand. This would be my first time to an outside baptism.

On the way I saw Sue Baker, the little coquette, standing on the mud path before her house. She used to make me blush tomato red. Today she stood still, looking. She saw me but she didn't show that whoop de doo like before.

The little creek that came from the natural spring that began on the top side of grandpa's farm mostly fed this creek. Here it swelled to an ideal place for a baptism for the church, which was just beyond the tree line and across Grove Road. We stood on the grassy slope above the creek and the hard-packed earth where the small congregation was beginning to gather. The minister stood, his back to the creek, facing the small gathering that included parents of those who were to be baptized. He held a red leather-bound Bible and wore white robes. On cue, they began to sing "Take Me to the Water" in that old Baptist way, slow and with great feeling. At the same time, eight children came from beyond the tree line, singing along. They were robed in hand-sewn white cloth. They carried crosses made from wood lath, tied with string and painted white. As they came closer to the water's edge where the minister stood, the singing seemed to get louder. They waded in the water and sang as the scene unfolded before us like a movie. We stood quietly and reverently, star struck by this emotional event.

The Family Homecoming

First, it was Papa's Model A Ford that pulled unto the grounds of Grandpa's farm, followed closely by two other jalopies, all filled to capacity, mostly with screaming, energetic children of all ages. They were filled with so much joy for the occasion they pushed and jostled with one another. Uncle Jake stepped in to hug each one, oblivious of the screaming and hollering, as he was deaf. He then retreated to a shady spot beside the door of his room at the rear of Grandpa's house.

There was a hustle and bustle as the tables were set up. The cookout fire had started earlier. After unloading the automobiles, Papa, Uncle Les, Uncle Bill, Uncle Tiller, and two of Grandpa's friends, Mr. Whitaker and Harrison Picket, seated themselves beneath the large tree closest to the picnic tables. First, the smoke, then the smell of hot food mingled with what was being put on the tables kept them in the area. There would be no activities, no baseball or horseshoe, until after the meal.

Uncle Fred was asked how he found such a good wife so soon after coming from the south. He answered with a long dialogue ending with his southern charm. Aunt Lucy, his wife, who was preparing the tables along with the other women, overheard him. She stepped out and said, "It's a depression and he had a job." Everyone laughed, including Uncle Fred.

After a dinner, which only Mama could have prepared along with her sisters, two of whom were professional cooks, the games began. Most all of the age groups played baseball. They then paired off for horseshoes. Along with the smaller ones, I began to run out of energy, so when the hide and seek began I ventured back beside Papa. I heard someone ask Grandpa what happened to his dog. "Well now," said Grandpa, "I keep corn and hay for the livestock.

146

The dog only wanted fresh meat, which is a scarce item around here, so I guess he's back in the wild if he is living at all."

Knowing Papa was fascinated with automobiles, he was asked about that new Ford which was commonly called a Tin Lizzy. Papa told them he met another Ford at a crossroad, whose driver seemed to want to challenge him on the open road. Papa, who was not a good storyteller, explained how he "dusted off" the fellow and his car in good fashion. "What time was it?" asked Mr. Harrison. He answered his own question with, "Tin after tin," laughing and patting Papa on the back.

Mr. Whitaker loudly cleared his throat with his gruff voice and began to talk. It's as if they were waiting for him. "You know," he began, "in the Civil War, the union army under General Sherman chased General Lee into Vicksburg, Tennessee. General Sherman's army was growing day by day with the freeing of the slaves. And don't you know, Lee's forces were dwindling by deserters who could clearly see the end was coming. Lee faced total destruction. That's when ole' Mossa was running, rifle in hand, across the field followed closely by his slave. 'Mossa, Mossa why do you run so?' called out the slave. 'I'm running 'cause I can't fly!' Mossa cried out.'" Though they had all heard the story many times, all laughed and some clapped as a compliment to Mr. Whitaker for being a great storyteller.

Uncle Les, a veteran of World War I, showed no sentiment for a war story. He had been mustard gassed by the Germans, was pensioned, and had a visible blemish from the effects. He simply advised and encouraged his and all kids.

Uncle Bill began to say, "In the spring I walked from Walnut Hills all the way to the Mill [the Cincinnati Milling Machine Company] looking for work. They took my name and told me to come back and I might be hired later. Hurt and with little choice, I turned toward home. On Lincoln Avenue, I saw a white fellow trying to fix a flat tire on his Ford. He did not know how to right the jack under the axle. I liked a white man having to listen to me. I had already told him I was looking for work, so when we finished he gave me a rightly good tip. Then, as if to be glad to get away from that colored neighborhood, he was gone. I looked at the tip, and as the time was yet early, I found my way to the racetrack." He hesitated. "Would you believe everything I bet on was a winner? When I got home, first off Lucy was steaming like a teakettle. I put the money on the kitchen table and she changed just like that," he said while snapping his fingers. Bet on a horse? I didn't understand that part. That is like when they say a man at a club was so disorderly the judge gave him two days and five dollars. How do you punish somebody by giving them time and money? I do not understand that either.

In Cincinnati, the late summer days are long, though on these occasions time goes like the wind. The sky darkens, the moon quickly rises. Everyone rises from their seats, knowing they must respect the time. Sleep is necessary for the children and the employed. While walking to their automobiles, they complimented each other on their previously prepared dishes. They ask for recipes while seemingly straining to remember them. They share words of advice and encouragement for the betterment of all. The agony of separation was being tempered by true joy of family. That was the feeling expressed by all and felt by even the smallest child.

As Papa was the first to arrive, we would certainly be the last to leave. We experienced all that was to be on this day from the beginning to the peaceful but agonizing end.

Soon we were out and down the road. Papa behind the wheel, Mama beside him, pregnant and holding the ninth child. Jeannette was on Mama's knees. Ralph Jr. sat between them, causing me envy. The others, Mabel, Cecelia, Francis, Della, and I were crowded on the back seat. Lillian, now twenty, was riding with Aunt Hattie. Already there were cries. "Your elbow is poking me, its hurting my stomach. Get your head up, you're hurting my arm. Scoot up, you are too heavy on my leg."

The many thoughts of the day passed as I looked back from the open window to see the small house, two small buildings and the huge tree, silhouetted against a starry summer sky. Going down along the Ohio River with Papa's brother, Uncle Bill, Aunt Lucy, and the girls—Della, May, and Laura—was fun. The church picnic at Burnette Woods was fun, but nothing came close to being at Grandpa's.

Papa, Mama, and Ralph Jr. are yet awake on the front seat. I alone strained to keep awake in the back seat, due to Papa's smooth, careful driving. I looked at Papa as he slightly relaxed himself behind the wheel after doing the gears and pedals. I wanted to ask if I could get in the front seat, but no, I would ask too many questions. Like, "Can I hold the wheel?" Papa was patient only to a point when questioned. "Why do you burn that tire patcher?"

"To melt and fuse the patch to the tube is why."

"What does it do when you push your foot down on the gas pedal?"

"It shoots gas into the carburetor," he would say, leaving me with more questions.

I turned to look at Mama, who was yet awake and holding Jeanette. I did not really know, but I gathered from the older women talking that Mama was swollen with another child. Mama would be going to the hospital for some nights. One of Mama's sisters would come to check on the little ones, though Mabel and Cecelia thought they could control them. Mama would come home with a new Boo. I know how it is when you are the Boo and mama comes home with a new Boo. You are not Mama's Boo anymore, and it hurts.

When jilted by the silence of being ignored, I retreated to the pile of warm, sleeping bodies on the back seat.

A Shy Guy

It's a late summer day. My birthday just passed. I'm thirteen. There was no party. No cake even. They just wished me a happy birthday. No anger or hard feelings, there now are ten siblings. There are just eight children at home now. I don't know about other families like those at church. Maybe they never have enough of many things, and especially money, like us. At thirteen I am scrutinizing every change taking place within me. I don't like being teased by my older sisters. Then I feel good and proud when I know they really want the best for me. When I feel down I go to my mama, volunteering to help with whatever she is doing, just longing to hear her comforting words. I sense a spirit-like closeness with her. She makes me feel special. Then some days I meet Papa at the garage where I find myself wanting to spend one-on-one time with him. There I recall the days going to the market or to the country in that limousine. Then I help him wipe down the car, or sit beside him on the front seat of the car, and I feel that same closeness to him. What is this I really feel? Is there a message? I don't really know. Is this my greatest time of life like my older sisters say? I don't think so.

"I reckon if you are going to that party, it's high time you get yourself ready," someone reminded me. Even at thirteen I'm not really excited about someone else's birthday party, especially this Mayday Pennington. Her mother is so bossy with everyone. Ralph has gone to some parties and he thinks they are great. He even danced with several of those who were known as celebrity types. He has stories to tell about what happened at those parties. Me, I don't know. I'm somehow not excited about this thing of a party. I don't know how to dance. Maybe that's it. I don't how know to be sociable like I'm expected even. My dominating sisters would agree, saying you are as green as grass, you are not ready.

I had prepared myself. I was to walk to Leonard's house on Rockdale Avenue. We would walk to the Pennington house on Beresford. After the party, though it would be late, I would catch the bus to Norwood.

When turning to say goodbye I felt a singling-out importance, a part of growing up. I could remember my older siblings saying goodbye to other family members on just this kind of occasion. Now I'm feeling it for the first time. Surprisingly it's a good feeling. Now having been told how to act and what to do by my elders who had experienced what I would be facing, my thoughts wandered. What was this party really going to be like?

Mrs. Pennington answered the door. Mayday, her daughter, was wearing an apron just like her mother. Monique, her cousin, was there also, helping with the preparations. They all recognized me, however Leonard's cordiality gained all their attention. I said "Hi." They motioned for us to go into the dining room where there were chairs. I noticed the table had been taken out, then took the farthest seat. Soon after, Mrs. Pennington came into the room to start a game that would assure the eight party participants would know each other by name. It rattled me when they called me Louis. I was accustomed to Slick or Tony at home. Sitting farthest from the kitchen, I was the last to be served. The ice cream and homemade chocolate cake was delicious. We all could have consumed more, even the girls. Then there was no one who could initiate a conversation that would include all eight party members.

Mrs. Pennington returned to the room holding one of those Mae West bottles named after that movie star, because of its shape. It was a six-ounce Coca Cola bottle. "Now that we know each other, we are going to play spin the bottle," announced Mrs. Pennington, as this was the focal point of the party. I just felt something when I saw the bottle. I heard about the game from my friend Julius. He said he liked it but I got goose pimples as soon as I saw what was coming. I have never played it but I knew what it was about. I was not ready for playing with girls like this at thirteen, either. It made me squeamish. I hoped the bottle never stopped at me. Oh, oh no, my goodness it was just the second time. It was that Betty Weathers, with the cold hands, who wore those short-skirted shirtwaist dresses. Her warmhearted smile made you forget things. My flesh crawled when she sat next to me. I backed off or at least I tried to without making a show of it. I leaned sideways, but the bottle was too directly pointed at me. I looked at her, but not directly. More like down at the floor. "Well," said Betty while I continued to look down at the floor, "you don't gotta do it." Her words did not relieve me or hide my blushing face. I felt every eye was on me. What were they thinking? I would never get over this. Like my big sister said, I'm just like a puppy dog. I follow people around and when they just stomp their foot I get scared away. Again I went to that farthest chair. I sulked I wanted to be alone. Why me? Why was I like this? I didn't want to be, really I didn't. I didn't like this society thing. God made people alike and they have to learn to be different. Or did He make people different and they have to learn to be alike? This is me, I think. This party is not fun. I'll be glad when it's over. Go home be with my family. It's what I like best.

Earl Selby

Mr. Earl Selby, machine shop instructor, walked into the school shop while the class stood in anticipation, carrying a two-foot piece of stainless steel one inch in diameter. "Listen up," he said, "this stainless steel can be cut into half-inch pieces. Students have made some beautiful rings here in the past, and the best will be put on display on the first floor during open house and there will be prizes."

Mr. Selby then went on to say each student must make one of three items for a grade and possible display for a prize. Louis stepped up for a piece of the stainless steel, already imagining how he could make a prize-winning ring. On the very first day, he drilled the hole with success, and then carried emery cloth home to smooth the hole. Filing and shaping was done at school because they needed to use a vise. The final shaping and smoothing of the surface was done whenever Louis could find a minute of time. He rubbed the ring with the emery cloth until he saw the shape exactly as he wanted. Then, taking a ball-peen hammer, he made indentations around the side of the ring and begun to buff it every day at school. He buffed that ring at every opportunity right up until he handed it over to Mr. Selby.

This Earl Selby was a teacher you needed to know. Before verbally disciplining any student, he would ask, "What's your name?" After discipline, he would always call you by name. If you called you kid, that was preferred over your name. Then there was skipper, a name he would call his best kid. Skipper, of course, was a navy reference to a small ship's captain. Selby, as he was always referred to, gave special privileges to his skipper. Like being allowed to use some of the machinery only he could use. Only one student would be a skipper in each class. Selby also had a facial expression with each way of addressing a student as kid, your name, or skipper.

You always knew how he felt, so when Louis handed him his ring and he said, "This looks good, kid, it's the best I've seen," Louis wasn't surprised. Louis had already seen every ring that was to be in competition. The time and energy he had put into his work was clearly visible and he expected a win.

Open house was on Friday evening. Louis usually worked Friday nights, and the family did not go to open houses. This one was no different. Neither Louis nor his family went to the open house. Machine shop was on Tuesday after lunch. Louis had heard nothing of the outcome of the competition. On the way to shop, Louis stopped at his locker to get his coat in order to leave for home at the end of class. Leaving his coat on the farthest workbench, he turned to see Selby motioning for him to come over where he was standing. As Louis approached him, Selby continued into his office. There was enough noise in the shop as to prevent anyone from hearing as he addressed Louis without closing the door.

Selby reached out and gave Louis his ring, saying, "You won second prize, kid." Louis could see uneasiness in Selby, and Selby could see hurt and anger in Louis. "I voted for yours, it was the best," said Selby. "I'm going to give you out of my pocket the money equal to first prize. It's only right. Let me tell you what happened. This prominent P.T.A. mother insisted her son's was the best. She was arrogant and pointed out that neither you nor your parents were there and you did not deserve first place. I'm sorry, Skipper, okay?"

Louis took the money, though it meant little to him. He was hurt and nearly in tears. Though this incident was not spoken of in any way indicating racism, in Louis's mind this had happened because this skinny, curly-haired kid was African American. Louis went to the bench where he had placed his coat and books, there he sat and did his homework in a remorseful way. From then on, Selby called Louis "Skipper" and introduced him to the operation of the lathe.

Grandpa Williams

We came to that place in the road where the trees were closer to the road, giving us some shade. We lessened our pace then came to a halt as out of nowhere we heard the sound of music. Now we had battery-powered car radios. Wonderful, turn it up! We stood and watched as the sound came closer and louder. The new sounds of gospel music now sweeping the nation filled the air. Oh! Do not spare the sound, turn it up! We watched the big Renfro Funeral Home Cadillac hearse slowly traveling the swells and valleys of the road. As it passed, we could see one of the Renfro sons driving along with a friend or another employee. They seemed to enjoy what they were doing. Why not? How else could they be driving a Cadillac of any kind in these days of hard times?

We were on our way to Grandpa's to be at his funeral service. The boys were in the lead. The girls were following in hollering distance as they went toward that third hickey in the road where Grandpa's farmhouse stood. The siblings had spent the night at Grandpa's house having night watch service. The embalmed body was kept overnight at watch service. The preacher came to the house to conduct the service.

Mama and Papa had talked it over and made plans as soon as the exact date was finalized. Mama would go to Grandpa's house while Papa would be home with the children. The next day would be the short service at the house where all would gather. All the siblings with their older children, that is. Papa would drop all the kids at the Waller's home, with the children of Mama's closest sister, Marie. From here on Springfield Pike, the older ones could then walk to Grandpa's house for the funeral service. The road from the Waller's home to Grandpa's home was a good mile and a half of ups and downs. Mostly ups, it seemed. Grandma used to walk this road and all the way from the end of the streetcar line down there on the Pike. I can still see her walking in my mind. She was tall and walked a steady pace as she went. Her long legs and swinging arms were positively hers. With a bony face and long flowing hair—signs of her Indian heritage. Grandpa brought the farm and moved here from Avondale, because her doctor said she would be better off in the country life. It did not look right! Well, yes, Grandpa worked hard while they lived on Irving Street. He saved the money to buy that farm. I know. They had cows, chickens, hogs, and a good garden, mostly what was needed, but there were extras you had to buy. Her work people declare she is the best cook. They cannot eat anybody else's cooking. At home, though, when she cooks, she doesn't have that fancy kitchen. She cooked for Grandpa on a wood stove. It is what he liked, though. They were a pair, hooked up for life is what I saw.

The boys were still leading the girls in two distinct groups, all cousins as they reached the last of the three rises in the road where they could now see the farm. They picked up the pace, as they now could see the hearse with its doors open standing on the lawn. They could again hear music coming from the car radio. Papa and Aunt Fannie with Uncle Bonne passed in their cars filled with adults. There was no room for the kids. It looked like Papa just flicked the ashes from his cigar and picked up speed when he saw us. He could have slowed down, we could have ridden the running boards from here to there. Little Walter was driving Aunt Hattie's car. He seemed to have stopped growing. Some call him Peewee in Walnut Hills, where they live. He played it so cool, with that smug look and a flip of the hand going by. We now could see all and clearly hear the music. We saw the siblings drawn outside and onto the lawn, half circling the hearse. We children pulled ourselves as close as possible behind those of our own. After the casket was aboard the hearse again, we asked the undertaker for prayer. This was done for the older children who would not be going to the burial. There was not enough passenger space. They prayed on the lawn, inside a large triangle formed by the house, the utility building, and the large trees. A breeze stirred, lifting the country sounds of birds, crickets, and farm animals. They smelled the many smells associated with the outdoors.

I remember so well. Grandpa had milk buckets in his hands and a towel over his shoulder. He took my hand and off to the barn we went. He sat on a three-legged stool, placing a pail between his legs. He wiped the cow's protuberance with the towel as I watched in awe. I remember the ringing sound as the first milk sprayed into that empty bucket. He then told me to come closer and to open my mouth. He accurately sprayed warm milk into my gap-toothed mouth. While wiping milk from my face and neck, I heard grandpa's deep, joyous, and infectious chuckling sound. We laughed aloud and repeatedly with great joy. I remember it well and he touched my heart. Until that day I must confess, I did not really know grandpa, but he knew all the children and he loved them all.

While the gospel music faded into the air, we turned to face again the long walk to Springfield Pike. We all had recurring memories warming our hearts and flashing within our minds. Each wanted to tell about their own experiences. When you are one of the younger ones, you get little respect and no attention in the conversation. You agree with all that is said. You sometimes realize you missed something the older ones gained from the teaching of grandparents. They all listen, they agree, and then wonder silently about their ancestry.

Grandpa Williams was raised near Lexington, Kentucky, in a large family of horsemen. They trained horses for show coaches and draft. Grandpa was best with workhorses. He could take one horse and plow a basement perfect in every dimension. In doing so, he put the horse through unlikely maneuvers. The two acted as one. The horse knew and followed Grandpa's commands by voice and a pat on the back or the buttocks. The animal followed a steady gate, never rushing but following every utterance Grandpa made in his low heavy voice. "Giddap, hup hup, and no no," he would say while steadily holding a loose rein. They teamed to perfection. Then Grandpa would pat the horse's brow, giving him water while the horse then stood tall and proud, as if to accept his due honors for a job well done.

"It was always that way," said Jesse Waller. He was named after our great grandfather, Jesse Oliver, whom we all are so proud to recall. We honored his name for volunteering to serve in the Civil War. Jesse Waller was respected as the oldest of the Waller family and having lived closer to Grandpa, he knew more about him.

Said another, "Remember when Grandpa's barn was about to collapse after a storm, roof and all? His many friends came with tools. Soon as Grandpa had some wood, they rebuilt that barn in two days. Grandpa had many friends; they say he would give the shirt off his back. He did not have to. His smile, his quiet confidence, and his joyous chuckle was contagious. He made friends with everyone he met. Grandpa never used a whip on his animals. He always gave Dad and Uncle Ralph the shotguns, and they would go hunting, but he did not go. Grandpa went anytime he wanted, by himself a lot. Mr. Mayview, who owns all that woods, let him. Grandpa's Mr. Mayview's nigger." They all laughed.

Little Charles crossed the drainage ditch when he saw a clump of blackberry bushes. The berries were either unripe or bird stained. He chose an unripe and bitter one and spit it out. We walked on, feeling a joyful togetherness we had not experienced before.

I remember coming from the barn with Grandpa and the boys. One of the boys would be trusted to carry the lantern, while he carried two buckets of milk. He took the milk to the kitchen and then called for Grandma to do the rest. He then took us into his bedroom. Beside his bed was a contraption we had not seen before. It was, as he explained, a super-heterodyne crystal set. We gathered around the small bedside table on our knees, while Grandpa reset the crystal and turned the two knobs, bringing in stations from far and wide. We heard music of many origins as well as foreign languages. We all wanted one. He laughed yet he explained nothing. Maybe that was his purpose just to introduce us to something new to us, but that was old science. Or was there just not enough time?

Grandma, on the other hand, had an accumulation of books, Negro authors mostly, including George Washington Williams, an Ohio native, whose name was like Grandpa's. He was called

"Wash" Williams. Grandma took the older girls to their room. They whispered. They giggled. They ran me out. I wish I could have stayed longer to hear them.

As we walked, they continued with the story of Jeff Cox and Grandpa. Jeff lived behind Mr. Whitaker. Jeff Cox was a friend of Grandpa's. Grandpa knew someone had been stealing his chickens and mentioned it to Jeff Cox. When questioned, Jeff explained to Grandpa how easy it was to take a chicken from its roost at night by grabbing it by its feet swinging it at arm's length. The chicken's blood, then rushing to its head, would prevent its ability to make sounds. Weeks later, Jeff Cox was seen running from the hen house with one of the chickens. "I was just trying to make a way for those children," he said.

"No, he was just stealing," said Grandma. "You think he is not going to eat that chicken? Hogwash. That is just a chicken-stealing scoundrel." Jeff Cox had a high-pitched voice that contrasted mightily against Grandpa's low chuckle, making their simplest conversation comical. He thought Jeff to be a firm believer. As a Christian trying to make a difference, Grandpa could not bring himself to condemn the man, much to grandma's chagrin. W

"Well, Jesse, but he only had one," Grandpa would say. Grandpa was somewhat of a philanthropist. Certainly not wealth in worldly goods by any means. He had, in his humble belief, prospered beyond his origin, and he felt blessed.

When Grandma died, a melancholy overtook Grandpa. He was no longer the same, though not all the family recognized the fact. He stayed inside nearly from sunup to sundown. The whole farm echoed his depression. That flock of chickens somehow was now nearly depleted. I wondered as to the condition of the cow, but did not inquire or venture to see, as weeds grew in abundance throughout the land. Those many and so appreciative friends faded away.

I will always remember going to visit Grandpa with my friend, Gene, on a hot summer day. We had bicycled our way from Norwood. We saw several pears on his tree before we arrived. We knocked on his door. I was shocked, though I should not have been,

Louis Gardner

to see him come to the door, glance out, and nearly get blinded by the sun, which he had probably not seen in several days.

"Hi Grandpa!" I said.

"Who are you?" he asked.

"I'm Louis," I said.

"Oh, you are Ada's son," was his response, holding his right hand in a saluting fashion above his eyebrows, sheltering his eyes from the intense sun. He stepped back from the door as I asked.

"Could we have some of the pears on that tree?" I asked, while pointing in the direction of the field where the tree stood.

"Sure," he said. "If any are left, have all you want." My friend Gene and I went to the pear tree on our way back. We stopped and had fun throwing rocks and sticks in efforts to break some of the few remaining pears from the tree. We had some success in dislodging the pears, yet little success in preventing their destruction as they hit the ground. Late in the season as it was, the pears were overripe and all we got were some well-bruised, overripe pears. I thought, *Grandpa is ill, and he's not himself. I must tell Mama.* From Woodlawn to Norwood is a long way on a bicycle, a trip I must and will endure. I was so happy I made the trip.

We were passing the Whitaker house, one of the few homes on Grove Road, between Grandpa's house and Springfield Pike. Grandpa's farm was the only real farm able to maintain cows. He could grow sufficient corn to sustain them as well as chickens and a vegetable garden that provided a saleable surplus. At Mr. Whitaker's, like many, they had a desire to produce as much as possible, on limited land, to provide for their needs. There was an unusually quiet atmosphere here on this day. A thin-bodied tiger cat slowly roamed the shaded area alongside the house. Farm animals were fed because of their future needs. They are the products. Farm pets, unlike city pets, have to scrounge for survival. This survivor peered at two blue jays on a long pile of stacked firewood. This cat had thus far survived on field mice, ridding the home of the pest, which was his purpose for being there. A group of leghorn chickens scratched at the earth in the background. The midday sun well displayed our surroundings in a bright, colorful manner, yet was unable to even dampen the mood as we went. Here lived the balding Mr. Whitaker, his daughter, and her two sons. Mr. Whitaker came to the farm one Sunday after church. That was before Mr. Tiller. He was introduced to Aunt Hattie. They all thought the two were a good match. The two talked very little.

Later, when asked why, Aunt Hattie just said he was born too soon. She didn't want to put him down by saying he was too old, though it really was the reason. She later said he could not get up to her and she would not get down to him. Again they laughed. Aunt Hattie was visibly attacked with that dreadful vitiligo, causing white spots. She still dressed in a flashy way and was witty and smart. The oldest of the girls in the family, she more than set the pace with her broad and engaging smile. The mood for the Negro at this time was move out move up. Aunt Hattie now lived alone in the house that once was the family home on Irving Street in Avondale, and she was doing just that. She kept herself well informed through the news, church, and other activities. Able to do so much more by having her own car was certainly a giant move upward for anyone, especially by a female Negro. Having traveled abroad with her employers, she had many a story to tell. It's no wonder that when she spoke, they listened. When the family gathered, she tried to outdo all others with her cooking. She brought more and was ready with something on her arrival. She didn't say wait. She always had sandwiches or something ready, which made her a champion for the kids and especially the teenagers, who knew she was also financial banker for Santa Claus. In the hearts and minds of the many nieces and nephews, she was the greatest.

We did not know the depth of gratitude we owed Grandpa for having bought the farm we all so joyously enjoyed. We did not know of this sacrifice, or part or what influence Grandma played. We simply took all for granted and enjoyed that it was there for us. We cherished the times. We played, we laughed, and we ate and even sang to the joy of it all. We filled ourselves with a lifetime of memories of the many days spent with a close-knit family. We never thought there would be an end to the joy of family. Yes, that was Grandpa in that passing hearse, as we stood again beneath the shade tree. We knew he was ours and we had lost him. We knew he had meant a lot. We knew he would be missed. But we did not know how greatly he would be missed. No more would we track the hillsides following the cows. No more would we feed watermelon rinds to the hogs, or kernels of corn to the chickens, or check their roosting places for eggs. No more catching fireflies, praying mantises, or June bugs. No more following the cows to their grazing hillside. No more damming the creek while knee-deep in mud. No horseshoes or hide and seek beneath that enormous tree, nor laughing at the chicken doo-doo on Grandpa's car. No outside tables filled with the best of food. No more would the aroma of the food drown out the normal farm odors. No more would we hear that deep and low chuckle that was solely Grandpa's. Hurt would come and pass, but it would not overcome the pleasure and love of a large and happy family.

Cousins and friendships would be separated, changing the paths of life for most, yet there was not yet the sadness that would surely come.

We crossed Springfield Pike in a group, eight in all. We reached the Waller's home, where we met "Bunny" Maynard and his sister, Ruthie, the youngest of the Waller children. "Where have you all been'" they questioned.

"We've been to Grandpa's," was the answer.

"Did you know he is dead?" we said. The two were shocked and saddened by this news, which also again saddened all within the group. They all took sitting positions around the perimeter of the raised concrete slab that was the front porch. They sat silently like a flock of birds on a cable line, until the three cars of the family came to retrieve each of its members.

ANOTHER SUNDAY

It was a typical Sunday, until immediately following dinner I saw my friend Julius coming up the walk to the house. I was shocked, as he regularly went to his sister's house to be with his family Saturday afternoons and stayed through Sundays. *What could have happened,* I thought? He showed a smile so it must not be too bad. I told him I was just readying myself to go to the matinee at the Beecher theatre. All he said was, "Well!"

"What happened?" I asked as we reached beyond earshot of the family.

"My brother Buss came and said for me to stay at the doctor's this weekend, 'cause the water is shut off at home."

"Wait a minute, Julius, don't tell me those people don't have the money."

Smiling again, he said, "Well, it is the depression, and when they say we're all in it, they must mean everybody."

"But you are going to the show? I mean, you got the money for a ticket?" I asked.

Julius said nothing, just rolled his eyes, like he couldn't believe I was asking him. "I've got it when you don't. I've got a regular job." In passing St Xavier's football stadium I picked up a two-cent deposit coke bottle and pitched it into some tall grass to be later retrieved on the way home.

"My mama said your sister Goldie is a jewel, stepping up and giving her all to keep your family together after your parents passed away. She prays for your family everyday."

"I know," said Julius. "When Papa got mad at them sisters, we had our hardest times. Mama said, 'I just don't know what we are going to do.' That was when everyone who was old enough did something. My older sisters ironed for the teachers or helped with their washing or cleaning. My brother and I were not able to do anything at the sister's to help Papa. We went to that Grace Methodist church with Mr. McDonald—he's the custodian there—to help with the cleaning up after their banquets. We cut the grass and watered the flowers at Mr. Mendel's house. We helped Mr. Elcho and ran errands, but that is not really much. Grandpa Williams sometimes gives us something, but very little as he has so little to sell. The things he has to have, like feed for the animals, costs money. Louis, you know I started working for the doctor last year when I was twelve. Well, I'm still twelve but it's not bad for me. My little brother Oscar is the only one without a job. We barely take care of ourselves. Goldie and Oscar need the help. Ralph, my big brother, helps though he is away. Sometimes Joe and Buster get into it. They think they are doing more than their share and that's when we miss our parents most. At least I do. It was better then."

Julius in my family, if you offended someone in the family, that's something mama is totally against. One day it was me and my sister Della. She said, "Come here, both of you. What is wrong? You don't do that here. Go hug her, say you are sorry."

"You, Della, go hug him say you are sorry." We had to do it, because, well, you always did what Mama said, because Papa's old time ways would back her up.

"Hug him, say you are sorry. Hug her, say you are sorry. Say it again, say it again. Hug 'em and say you are sorry, then say you love him. Say it, let me hear you." After repeating this several times, she would look into each face to see if we were truly sorry. I don't know how, but she could surely tell. If she didn't see a change, we had to continue. At first you would feel silly. Then you would come to tears and you really did feel sorry. Sorry for everything that happened. Sorry for the one you hurt. Sorry for having to go through the whole ordeal and so, so sorry that you have so disappointed Mama. After that you feel so much better. At bedtime I went up to Mama, and while standing there she put her hands on my shoulders. She turned me around and said in a heavy voice, "Goodnight son."

Julius and I came from the matinee at the Beecher Theater. The featured movie was a Charlie Chan mystery. I did not get all the detailed implications that solved the mystery, and besides I didn't really care that much. Just another Hollywood flick to get my little spending money. They showed a news clip of the German dirigible, the Hindenburg, bursting into flame on its hanger and burning completely within one minute as it fell to the ground. This brought to realization the photographs we had seen in the newspapers and the stories. Then, as if to fill in for the low-rated movie thrown at us, they showed a short comedy of a Negro confronted by a bear scavenging for food beside him. They showed the frightened Negro with bulging eyes and mouth gaping open. Without a zoom lens, they flashed a blown-up, still picture of a more frightening view of the Negro with bulging eyes, sweat pouring from a monkey-like face. I looked around at the nearly filled theater to see most occupants laughing heartily. This did not sit well with me. Already I'd been taken full fare with a second rate movie. Now, having taken my fare, they were mocking my people. They created these movies, made their money, then put me down.

On leaving the show I noticed the yet clear sky on a spring day. We would walk home before dark. Julius to his job, me to my family. As we walked, I watched Julius's face, knowing he would make a remark about that comic strip. I could see it coming.

"No, Julius, I don't want to hear that." Julius laughed heartily. I said nothing. He had to stop at the sweet shop for spearmint chewing gum and a Baby Ruth candy bar. Cheaper than at the show. At night at the doctor's house, he would become bored and go for the chewing gum and candy. He was not fat, but he's working on it. Without even a radio in his room, as a radio would interfere when he was called to serve, I suggested books, but he read very little, mostly pictured stuff. I urged Julius to look back at three Negros standing beside an old, well-worn Dodge automobile, completely dressed in riding gear as if returning from a day of horse riding. "This is still the depression, Julius," I said. "They don't need to be out here making a front. They are not the wealthy. Next week they will be in golfing clothes, complete with bags. They are not fooling anybody. Some of these guys played ball with my Papa. I know about them.

"Well, Louis, you need to have some fun, you need to laugh sometimes, too. Maybe they are not the wealthy, but they can do what the wealthy do. Have some fun."

"No, it's all pretending. Pretend you got it when you don't. Pretend you are happy when you're blue. You think if you ignore what they do, like in a movie, it will all go away, but you are wrong, Julius. My past of going to Norwood High and working at that barbershop tells me there are things the whites must face, and we must not waste time. We must avail ourselves of every opportunity as well as sacrifice. It's the only way I see. We don't need to be pretenders; we don't need to clown our way. We need to get down with some serious thought as to who we are and where we are. We are at the bottom of the ladder to a better living. We need to dedicate ourselves. Take advantage of every opportunity to improve our condition. Hard work and sacrifice."

"Hard work and sacrifice? You'd fail a Sunday school class talking like that. There ain't no jobs and sacrifice is every day. It's still the depression."

"Well, you are talking plantation talk."

"Louis, what do your parents say?"

I thought long and hard about the whole subject. *Sometimes our parents did not want to talk about the past because of its painful stories,* I thought. "They want to spare us a painful history, but we children want to know. We need to know. But, my Mama says, 'The Lord will make a way.' Then my sister Lil says, 'You just have to know what you want and where it's at.'"

We reached our final breaking-off point. We saluted each in our own way. Our thoughts went inward. Oh, thank God I was born within this Christian family. Taught to embrace the Christian faith. Drenched in the sounds of gospel and uplifted by spirituals that cut soul-deep. Taught to be first faithful to God and country. Though often race consciousness followed closely behind our Christian faith, we supported its every cause. But what will sustain me is the love that abounds within the family and every heart that beats within. That will last as long as life itself.

Wet Behind the Ears

After a busy Saturday of chores, a bath, and a change into summer casuals, he couldn't resist a stroll through his sister's room, where he could gaze into the long vanity mirror, and observe his full body image. Louis stood tall, his hands in his front pants pockets, while slowly turning first right then left. Then again with palms outward, he placed his fingers into his back pockets and repeated his left and right, turning while carefully observing himself. Maybe he would clip that Charles Atlas coupon from *Popular Mechanics* magazine, send it, and get into building his body. *No*, he thought, *that's too much work, requires exercise equipment, and being a Negro he would not be judged fairly in competitions.* Yes he was skinny and tall. He liked the tall part. Louis stepped closer to the mirror and gazed into his own eyes and made faces. He could see a resemblance to an earlier picture of Papa. *A real haircut at the barbershop would help*, he thought. *The big eyes, the smooth skin, and original smile that Papa says he'd seen too much of already, are okay by me*, he thought. The smile is what he thought caused some to say he's cute, but cute is not what he wants to hear at fifteen. Well, a few facial hairs would make him . . . *Wait a minute*, he thought, *what is this all about, why am I thinking about this?* He quickly moved toward the kitchen. If seen he would have been embarrassed to a blush.

Louis was of late taking days when he wants to walk. There is no air conditioning, so a walk in the evening air was a relief from the heat and tension. As he walked the familiar streets he knew each resident as he passed, and they would speak to him or acknowledge him when he spoke. As he walked the familiar streets he recalled many memories of the past. That time as an eighth grader when he with his friend Gene rode their bikes to the high school athletic field. There from a short distance they could clearly see and hear as the head coach brought the team into a closing huddle, warning them there would be a nigger or two on the opponent's team on Saturday. "They do play hard," said the coach. "You'd better bring your best game, hit 'em hard, and show 'em you came to play."

He remembered his past years working at the barber shop where he shined shoes and cleaned the shop. The shop owner was often saying, "Save your money, 'cause when you get married you can never have too much money." This was never a concern for Louis at thirteen and fourteen, so why now?

On a hot summer evening, when passing Shapiro's drugstore, many of Norwood High's students were coming from or going to the ice cream and soda bar. They all spoke when recognizing him and he noticed who was with whom as they passed. There were mixed male and female couples or groups.

Passing the Buick dealers well-lit show room again, he looked at the latest roadster in the window and imagined what he would do if it were his.

At the next corner he felt a rush of memories, for this was the streetcar stop closest to home where he had met Mama on her return from shopping downtown so many times. He had met relatives and church friends here, some for the first time. On this day his thoughts reverted to Amy. Louis had worked his last day at the barbershop and was catching the streetcar for his first work assignment at Stones Bowling Alley. Amy, a student at Norwood High, recognized Louis. She grinned as she continued to talk. She too was going to Stones. Amy's mother ran the concession stand at Stones. Amy had waited at home with her little brother until father got home before she could leave. Amy was quite typical of students at Norwood, but she was exceptionally friendly. Though his words were few, Louis felt he had never had a conversation as memorable as that one, yet he avoided Amy on the bus as well as the later hours when they would be leaving work or when she waited for her mother in the lobby. Strangely, he was happy to have met Amy. They smiled and spoke to each other on only a few occasions unavoidable by him. Thankfully the devil did not get involved. Thought Louis, *there's nothing wrong with the whites, but this town is not ready for that.* Then suddenly it started. Why? Why am I thinking about these things?

Again Louis sneaked through his sister's room to view himself in that long vanity mirror. He stopped momentarily, then he heard a voice that he knew too well. "Oh, him's so cute, where you think you're going, big man?" As he turned in the direction of the voice, he was confronted with his two oldest sisters, Lillian and Mabel. He was shy and somewhat embarrassed having been caught unaware of them, while styling in front of their mirror. He knew their teasing and criticizing was to teach and prepare him for any event he would face.

"Cousin Jet's going to pick me up and we're going slumming."

"Slumming?" was a quick reply.

"Slumming is what rich people do when they cross the tracks into our neighborhoods. Boy, you're going to a club. Ain't you?"

"Yes," said Louis. A club would be a bar with a jukebox for recorded music with a small space for dancing.

"You don't know it, but you are not ready for that. You are still wet behind the ears. You are not the witty kiddie from the city you think you are, you're green as grass," said one.

"You are not so slick you can't stand a little greasing," said the other.

Suddenly there was the sound of an automobile horn, and Louis turned to leave, catching the last words from Lillian and Mabel. "Be careful. Listen and be careful. Don't make quick judgments. Don't take any wooden nickels," which meant nearly the same thing. As he rushed through the house, then out into the fall air, he could feel the concern shown by his sisters and the love that his family had so often shown in his growing up. He did not know the great value of his family experiences, but he could feel a calming peace and confidence that all was well. His personal desires were changing and he could fell maturity within but chose to not dwell on the thought. His thoughts ran to the venturous, unraveled, unknown world beyond.

She came to the booth with a forced smile and was greeted only with an order, "One quart of beer, three glasses."

"I know him," she said as she pointed to Veppie. "I'm Tommie, and as you can see all the city is at the Cotton Club's blue Monday," she said. "I'm not really working, but since I'm here I'll be glad to serve you."

Veppie seized the chance. "Then if you are not working, sit here with us. We don't bite." Tommie sat on the end of the booth on Louis's side as the conversation went quickly to street talk. Louis became shy and apprehensive. Sitting in a club with the best and latest music and beer was what he expected. The girl sitting beside him had not been expected. It caused him anguish; his immediate feeling was if he were a mole he would go into a hole. Then he thought, *I'm given this part to play, so be it, I'll handle it.* Meanwhile, his thoughts drifted far from the conversation the others were engaged in. While his eyes covered Tommie inch by inch as much as he could observe, his mind asked questions and sometimes found answers. Her hair had been recently done (pressed and curled), and seeing what first appeared to be a birthmark behind her left ear, his mind said no, that's a hot comb burn. She had a short hairstyle with much of her forehead covered, causing her face to appear wider than it was. She wore no makeup, not even five and dime store. Her greatest thing was her honey-browned complexion and winning smile. Her smile was one you could not break down, meaning you could not be for certain she was happy or pretending. Somehow, that smile caused most to want to please her. Louis felt likewise as he continued to observe Tommie's hands and upper body.

While eyeballing Tommie, Louis only pretended to drink his beer. Beer was not something he liked. Tommie suddenly excused herself and went to say something to the club owner. Then nature and the beer caused Veppie and Jet to go to the men's room. Tommie returned first, asking Louis if he liked music. "Of course," was the response.

He quickly came up with some change, saying, "Play after hours, then whatever you like." When Tommie went to the jukebox, he seized the opportunity to observe all that he had not been able to see while she sat beside him. She wore a pleated skirt that complemented the fuzzy sweater. Her shoes were pumps with laces behind the ankle. Her body was well rounded to match her face. Louis gazed as she wheeled from the jukebox, gave a dance move, snapped her fingers, and returned to sit opposite him. She leaned across the table and in a low voice uttered, "You're a handsome guy." His shy innocence couldn't stand such an aggressive behavior and he was much relieved with the return of Jet and Veppie.

It soon became obvious the night was a dull one at the Century Club. There would be no crowd, not even a small one. On leaving the club, Tommie, as well as the owner—a white man with a Negro wife, not present due to an unexpected lack of patrons—bade a fond farewell to Louis, Veppie (Sylvester), and Jet (Justion).

As he slouched on the back seat of the car, the memories of the evening hung over him like a cloud and followed him like a lost kitten. The conversation between Jet and Veppie went unheard. His visions were of a warm smile from a plump, seemingly happy face. Lips that curled and eyes that suggested, and left lasting memories. Heavy on the back side, does this indicate a young woman capable of child bearing? What was he thinking about? Again, she didn't say cute, she said handsome, which was exactly what he would like her to say. Louis had been won over completely, he could follow this woman's lead wherever its destiny, only he was not eighteen. He found the composure to say, "I'm not in love and have full control over my destiny."

While slouched on the back car seat, his mind again far from the scene, Louis recognized again the voice of Veppie. "Louis, you know the man at the place we go on Sundays, Burnard? He said you all who live in Norwood think you all are better than other people."

Louis answered, "All people are not the same."

"Everybody's the same," said Veppie.

"No, that's in God's way," said Louis. He stopped short to hold onto and enjoy his thoughts of Tommie and wondered what was happening to him.

Again Veppie intervened, "You out here trying to make these girls and that's not right." "Look, I have eight sisters, and I'll never do anything to any woman I would not want done to them," answered

Louis. There was a long silence, then a friendly good night as he quickly returned to the basement at home to grab a recording by Billy Eckstine (the one who so greatly resembled his brother Ralph), and listened to one song in particular. It was called "Coquette." As he listened the words of the song it helped him understand what he was going through.

He listened and he listened. He began to understand. Different people have different intentions, purposes, and reasons for being. This girl was on a mission to be well known and well liked. "Yes she was clean and in these times clean meant more than soap and water clean. Clean meant also clear of bed bugs, lice, and venereal diseases as well. If we are all here to make this world a better place, she was ahead of the rest, she spread joy in her way. "Again and again he listened to the words of the song, written by John W. Green, Carmen Lombardo, and Gus Kahn.

Tell me why you keep fooling little
Coquette making fun of the ones who love you breaking hearts
you are ruling little
Coquette, true hearts tenderly dreaming of you.

Some day you'll fall in love as I fell in love with you, maybe
someone you love will just be fooling then when you're all alone
with only regrets.
You'll know little Coquette I loved you

Chorus.
And when you're all alone with only regret
You'll know little Coquette, I love you.

Hound

In Cincinnati, Ohio, two of the four seasons are miserable. Summers are hot and humid, and there are no lakes or beaches, thus the misery. Even more miserable is be winter. Its snow and ice constantly threatens the life of anyone who dares to travel in it by any means. Springs is exciting with its signs of renewed life, but fall is most beautiful. The humidity subsides with the coming of fall, restoring the lushness of spring. Then the light rains bring fall flowers, adding their colors to the landscape ahead of the coloring trees. Squirrels scurry around preparing for the winter along with all the other creatures, such as rabbits, chipmunks, opossums, raccoons, and others that are seen less often. Fall in Cincinnati is so invigorating it causes one to stare out the windows at home, or when traveling by car or bus. The weather would also cause one to detour up or down the river or in any direction to view the landscape. One can then see or feel his or her own importance in the ecosystem.

In the year 1940, World War II raged in Europe. There were those who highly expected war would reach our shores, or at least that we would be drawn into the conflict soon, because Hitler was so well prepared. War, however, brought a much-needed prosperity to the region. The new prosperity did not improve the lot of those African-Americans (AAs) who populated the city. The depression of the thirties had relegated and confined many to the most meager of jobs. Many were domestics. Those above this category were janitors, foundry workers, and common labor. The larger companies restricted AAs to such positions. Some large local companies refused to hire AAs in any capacity.

There were AAs who succeeded in the businesses restricted to their own clientele, such as undertakers and beauty and barber shops. There were a few doctors, lawyers, and one real estate broker.

AAs also operated a hotel and taxi cab service. There were several night clubs as well as the nationally syndicated Cotton Club. AAs, however, were refused admission to all movie houses except two, which were operated by AA's but owned by whites. Most were second class and some bore restrictions. AA cabs could not pick up passengers downtown. AAs were restricted from downtown hotels. Thus, we saw the first integrated jazz bands as well as the first integrated national sports teams. AA players were housed in the AA's own hotel or housed in some AA's home.

Cincinnati schools were integrated, though again some restrictions were in place. Whites and AAs were not permitted to combine use of the swimming pools. AAs were often put "in their place" by school masters and sometime denied their just dues and honors. However, a fortunate child whose family was able to acquire a home in the right neighborhood could sit in a classroom alongside some of the city's most prominent sons and daughters.

On the city's police force were not more than four AA officers who patrolled the AA's neighborhoods. Other than garbage collectors, few city employees were AAs. The National Association of Colored People was alive but struggling without much success in Cincinnati. Much of the population was ready to force a change, but lack of economic opportunities brought hopelessness to many. Some change would come with the war effort.

The suburb of Avondale was the biggest suburb of Cincinnati at this time. It was occupied mostly by Jews, who during the early twenties ran Cincinnati. They were wealthy. They owned the largest factories, banks, and businesses. They were the lawyers, judges, and politicians who had to be reckoned with. They were rebelled against and were forced out of politics but retained their wealth quite visibly. Nestled alongside this affluent community, lay a contingent of AAs. Being within this community known to be inhabited by the wealthy and often envied Jews, these AAs felt somewhat comforted. An AA youth could take a chauffer's job and sometimes parlay it into a much better position at his boss's place of business. At any rate, the job was not hard. The boss was not mean. For most it was exciting to drive one of those fancy cars, when so few families had a car.

In 1940 nearly all homes had radios. Most, however, had no phones. Few had audios for recorded music. Jazz, and any other AA-preferred music could be heard only late at night and on certain radio stations. Newberrys and Woolworth's downtown had AA employees at their lunch counters. They served all races, because many AAs who worked downtown ate at their counters. Cincinnati had Castle Farm and Kentucky had Beverly Hills. These night clubs served only whites, even when starring top AA entertainers. Those entertainers, however, would perform for AAs at the only AA Greystone Ballroom, which was called the Greystone only to distinguish it as an AA's affair. Cincinnati also had its Cotton Club, which was owned and operated by AAs, although it was a syndication of Cotton Clubs across the nation. Newport, Kentucky was a sin city that featured live music on weekends as well as open gambling. Nineteen and sometimes twenty year olds were turned away without question. After-hour joints (as they were referred to) also turned away young people at will.

For the young, there would be an occasional dance at the Greystone. As only set-ups were sold, there was little problem of age. The Catholic Church had Friday and Saturday dances. The younger girls stayed away, and the watchful eyes of the fathers turned away the loud or mischievous guys. Since you did not dance in the basement of your own church, why would you dance in someone else's?

When Louis climbed into the middle of the rear seat of this black Buick deluxe sedan, it was a Sunday night. Not late, however, as most of the occupants had a day job or had a curfew. It was a beautiful but slightly breezy September night. The fall season was everywhere. The heavy car with its eight cylinder engine churned the loose gravel as he left the driveway. In the country air was the smell of fresh fruits and hay and the odor of horse manure, outhouses, and skunks. All beneath a darkening blue, red, and orange streaked sky. Earlier rains had quieted the birds and crickets, normally heard at this time. In the late evening it was quiet enough to hear the hum of the car's engine. Louis heard the distant sound of a train whistle along with the distinct patter of rubber tires on a smooth asphalt road surface.

Louis, sitting in the rear middle seat, was in a melancholy mood. He sunk into the plush seat, dropped his head, and feigned sleeping while the car treaded along at the speed limit. At seventeen he had great dreams of being a success in the business would. Just like the people he had worked for after school. People, who from meager beginnings such as he, had become quite successful. On occasion he had run errands to their homes. He loved the way they lived and made a personal vow that he would one day live as they lived. Sinking deeper and deeper into despair, as he thought of his family, who earnestly and eagerly advised and supported him. Most disappointing to his mother and father he had dropped out of school. Ralph and Ada Gardner gave their children freedom to choose at any early age. The guilt and hurt overwhelmed him. Louis was distraught. He had been less than what was expected of him; much less.

Occupying this car were his contemporaries, and they will not be named except "Hound," who drove. Their parents were church people and knew each other by name. They were nineteen or under. This was a Sunday, and most had been to church earlier. Because even expensive cars in 1940 came without radios, the occupants went to their back porch harmony thing. That is, together they made the sounds of the music they would have heard late on Saturday night. They could make the sounds unbelievably real. Each instrumental sound was duplicated by one of the occupants. After the sounds ceased, they began to raise their voices, each professing to know more about the song, their artist, and writers.

During the evening there had been many discussions; some meaningful, some worthless. Some skirted the war topic. Some were so opposed to the war on racial grounds they talked about how to avoid the draft. They gave examples of how to avoid the draft, such as feigned illness and even eating soap to gain a physical exemption. "Foolish," said someone.

Another said, "I hate all the history but I love this country. I really don't want to be a hero. I just want to be the big guy who beats the snot out of the little guy. I'll go and I—like General McArthur—shall return."

Another said, "If you're a Negro in this country, you gotta take hind tit."

Another said, "Hind tit is all you get, but some place there's more hogs than tits. Paul Robeson, Marion Anderson, the Duke and them don't take no hind tit, they got it all."

Another said, "Enlightened people deal in their own best interest, remember that son. You do have a tit. Some in other places don't."

None of the enlightening talk or foolish attempts to make jokes changed Louis, however. His anxiety for the moment was to get home and away from these street wise but in some ways degenerate people. Why had he even left home? No girls his age and liking would be in the places they went. The music was good but he had the same recordings at home.

"Yesterday I sang a love song. But tonight I sing the blues," thought Louis, remembering an old song. They told preacher and the chicken jokes. They talked about girls of every kind, body types, colors, their likes and ways, charity girls, goodie goodie girls, and descriptions not worthy to mention. They talked about the Cincinnati cops, especially the two AAs at District Four in Walnut Hills. "They beat that boy like he was a piñata," said one, "all because he was driving a car they thought he could not afford."

Suddenly there was a momentary silence. "Did you see them two white cops pass? They was looking hard, too, man, wasn't they Hound?"

Said another voice, "Why are you driving like you stole something?"

"You know this ain't my car," said Hound.

Louis raised up from his slouched position, muttering "My God." As bad as things were, they had suddenly became worse. He blamed himself. He did not have to be in this position. "Lord forgive me, never again!" he said to himself. Too afraid to look out the rear window to see if the cops were really going to give a chase, he simply dropped his head. Louis was stricken with fear. "Lord deliver me!" he moaned. He could not ascertain the consequences of being arrested in a stolen car. "Lord, let me survive this. This will not happen again, ever. I'll get my own car, I will!

Hound drove that big Buick loaded with five teenagers in a masterful fashion. He took curves at a speed above the safe limits, yet with minimal squealing of tires. Hound obviously had made his own decision as to how to handle the situation. The others were all at his risk. Being the perpetrator, Hound had become quite fearful himself. Now with no sound of sirens, the greater fear was for an accident. Hound was taking the center of the street, when traffic was light, then turning left or right from that angle. Minutes later two vicious left turns of this nature brought the car to a lot where gravel and coal trucks were parked.

Hound said, "Go for it, guys, this is where I'm leaving this car." Five well-dressed teens were forced to distance themselves from this car through a muddy lot, then a leaf-covered and muddy hillside.

Louis was farther from home than the others who lived in Avondale. However, Louis was no more than a block from his closest street car stop. Bewildered and with a pall of uneasiness, he was soon back at home.

Fight Time

I don't know when it started, but suddenly the sport of boxing was a part of nearly every newscast on the radio. A Golden Glove champion by the name of Joe Louis hit the news with a bang. His story about coming from Alabama to Detroit as a youth was constantly repeated. We gloried at the mention of his name, which lifted our racial pride. We listened to the news in silence, trying to gather every detail, as this would be the talk in the neighborhood at church and Sunday school. Though at our school there were those who were not ready for this kind of progress for the Negro. They would rather see the past fighters continue to dominate the sport. Those, mostly whites, saddened at the mention of a colored fighter as threatening as he. We took notice of his every success. We bought the *Pittsburgh Courier* or *Chicago Defender* (the Negro newspapers) for their special coverage and pictures. Our pride swelled seeing his good looks and celebrity. We wanted to initiate conversation wherever we went, and boxing was the first topic at any event. Many, employed at the homes of whites, had few opportunities to converse with their contemporaries on a daily basis. They would just let loose at a gathering of their race. They made fun of the "get back at 'em" feeling they shared when hearing of this young Negro phenomenon exerting his dominance in this the manliest of sports. "Go get 'em Joe," was the cry.

As exciting, as the news of Joe Louis was, there came a counter punch. His name was Ezzard Charles. He quickly became our fighter, though he rarely made the news radio or the dailies. We knew where he lived where he went to school, and where he was reported to be working after school. While attending our Woodward High School, normally out of his west end district, he fought ranking amateurs with tremendous success. He was glorified locally and mostly by his contemporaries. We nearly paraded his home on Lincoln Park Drive, the school, and the clothing store on Central Avenue where he was said to be working, just to make our conversations creditable. He dressed with a certain flair when pictured coming from any of his activities. We, the youth of the times, were enjoying exciting jazz music. Some of the clothes were even designed and initiated by our own, like Billy Eckstine's "Mr. B," a wide collar, long lapel shirts with square knot ties. Following their lead, we were exuberated by these happenings. These were our times. We could feel a part of the present as well as the rising tide of the future.

What was so astonishing about this rise of the Negro in this manner? In olden days they had picked cotton fast-paced and with strong hands bailed and loaded those bails with their strong arms and backs and often left Massa's hounds in the dust. Why then would he not have the skills and stamina to champion anyone's challenge as a fighter, even without the revenge factor?

These times motivated us all to try our skills in the art of boxing. We wanted to know where we fit in. Did we have the body and the skills, and could we mentally survive the challenge? Since Jack Johnson none had been given the opportunity. This Joe Louis had opened the gate and there would be a flood of challengers. There was no doubt our African American fighters would dominate from then on.

On a rare occasion I had after-school detention, I crossed Allison Street in front of the school. The school patrol officer had left his position. On the corner of Allison and Courtland Street there stood a vacant lot overgrown with shrubs and trees. One large apple tree stood beside the nearly bare spot where the original home once stood. A spot so isolated as to prevent passersby from seeing what went on in that bare spot.

I met Ralph Timberding on his way to just that spot carrying a set of boxing gloves. He urged me to come along for some fun. He wanted to put the gloves on me as soon as we arrived. At first I declined, knowing I would have to explain for the reason for being late at home. Still, I was drawn to this thing of boxing. I watched Ralph lace up the gloves on two of his neighborhood friends. I watched their brief match. *I could have easily have beaten either of them*, I thought. Without questioning me, he laced me up against who he thought was the best. He stood in my corner constantly giving me advice. There was no need to encourage me. I somehow came motivated to win. After a quick win, I told Ralph to unlace me.

"I must go home, I'm late," I told him. Ralph Timberding was the son of a former boxer, now employed at the Chevrolet plant. Ralph himself loved the sport but wanted only to manage and guide others. He seemed to have chosen me as a protégé.

"Great, but I'll see you later," he said. On the few occasions I stopped at the lot it was always the same. Ralph was my corner man.

Wednesday after school, the barbershop would be closed. My chance had come to go to the bowling alley with my brother. We met Smitty, the man in charge. He was in charge of the business as far as pin-boys were concerned. He was being the right hand man of William Stone, who owned the business.

"Oh, Little Norwood," he addressed me when we were introduced. My brother Ralph had been called Norwood, as he was the only pin boy from the city. All others were from the west end of Cincinnati. Smitty asked my age. When I answered fifteen, he told me to go downtown to the social security office in the federal building. "Tell them you need a card. They want sixteen, but you just go down there tell them when your birthday is. They will ask what year and you just say 1922 instead of 1923. Okay? Just remember that and you will be fine. You don't want to be working shining shoes in no barbershop. You can work here and make more money. Ain't that right, Norwood?"

Having been instructed as to what I was to do, yet not occupying the position, I watched. Somewhat bored, I went to the pin-boys' room, a first-floor basement-type room at the end of the building. The walls were concrete and joined a seldom used parking lot. The room reeked with a mixture of foul odors. A picnic type table occupied most of the room. There was but one light bulb that hung midway of the room. Ralph Jr. and I rarely used this room, except in extreme bad weather. We arrived on time for our games and left. The first time I went into the room, two pin-boys were in an argument, both with knives drawn while I looked on. This was so new to me I nearly went into shock. I backed from the room. I heard someone call out, "Smitty, they're at it in there."

Smitty came running. He knew just who was there. Amazingly, he separated the two. His threatening words were, "You are not in the west end, you are in Norwood, and these folks will put you behind bars. You'd better listen to me. I know ya'll don't want that kind of trouble. Sit down, just calm down," he said to one. Then to the other he said, "Go home, just go home. You know we are not gonna have that kind of behavior here. Go home and get yourself sober. You've been drinking." Then he held the door for the man.

God, I thought. *How could my brother have been here at an early age and survived this place?*

Again, I walked into the pin-boys' room at Stone's bowling alley where Ralph Jr. and I worked. This was a Saturday, and there was a new excitement. While waiting for game time, the pin-boys decided to occupy their time by some boxing in the small lot outside the meeting room. Ralph Jr. was putting on the gloves. Immediately I feared for him. I knew him to be a great athlete quick of hands and feet. However, these were down and out athletes of the past, here to make it through these hard times. Some, such as Shuffling Billy Baker, were known far beyond this town for their fighting skills. I cringe with each flurry as they entangled. I begin to perspire along with them. Ralph Jr. proved himself a formidable opponent. I stood back, listening with pride while they pointed out his excellent points. It was then that I realized this was a point game. Points for the most hits scored their variation, defense, and the beauty of it all. They emphasized the art. This is the golden age of boxing.

Finally, as other schools were doing, Norwood High had a former boxer come to the school to teach the martial arts. Coach Shoenburger was in charge. We were instructed in the many exercises, including skipping rope, punching the bag large and small, and shadow boxing, along with many other exercises. When not being instructed, we ran indoor track. Coach announced. "Find an opponent and line up." These were not fights, per se. We were reminded that these were just drills. "All you guys not participating go back and run the track," said coach. This I did without choice, as I was not ready with willing opponent. When Coach Shoenburger stopped those running the track, he asked me directly why I did not want to box. I answered by a shrug of the shoulders indicating indifference. He quickly picked one of his better athletes to oppose me. Ralph Timberding quickly came to assist me in lacing up my gloves. He would be in my corner, though I was fully confident there were no real opponents for me in this class. I literally warmed up on the first opponent. Coach then hand-picked another. Though the weight difference was limited to five pounds or under, I think he tipped the scales against me. I listened to Ralph. "Continue to mix it up, a series of hard left jabs then the crusher," he said. "Keep moving, keep him on the defense." I followed his word. The second opponent took only several seconds more than the first. Coach then asked me why did I act as though my life was at stake when in the ring. I again shrugged my shoulders. Again, he called one of his wrestlers. I accepted the challenge, though I knew nothing of the sport or its rules or even its point system. I was quickly pinned and defeated. Coach must have felt vindicated. I had no shame. Surely had I known anything about wrestling, I would have won.

This all began one day in Ms. Baumgardener's class. She came into the schoolroom with a bag containing some cotton balls along with the pods they grew from. She showed us a picture of how the fields looked, and how the cotton stood waist high. How the pods would burst open when in full bloom and ready to be picked. She explained how this would be a sun up to sun down, backbreaking job to pick these mile-long rows of cotton. How the invention of the cotton gin only increased the need for more hands, forcing the use of children to work the fields at the earliest age. "That's why the nigger . . ." Suddenly she halted, then she nearly stammered in a way we had not seen before. She looked at me, attempting to soften what she had said by saying, "Well, that's the word they all use. It's not meant to harm." Her crude explanation did nothing for me. My thoughts were, *how can I defend against this hatred. How can I get my rightful revenge?* I must somehow find an outlet for this anger that filled me to overflowing. No sooner than crossing the street at Allison and Courtland, it happened. Then and there, the revenge thing began for me at least. No finesse, no art, just an all-out attempt to defeat. Ralph Timberding and I carried it out, but maybe he didn't know.

Julia and Sarah

U ntil Abe Dernham's assets were totaled, Julia and Sara were given money to cover burial expenses as well as necessary living expenses for themselves and the needs of Eva at the rest home. When all the assets were totaled, the sum then would be in the hands of Julia and Sarah alone, with Julia the provider as prescribed by their faith. These assets would of course be mostly stocks and some bonds. That was Abe's business. This was one year after the fall of the stock market, making the totaling of his portfolio difficult and time consuming. Thus, Julia and Sarah's real financial condition was in the balance. It was hope for the best and prepare for the worst of times. At worst they would have a small apartment such as the one they occupied with bare necessities. At best, a home of their own with low expenses, enabling comfort for their last days. As time went by they pondered many questions. How long or how often would they be able to visit and care for their poor sister Eva, who never recovered from shock sustained in that streetcar accident. How would they provide their own needs? These sisters had always depended on Abe with Ralph's services to provide their every need. These sisters had always been so close as to have made no friends since coming to America. They visited the synagogue only a few times in eight years. Under Dr. Wise's reform they hardly fit in at the Plum Street Temple, yet they continued their support. They had some difficulty with the English language and were frightened by the daily news of violence in America. They really knew no one and fully trusted only Ralph. They needed him now. They anxiously awaited a word, something implicating a settlement that would help them afford Ralph.

Ralph Jr. and Louis would go to the garage to meet Papa when he returned home from work. In doing so, they learned that Mama and Papa's first conversations were the most revealing. They listened as Papa spoke first. "I'm still going to have Mr. Mendel to take here and there. That will take care of the mortgage and some automobile repair work here and there sure would help. I'm sure something will happen soon. I'm looking every day and asking everyone what places are hiring. I need something steady."

Said Mama, "I hear there are few jobs and many are being laid off. Things continue to get worse. It's the depression, they say. I'm praying you can get past that working under automobiles in the winter, Ralph. There must be something in our future."

The phone rang, there was a silence. Mabel, who was fourteen, answered. "Papa, it's for you," she said.

"Who is it?" asked Papa.

"It's a white lady," said Mabel. After taking the phone, Papa returned to the kitchen. "That was Abe's sister, Julia, those bitties. How do they have the nerve to ask me to work for them? Can you imagine that? They are too pesky. They want you to do everything imaginable. Go here, go there, always in need of something they don't have. And besides, they don't have a dime. Abe did everything for them. They have nothing and they know that; besides, nobody could ever please them. Never," said Papa. "I'll walk the streets. I'll not work for them old bitties."

This Great Depression was now worldwide and known by all and suffered by all in some way. Those with a breadwinner who was unemployed knew it painfully well and from the heart. Hardships can draw people together like beetles around an outside light in the summer. This family would gather at the kitchen table for dinner, staying there until bedtime, so as not to have to heat up the bedrooms before bedtime. They talked, they sang, occasionally they joked, and they did homemade or make-up crafts. They played cards, checkers, and drew and colored with crayons or watercolors. They made popcorn, cookies, and candy. There was homework, too, as well as help for anyone who needed help. The atmosphere was jovial, or at least congenial. Mama saw to that. Christmas came with great joy and expectations, yet leaving some quite bewildered. Some were disappointed and let down. The New Year again promised hope for a long-term solution.

Julia called twice more, determined to get Papa to reconsider. Papa refused to talk, virtually hanging up the phone saying, "I'm sorry, but I cannot accept the job. I need something better." Still determined to engage the services of Papa for her and Sarah, she turned again to the bank manager for assistance. The bank manager agreed to call Papa.

On returning home, Papa was told that the man from the bank called and wanted to meet him before noon at the bank. "What could he possibly want?" asked Papa. Papa also kept a small savings account at the same bank and wondered what could be the purpose of the call. His thoughts were, "I don't have any loans except the mortgage, and that's paid. I only have a few dollars in my account." He made no connection with the bank and the bitties, as he called them. At the time Papa arrived home the bank had already closed. Papa would have to wait until the morning to know what the problem was.

On his arrival, Papa was ushered directly into Ben Campbell's office. Ben went directly to the point. "Ralph," he began, "Julia and Sarah Dernham can now be considered millionaires. We've just completed a totalizing of all the assets of their inheritance. Abe Dernham was a wise and prudent man as well as tremendous business manager. As you are well aware, I've talked with Julia about your services and the matter of wages. We agreed you should be paid as well as the best are paid. You should seriously consider this, Ralph, it's a darn good offer. You might want to talk to Julia on the other issues such as hours and other working conditions."

"I know them from the past," said Papa. "They want a flunkies to do this and do everything around that apartment. All hours, just like they did when Abe was living, only it was me running here and there." He wanted something better, but he started to think how badly he needed the offer of a steady wage now with eight children. He had cleared what was on his mind spoke his piece. Then a short discussion with Julia and Papa was back chauffeuring,

Papa sat in his favorite chair in the kitchen at home. Louis was standing beside him. Louis was anxious to hear Mama and Papa in conversation, because there seemed to be something brewing within the family. Though they were in a good mood, he was not hearing any real news. He soon gathered that Papa had been home at noon following an important meeting to have coffee with Mama. Papa had stopped at their favorite bakery on this day and brought a piece of cheesecake to share. As Mama started up singing, "Blessed Assurance, Jesus is Mine," Louis became more bemused.

"What's that?" asked Louis, pointing to a piece of newspaper protruding from Papa's shirt pocket.

Papa pulled the paper from his pocket, ran his fingers over it as he would a wrinkled dollar bill, and said, "This is the car I'll be driving." The picture was one familiar to many as it showed former President Woodrow Wilson in his Pierce Arrow automobile.

"Whoo-wee, what an automobile! Did you see that, Mama?"

"Yes," said Mama. *So!* thought Louis. Mama and Papa had made their decision about the job with the sisters. Papa was an honorable person, prompt in his appointments and trustworthy, as proven in the past dealings with the Dernham family. He did every task asked of him with a smile and to his best abilities around the house, the yard, or with the car. To drive and to service the car was his passion. Other things like shopping for the house in bad weather when Julia and Sarah stayed home he found enjoyable. On the other hand, there were the pesky, demeaning, annoying calls late in evenings. They heard noises, the sink or toilet was stopped up, the window would not open or shut. There was a mouse in the basement, a bat in the upstairs. After calling him from home, they would take hours to explain or to get ready. Abe, their brother, was as prompt as sunrise. They lose keys and get locked out on the porch. Because of this, they gave him a set of keys, which did nothing to eliminate the problem. These calls presented another problem for Papa, as they sometimes came when he was working on someone's car. These things greatly disturbed Papa.

Within the Gardner family there was happiness, even with the severity of the nationwide depression and its joblessness. They had unity. There came some aid to families now in the form of government surplus of rice and flour. Some potatoes, margarine, and peanut butter. This was a help but not survival for the unemployed. While Papa worked more than many, he and his family had yet to recover from the loss of wages when Abe died. Added to this was the greater and more visible problem that their family had now grown to ten siblings. The poor little house at 1709 Hopkins was overcrowded. The need for space was stifling.

These problems overwhelmed papa. There seemed to be no progress, simply a hanging on. Every family in the neighborhood, or those we knew elsewhere, were on low wages—if they had an income—and all were in need. Maybe having worked for Abe Dernham, Papa had learned to spot the signs of progress, but this was the Great Depression. The few Papa saw not working seemingly were no worse than he. Then one day out of aggravated, pinned-up feelings, Papa left Julia and Sarah in anger, vowing to hit the street until he found something better. What he found was that most were as bad off as he and many much worse than he. Some had been unemployed as long as four years. Some were homeless, some virtually homeless while living in attics or basements of relatives. Some worked in exchange for meager living conditions. The newspapers showed pictures and told stories of once wealthy people who became penniless when the stock market crashed, and those who jumped from bridges to ease their troubled minds. Many working classes lost their homes. Some walked off from families in shame and frustration when unable to provide the necessities. What kept Papa? Was it Mama's singing of gospel tunes? They all had a message. Was it Mama's undying faith? Did he feel he had something to prove like his true faith as a man? The real answer will never be known.

The first calls from Julia Dernham were of course ignored. Later someone had seen a younger Caucasian driving the Pierre Arrow. Papa's words were, "Those bitties will never be satisfied with any other person, they only trust me. Nobody can do all the things I have done and can do for them. I'm not going back; they are not going to pay me equal to what I need." Maybe six months later, Ben Campbell at the bank called.

"Come over, Ralph, let's talk," he said.

"Well, okay, I'll be over in the morning," we heard Papa say, which brought some joy to the roving eyes of those siblings present. Julia and Sarah were aging and becoming more and more dependant on others for service and care. The bank manager again called Julia to relay Papa's reflections. He needed more income to satisfy the conditions at 1709 Hopkins Avenue. He needed at least one full day free, for which he did not elaborate, but it was for other opportunities to employ himself for financial gain.

Papa held out, knowing the new chauffeur had accidents with the car and was accused of drinking. The repairs as well were likely due to improper care. When Ben Campbell hung up and turned again to Ralph, he said, "Ralph, Julia wants you to work for her as she always has. Just tell me what your legitimate needs are, I'm sure we can reach a settlement that will be good for you as well as for them."

Ralph answered, "My house is number one, but that's not their problem, only more income one way or another can correct that. The time off is really for the same purpose to work on automobiles and my chauffeuring, mainly Mr. Mendel. I have worked for him for several years now. I have a mortgage obligation that comes first. Then we have ten children now."

Ben said, "I'm well aware of that concern, Ralph. Listen, Julia has not spent anything equal to what her assets are. They have increased in value in the past years. Suppose," said the manager, "that she agrees to a Sunday that is free and at least one half day on Saturdays, except for emergencies. Emergencies will happen, and we know that this is fair and she will no doubt agree. Ralph, we are talking about two elderly women without the energy to perform daily tasks. They need help on every hand. Though they have finances beyond their needs, they stress themselves managing it, however, and that's a benefit to you. Let me make an offer that will satisfy your needs as far as your house is concerned. Suppose I write up an offer? She will guarantee a loan that will pay off your existing mortgage, and cover the add-ons to your home, including converting that coal furnace to gas and adding a bath with a hot water heater. We will not add on the minimal office expense of one and one half percent. Of course, this will extend the loan another two years. So long as the regular payment is made on time, there will be no interest charge. That is a favor from Julia. Now how could any thing be more fair and equitable?"

Papa said, "That sounds good." The deal was written, offered to Julia, and was accepted the following day. Papa was again driving for Julia and Sarah Dernham.

This represented a new beginning between Papa and the sisters. Julia gave Papa the rights to negotiate a deal to buy a new car, which he chose only when given a piece of the salesperson's commission. He chose again a new Pierre Arrow to be shipped from New York. Papa seemed to accept his responsibilities with a new dedication. The sisters spent more time out and about in the new car and all seemed to appreciate each other. They went up and down the river on both sides. They went beyond Hamilton, north of Cincinnati and south toward Lexington. They met farmers who sold produce wherever they went. They ordered only kosher foods from select stores, and a Jewish bakery delivered. A Jewish doctor made regular house calls. They received literature by mail from the temple. Eva no longer recognized her sisters, but she was in good hands at the rest home. Julia and Sarah no longer visited. They began to stay at home. Papa went to the bank with a blank check to present to Ben Campbell, the bank manager, who allowed Papa to sign for a weekly draw of cash to cover wages and normal household expenses. The two became feeble. It sometimes appeared one of the two was improving, then again it was the other who was improving. The doctor began visiting three times a week. They had visitors from the temple. There was not the usual gift of turkey for the 1937 holidays. Julia and Sarah were bedridden. All attempts by Marie, the cook, to feed and nurture them failed. Seemingly with little pain, Julia Dernham passed away on January 13, 1938. She was seventy-eight years of age. In the same fashion as her sister, Julia, Sarah passed away on March 24, 1938 at the age of eighty.

The end of an era had come. Memories began to build and become more vivid. That guaranteed, interest-free loan had given the family all they needed in a home with a loan that virtually guaranteed financial security for the future. Papa was convinced there would be another job he would have to fit in. We all had fond memories of the stories told about the sisters. We remembered things they sent us—turkeys, cookies, candles, and sometimes even toys. On occasion we used the limousine with great joy, leaving fond memories at their home. We wiped the car, we raked the leaves, cut the grass, helped plant flowers and water them. We carried the potted plants inside for the winter, we shoveled the snow, and on every occasion there were refreshments. We watched the doctor coming and going with his leather case who walked from the Belvedere. People came to the parked limousine to ask questions. Sometimes a market vendor offered a fruit or handful of grapes. The sisters were little women—less than five feet tall and likely less than eighty pounds. How Papa tired of waiting, holding the door. He sometimes just picked Sarah up and placed her inside the car, then reached inside to make sure the door was locked for her safety. They were buried at the United Jewish Cemetery in Evanston, nearby their brother, Abe L. Dernham, and their Uncle Max. Strangely, of the five, Abe, Julia, Sarah, Flora, and Eva, none was ever married. The death of Julia and Sarah Dernham brought an end to an era that began with Ralph Gardner (Papa) and Abe Dernham and lasted twenty-eight years through World War I, the period of prosperity that followed, then the Great Depression that lasted into the beginning of World War II. This era depicted the life and times of one wealthy Jewish German-American family and the Gardners, an African American family.

This picture shows from left to right, Marie Wagner, Julia Durnham, and Kitti Huffman. Sara Durnham is most likely the photographer. Over Marie's right shoulder, inside the car, there can be seen the outline of Papa's white summer hat. Inside the cozy window is the reflection of Papa's watch, as his left hand is draped over the steering wheel. Papa did not like wearing a hat, as was required on most chauffeuring jobs. Here it was not required. In fact, Papa had little of the duties expected of most chauffeurs. There were night trips, in or out of town, vacations, take the kids or walk the dog, these things never happened.

Papa arrived promptly at 8 AM, parked, and entered the house. He greeted all who were there, mainly Marie, the cook, who was the senior member of the staff after him. He inquired of the sisters, offered his services, then retired to the garage. The garage was a formal coach house complete with stable area for six horses, two coaches, a wash-down area complete with drains. Above this were three rooms and bath for a live-in coachmen beside a storage area for feed. This building was Papa's domain, and he kept it well. In fact, the garage, the car, the yard, and the porches were show places. Never was the car out of service nor was any car owned by him or his employer. He kept them in perfect running condition. He kept them fit and finished so as to be envied by others.

The Parade

Having just completed and still holding the book *For Whom the Bell Tolls* in my hand, I saw my friend Julius turn onto the sidewalk to our house. Not wanting to leave the book in the kitchen, I ran to my room, pitched it onto my bed, and rushed back to the door to meet him. The thought, *oh, what a wonderful story,* filled my mind and lingered. Like the song has ended but the melody lingered on and on. So did the story.

Julius was my friend. He was six months older than me. He once lived in the house joining us in the rear. We first met when we were in preschool. At kindergarten we were in separate groups because of he was six months older. His parents passed the following year. From that time we had not seen each other until he returned to work for Dr. Silverstein, who lived only four blocks from us in the neighboring wealthy section of Avondale. Now, having reunited and into the third year, we had become quite understanding of each other. Julius, while working at the doctor's home, was supposedly home taught. My mind told me this was purely a case of one family taking unfair advantage of another family's unfortunate situation. I wish I could go on, but that is another story. He was always he was neat and dressed properly for the occasion. He wore short-sleeved golfers' type knit shirts and pressed cotton trousers with polished shoes. He always had his hair trimmed, maybe because of his job, as he did almost everything. He even did some cooking, which he enjoyed. He washed, ironed, did yard work, and would soon learn to drive a car. Once Julius was bigger than me, but now I've become taller. He once told me he was part American Indian. I told him I was too, but I said, "You don't look red."

"Well, Indians don't shave, nobody in my family shaves and I won't either," he said. Julius had a dimple on one side of a plump face from which there was most always a smile. He never frowned. Maybe he couldn't make one. Though he smoked at an early age he was yet a good friend. Now he wanted to know if I saw the news reel at the show, how the airplanes were dropping bombs on Madrid. I had to tell him about the book I had just read and could hardly shake from my mind. That revolution was now four years old, and the book was about that war. This young man is given an assignment to blow up a certain bridge leading to his town. He is given the explosives, told how to place them, and where. He is to blow the bridge up when told the enemy is near. Without the bridge, the enemy will be held back, allowing reinforcements to arrive to hold back the attackers. The young man then meets a girl, falls in love, strays from his position, then fails to get notification and fails to blow up the bridge. He is apprehended and taken to the city square, this is where the bell tolls when there is an execution. When he hears the bell, he asks, tell me for whom the bell tolls? "It tolls for thee," he is told. "The bell tolls for thee."

The sun beat down early on this July day. It was going to be hot, I could tell. With much curiosity, I listened to Julius, as we seldom went on these kinds of trips. I worked after school now, when he would normally be off work. He started out saying that Reverend Page of Southern Baptist Church said, "There will always be wars." It's nearly twenty years since the Great War, and that's most unusual. I told him my Uncle Lesley was gassed in that war. He's skinny, looks real bad, and when he coughs hard I can tell he hurts. Like I did when I had the whooping cough. We walked on and headed for the heart of Norwood. We would be there to watch the parade, a once-a-year celebration sponsored by the business men of the city. It was a Wednesday; normally stores would close at noon, that day all stores were closed for the celebration and parade. I would normally work every other Wednesday, scrubbing the floor at the barbershop of Clarence Saunders, who was also heavily into the businessmen associations. He was a poor and struggling Scotch Irish, second-generation owner of a barbershop, manager of a semi-pro baseball league, as well as financial management assistant at Oakmont Savings and Loan. He would describe himself to everyone in that way.

Julius stopped to gaze through the window of the Thom McKann shoe store to point out some shoes he liked. "I'm going to get them," he told me, "they are called wing tips. I'm gonna get cordovan brown," was his word. "At Union Baptist we do go sharp now, we dress. We all go sharp, now you know I do. I'm gonna get them Friday."

"So what, Julius?" I told him. "What's the big deal? All God's chillin got shoo-oos," I said as I walked on ahead.

"Wait a minute, you forget something," was his remark. I hesitated while he answered.

"All God's chillin can't sing," he said.

When we approached the gathering crowds along the parade route, I pointed out Shapiro's drugstore, which looked strange to be closed. Julius wanted to know how I felt on a daily basis going among so many prejudiced white people. I told him some days I felt like a piece of shit, but more often I felt by God's word and promise that I have no reason to feel inferior or threatened. As usual he did not answer. He gave little expression, just that tired old devil-like grin. I like to watch expressions. I like to judge people's reactions, their feelings. Without an opinion from Julius, I went to the steps of city hall for a good view of the parade. While standing on the steps awaiting the parade, he questioned me. Why had I spoken to so few when certainly most all went to Norwood High? Certainly we all are from Norwood High.

"I speak to those who are my friends, or I want to befriend. They do the same," I said. "That's the way in our school," I told him. "We Gardner's are the school's only Negros right now." He wouldn't like that, he couldn't stand it, he remarked. "You stay with that doctor's family and you sleep there at their house," I told him. Again he gave me that ill-defined grin. Again, in answer to his question, I said, "No, we don't go to that show, we go to the Beecher in Walnut Hills. You know that," I said, which compromised his grin. Then, as a friend would, I told him some of the things I did on my job at the barbershop where I also shined shoes at ten cents per whop. I told him how three veterans (when leaving the shop headed for a meeting at the Veteran's Hall) stopped to address a complaint. The complaint was that last year one Negro had stood up in a speech saying there had been no progress for us since World War I. The man was outraged by this and seemed sincerely ignorant of the Negro's true complaint.

"We have all progressed, how can he not see that, when all the whole country has grown and progressed?" said the man. The sounds and sight of the oncoming parade denied me an opportunity to again judge the one dimpled smile when Julius heard this.

The crowd cheered the first arriving shiny new patrol car. The police on horseback were followed by the mayor and city officials, then the NHS band, complete with drum major and cheerleaders. An unexpected feeling of pride went through me as I watched. There were other dignitaries and notables that I did not recognize. There were the Owls, the marching Columbians, and Shriners group on unicycles. The first floats appeared with a man and woman unknown to me. Then a float from the bank with none other than Vera Ellen, who would become an actress, and play alongside Rosemary Clooney (from nearby Kentucky). I had to tell Julius how she would come into study hall and sit on a seat in front of me because she knew I would not humiliate or harass her as others did. She was a mother's child, controlled and pampered. She took classes in one of the professional drama studios. She was the only girl in class who had a perm and who wore a brassiere and makeup. Soon came the Shapiro Float with the Bloom sisters, June and Billie Bloom. In her senior year, Billie won a *Pick Magazine* contest. The runner up, June, danced ballet and also went to a school for drama. June was also in my class at Allison Street Elementary as well as Norwood High. Their father came to the barbershop.

Looking ahead I could see a float with the familiar colors of purple and yellow. The same name and colors of Pierre's party goods, that store right over there. I pointed to the sign nearly directly across from where we stood. Pierre sold party goods and supplies, hardly expected to be a successful business as we were in a depression. Who could even afford a party? Pierre sold goods for all or any kind of party and much more. Fruit punch base, just add the water. Blenders, bar equipment, novelty gifts, games, dirty books, and adult sex toys. He seemingly sold everything. With his travel experience he could import things not available elsewhere. Passersby could not resist cruising his store. Pierre was from Algiers—he was a mixed French Algerian. He came to this country having been educated in Paris, France. While in London, he was successful in selling large engineering projects. He settled in Norwood with his wife and son several years ago, and he opened that store seemingly as something to do. They were quite secure with other investments. Everyone liked Pierre. He literally stunned people with his presence. They lived in Pleasant Ridge, in one of those beautiful homes near Montgomery Road. He came into the barbershop, and Clarence, the owner, made sure he got his choice seat in the extra barber's chair. Everyone noticed him and seemingly wondered who he was with his tawny brown skin. Having been a well traveled man he knew his clothes and where to get them. Clearly, he loved shirts just as I did. Everything he wore was like nothing we had ever seen before. For some reason his wife did not like Norwood and wanted to return to Paris, her home. Pierre persisted and was able to keep Chauncey, their only child, here with him. Now he had that Rita, the beauty shop operator, into that new perm stuff.

"There's Chauncey. He's my friend," I said, knowing he did not recognize me even when surrounded by the many Caucasians. "He's my friend, Julius." Julius's face did not jibe with my pronouncement. "Just keep it to yourself, Julius," I said. "I don't want to hear it. You don't think he and I could really be friends, that's because you don't know. Look, we met on the stairs to the gym and he asked me why I didn't swim. I didn't want to, I said which was a lie." "You didn't want to last week, you were not there," he said.

"Well, I told him, it is the coach who said if I go swimming he doesn't know what might happen."

"Because you are colored, and some parents don't want their kids swimming with colored. Well, I think it would be better that you don't. Now I'll let you come in on a Friday after school and swim. We drain the pool on Saturdays. I'll go with you on Fridays," said Chauncey.

"No, Chauncey, it's okay. I'll be okay."

"Are you sure? I want you to know I'm not like that, I'm your friend."

"Julius, I know what you are saying," I said. "You are my friend, have always been and always will be. Chauncey is a different kind of friend. Not better than you—of course not. I hope you have a friend wherever you go and I believe you do. Places like church and at your sister's house when you go there after church. Are you not happy at the doctor's, even though its work? Chauncey wants very much to be like his father but he is not. Yes, he pushes hard to be but he is not. Yet he is a good friend. I've never had a friend with his social or financial position. His daddy, Pierre, is celebrity-classed. Chauncey and I plan to go to the Greystone as soon as one of the top bands is there. Honestly I hope I can be as good a friend as he has been."

The many floats had passed. Nearly every business on Montgomery Road had some kind of representation. The best was over, now came that fondly-anticipated group of Veterans of Foreign Wars. The sun shown brilliantly on the honor guard as they passed before the larger crowd on the city hall steps, followed closely by the veterans themselves. The crowd let out its loudest cheer for a rag-tag group of veterans said to be of the Civil War and World War I. I could not determine which were of either war by their uniform. I guessed by their ages. These soldiers looked as if they had been taken from a history book. Or maybe it was the other way around; they should be pictured in the history book. They were history for real. They seemed to go by a different rhythm, a different beat. They had done this for a long time nineteen years and more.

"Thank God," said a voice in the crowd. "Thank God for those who fought that war to end all wars. Never again! Never again will our sons be subjected." This was 1937. Hitler would annex Austria in 1938 and invade Poland in 1939, and World War II would begin.

Tupelo

It was right after Loby came to work at Stones Bowling alley in Norwood. Loby made the job of pin setting enjoyable, especially between games. Together we listened to the stories told by the older city slicks we worked with, whose lives were so different than our own. These men, who ranged in age from late twenties to mid-fifties, were trying hard to make a life for themselves and their families. The country was yet in a depression and the going was rough for those who came to the city looking to find gainful employment. With the Chevrolet plant and the many other industries, there was a flow of outsiders. The limits placed on jobs offered to Negroes put many into bowling alleys, as meager as the pay was. They attempted to break the agony of their situation by joking and telling stories of their past and present. They nicknamed everyone. Cowboy loved cowboy movies, and talked about the latest ones and walked with a swagger. Dead Man was tall and extremely thin. Hoppy walked with a limp. Punchy was a punch drunk former boxer. My brother was the first ever pin setter from the city of Norwood. They called him Norwood. Then I became Little Norwood. Then there was Tupelo, which sounded like two-below when they said it, who came from Tupelo, Mississippi. At least that is what he said.

One day it came to the minds of some of the pin-boys that the bowling alley owner was once said to be from Tupelo. They formed an opinion that Tupelo was too small for one not to know about the other's past. A group formed in the pin-boys' room shortly after Tupelo entered.

It was Cowboy, who first spoke stuttering, "I know Mister Stone is from Tupelo and you are too, ain't that right?" Tupelo said nothing while Cowboy continued. "That town's so small, everybody must knows something about the others. Did you know Mister Stone?

He seems to favor you when you want some extra work. In a town like that, colored and white don't mix, but they knows things."

Tupelo then stood up behind the park bench table. He held both hands out, palms up, in a "what can I say?" expression. "Yes, I am from Tupelo, Mississippi, and it do not matter about what white folks do. We are better not knowing. At the city square one day, I heard loud talk and white folks gathered around. I only heard some. They talked about Mister Stone. They did. I could not get close for fear of those who were full of hate 'cause this was all about white folks. I just remember some talk was on Mister Stone. There was no talk on lynching, but they just wanted to question some in the morning. When the morning came there was no Mister Stone, he was gone. I did not know Mister Stone or what they had against him, but I began to have some fear for my own safety. I had no job, anyway. I left Tupelo a day later. I heard, too, there are jobs in Cincinnati and when I got to Cincinnati I heard Norwood. When I crossed that railroad track out yonder I saw Stone's on that big sign. I walked in and that Mister Foster put me to work most in sympathy, 'cause I was really down. Shortly I met Mister Stone. He knows I'm from Tupelo but that's all we surely know. He is a righteous man, I know that. He's done a lot for us. Are you with me?" There were some amens, and then Tupelo went on. "When Mister Stone bought this place it was already Stone's Bowling Alley, just as you see, and he carried on the same. Stone is not his name and my name is not Tupelo, even if y'all do call me that."

Pre-War Time

As compelling as the newsreels were, indicating the dire predicament of our allies in the ongoing war, we teenage African American souls gave little thought to the meaning thereof. Our everyday living and progress therein was our daily concern. Who made the dance? Who had the clothes, watches, shoes? Who could drive, who had something to drive, and the freedom to go was the utmost. Oh yes, you must also claim one of the neighborhood girls and she must concur. Don't, however, go into the west end in an argumentative way. You will be run out. Get to know the bartender or manager. Try to know the owner at least by name, use it. Introduce yourself loudly. Be cool, sit up front, as to be seen incoming or outgoing. Park close, illegally if you must. Join in, buy little but buy the best to impress. This is your day, at least that is the front. If the front collapses and you must leave, then all of Avondale must leave together even when involving more than one car. Safety first.

Hughes High School was at this time has nearly twenty percent colored. More than any of the other integrated Cincinnati public schools. George and I would park in front of the school, single out one or two, and offer a ride. This never resulted in a relationship, which was not our intent. We only wanted to be wider known. One winter day with two or three inches of snow, we drove our cars down to Lincoln and Gilbert Avenues. Here, in front of Brother's Chili, a restaurant popular with the teenagers, we would speed up make a quick turn then spin dangerously to the curb. By this we displayed our ability to control our cars on slippery streets. Some thought this exciting, others thought we were fools. I would sometimes put my convertible top up at home. Then, in front of my destination—the school, park, ballgame, or whatever—I would put it down again for show. These were our attention-getters. We wanted to be seen and remembered, mostly by the girls.

Several of the Avondale boys were now chauffeurs, at least part time. They were often allowed to use the car on Sunday afternoons. Why not? They were insured. During the first year we did not cross the Ohio River into Kentucky. Instead, George and I scouted every neighborhood where we knew or heard Negroes lived. When my cousin Loby was along, there was this North Carolinian, a Kentuckian, and a Norwoodite—a strange-sounding trio. Few places we visited had bars. Some neighborhoods had homes where people partied evenings and late at night. Our nights were short just like our money. Neither of us drank and spent money for little more than gasoline. We bought pop and sometimes stood beside our cars trying to make conversation with locals. George did all the talking while I watched. He liked the part he played. I was comfortable. In these small communities we found kids in their late teens with our common background and interests. They went to schools just like Norwood. They came from close-knit church families.

In 1940, President Roosevelt signed into law the selective service and training act, to set up the first peacetime military draft in U.S. history. We, however, continued on as usual until someone close to us was drafted. We lived for the day.

HOMECOMING

"I'm going to show you where it is," said Loby as he jumped into the car. "It's right by your church. I don't know the name of the street, but you will see. They will be there jamming like crazy. You know those guys from Avondale, George Lamar and Veppie. They love to jam to some jazz music and that girl sure can play that piano. I mean she really messes with them keys. I swanee—you'll see."

This was one of the few days I drove my car to work at the bowling alley and one of the few times I would take Loby home. This being a Monday, I had no intention of being up late. When I reached the corner of Altoona and Mathers, I turned onto Mathers and stopped directly in front of Loby's intended location. We heard the music loud and clear with a background of clapping and shouting in a joyful rhythm. Yes, those were the guys from Avondale and they were into their thing. Thank goodness the neighboring ice house and church were closed and dark. The only other neighbors were the occupants of this townhouse of four, who seemed to have no objection to the loud music. Rose Calloway played to a beautiful rhythm and with great energy rocking side to side, stomping one foot, then turning sideways and turning to the other foot. She at times seemed to play more with her left hand. "That's the rhythm side," she would later say. We momentarily enjoyed the music from the car. Then without words we both were out and in front of the porch where Veppie George and Lamar were getting with the rhythm of the piano now in serious boogie woogie. We stood and listened until Rose suddenly ended her fiery twenty-minute show. She wiped the sweat from her upper body while holding onto the hand of one young male not of Avondale. He would be her prize, we all knew. Some called her everything but a harlot. To our generation she was an enigma initiating good times.

The ever-boastful Veppie spoke out. "It's Monday and they are having blue Monday at the Cotton Club tonight. A darn good band too the Skat Man. But I'm not going to go. This Saturday is the homecoming at Wilberforce. I'm gonna get my vine out of the pawnshop and I'm gonna be ready Freddie. That is going to be the real deal. We are going to ball. Fine chicks. Jimmie Lunceford's orchestra. I'm gonna be there big time, razor sharp. Y'all know me, hey—hey."

Loby and I, having never been before, decided we would go together. We would also dress our best.

As always, I wanted to get as close as possible to where the band was performing. I squeezed myself between the dancers and along the perimeter of the gym. I never reached the position I wanted. There were no separation ropes as normally seen. The bandstand was slightly raised and the dancers so crowded the floor as to prevent my standing before the elevated stage. I continued circling the floor. I felt myself a complete misfit. No girls came with us, as usual. I had not the nerve to ask for a dance from a total stranger. My no-dancing self would embarrass myself and whoever I danced with.

Not nearly having the joy of listening and closely watching the band as I had expected, I again circled the floor. I saw Hound and in his soft but firm and excited voice he said, "There's going to be a fight." I did not question him directly. I just hoped and went on thinking that's just Hound. A fight is what he would like, that's just him. I looked around but could see very little on the crowded floor.

Suddenly, a louder heavier voice cried out sharply, "The niggers got a gun!" Everyone who heard the warning began to exit the gym. Most were in their cars, except for those who might have known the involved parties.

We sat in our car for nearly thirty minutes. Then seeing others return, we slowly ventured to the gym door. We were rejected. We had no proof we had paid. We were not students. The doorman let in those he knew. I was not sure I wanted to return. What really happened? Who had the gun? Was he gone? I saw no indication of what really happened. The night was destroyed. Who to blame? The school? Who? The crowd was too much for the gym. They sold tickets without regard to capacity. No one set or enforced rules that might have prevented this. No one even took advantage by selling food or drinks. Yes, this night we spent more than a week in preparation for was over. We would not return and pay the price of another ticket. There might not be a show worth the second price, or there could be another fight. No, at least for Loby and me, it's home again.

While we sat in the car, Lamar and Veppie came up to us. They sat in the back. In disgust I spoke up, since I was the driver. "I've got other and better things to do. We can't just sit here waiting for that crowd to leave. Let's just get the heck out of here."

Questioned Veppie, "How are you going to get out of this mess the way these cars are parked all crazy?"

"Just move 'em," I answered. "Just like you're going to steal one. Hound can do it." They laughed.

I didn't understand how this had happened. I thought this was a good school. My sister went here when I was eight. It never was like this. I couldn't believe this. They can ditch this place and start all over again. No rules, who's in charge. The students?

"It's not like that," said Veppie. "Come here on another day you'd see the real Wilberforce. I've not been a student here, but I know the church that supports it. This school is the brainchild of our fathers. Who never had a chance themselves, but they sacrificed for us. And don't worry, this school will be here for your children, their children, and mine. Those older church members will never see this school fail. This school will be here. This day is given to the students but it's their only day. Monday you will see ministers, teachers, and student ministers leading by example. I wish I were coming out of here with a degree! 'Cause then you are equipped with an education and no one can take that away from you. No, the battle is not over then and there. You gotta prove yourself, show you can do your thing, or you will be put back into the ditch where the one who wants it the most gets it. Like our ball team that went to

Walnut Hills. Walnut Hills had uniforms, more players, and bigger players. They had everything we didn't have. But I knew when their best pitcher, with his long, lanky, left-handed self, came out throwing nothing but heat, the game was in our hands. I've never seen a high school pitcher with a fast ball I couldn't hit. I hit the big home run early, then we shut them down. You gotta believe and be hungry. You must want it more than the others. Home, James!" he said, referencing a recent movie.

North Carolina

President Roosevelt was nearing the end of his second term. He had kept us out of the war in Europe thus far, and now the people could see some improvement on the job front. Papa was no longer driving for a living. With prospects for higher pay, he again negotiated a mortgage loan to buy a new car. This time he wanted a 1941 Chevrolet. His first venture beyond a Ford factory-produced car. By paying cash at the dealers, he got a cut into the salesman's commission. This was the best way to buy a car in his words. As expected by all, next would be another trip to North Carolina. This time it would be his boys again. On this trip he would go a little later in the season in order to bring as much food as possible. Mama would like some of the late crops suitable for canning—any fruit, including grapes, peaches, and honey. This time we were also instructed to return with one of those cotton candlewick patterned bedspreads sold along Route 25.

The new Chevrolet was a little larger than the Ford. We traveled faster and took the hills and curves with more grace on improved roads. Papa seemed more relaxed than before, indicating a more enjoyable trip. We did not need to stop at Nashville, though at times it was considered. We cruised through most of the small towns without interference. The scenery was beautiful as ever, however, at Aunt Lillie's we again stopped for the night. We slept in the car as we did before. Cecelia slept with the girls, Helen and Vaudie Mae. We all greatly enjoyed our one day with the family. We again negotiated the climb to the homestead. Papa once more feared he would damage his new car, so he cautiously climbed the mountainside to the homestead. Fondness and joy surrounded us when greeted by our cousins, uncles, and aunts. We ate our fill of those big fluffy biscuits along with all the other goodies spread out at breakfast.

On this trip, Loby and I went more directly to the homes of our relatives. Having a camera belonging to my sister, Mabel, I took many pictures as we traveled. Many of the relatives I could not name after the pictures were developed. While in front of the post office, a car pulled up and stopped. Within the car was a close friend of Loby's, driving. He stopped, asking Loby about going to Forest City. "No," said Loby. "I'm with my cousin and you don't have room. I'll see you all later." Loby again looked at the passengers in the back seat. When seeing Daisy McIntyre, he asked if she remembered me. She bobbed her head as if to acknowledge, but said nothing while the car sped off towards Forest City. We went again to the church. We again listened to the testifying and singing of the Holy Rollers and left the church as before.

On our second day, Alfred Forney came to get the three of us. He would take us to Forest city to a movie. We went in his 1930 Ford complete with a rumble seat. An open air seat folded into the car's rear deck. We first went to a restaurant where we gave an order to a colored employee at the back door. Our order was so long coming, we were forced to forgo the movie. The following day we all came up sick.

We traveled to as many places as time would allow, meeting most of our relatives. The greater knowledge of our people we enjoyed immensely, yet it is the first of anything that is the most exciting and memorable. This trip was a greater learning experience because of our age and prior knowledge. We brought our eight-year-old cousin Sue with us, who turned out to be a tremendous joy. We brought that bedspread for Mama. It was just the one she wanted, and we knew she would be delighted.

CHAUNCEY

It was the year 1939. Grandpa and Grandma were gone. Julia and Sarah Dernham were gone. Papa, who was without a job, had temporarily gone to Delco, an auto parts supplier now and soon to be a supplier of military hardware. Our county was still in a depression. We did not know the great need faced by our future allies in the war that was so immanent. Norwood's largest employer, the Chevrolet plant, was at about half its capacity. It was the same with all the other manufacturing plants in Norwood. My brother, Ralph Jr., would graduate and make an effort to land a career job. Because of the times, he decided on college, and with great effort he landed at the West Virginia State Teacher's College, for which I was extremely proud. My great friend Julius had turned over his job of housekeeper for the doctor to his younger brother. This left me without a friend because of the age difference. Now all industrial effort was spent trying to find a way out of this depression by some new product or re-engineering some kind of military product. At this time, the Gardner's were the only African American family at Norwood High. Ralph was away and Della was not yet ready for high school, which meant I was the only African American at the school.

At times, I felt loneliness, which I fought daily at first. I realized my routine made things difficult when I worked at the barbershop. However, the owner often stated his willingness to cooperate if I wanted to participate in sports at the school. I, however, had little desire to involve myself with a coach I had determined was prejudiced. Still, socializing with other students was nil.

When Chauncey asked if I would get tickets for a big show at the Greystone, I was not very surprised. He had often mentioned his love for jazz music. Then again, he expressed his desire to see a performance at one of the future Greystone dances. His offer to pay for the tickets made sure I would go. Most everyone knew the Greystone was the music hall ballroom which catering to Negroes. The same facility was the Toppers Ballroom when used for white affairs. The day came. Chauncey already had the tickets. I would be ready. He would pick me up at seven thirty. He knew exactly where I lived, though he had never been to my house. Ditto for all of my school friends and acquaintances. However, Chauncey's daddy, Pierre, came to the barbershop where I worked last year and was known from his business and his participation in as many activities as he could. Chauncey stood out by his ancestry. His father was Algerian and not at all like the pink-skinned Europeans, like nearly all the locals. Chauncey was a natural to bring enthusiasm to any group, and he usually did. Some thought he was too brash, but most loved him and were eager to be in his company or surroundings. Chuancey did not have the presence his daddy enjoyed. He seemingly forced his way by an aggressive friendliness and his ability to make people listen. He led nearly all conversations. When in his presence I was never embarrassed. He was a way maker.

This was my first time going to any event with Chauncey. I was not at all expecting he would be so prompt. As I walked from my two older sisters, Lillian and Mabel, they lit into me. "Where do you think you are going?" they asked.

"To the Greystone, of course, to see the Hawk—Erskin Hawkins."

"Who's ya hootie?"

"I ain't got no hootie. You don't know Chauncey, but he's going to pick me up. He is a white boy from Norwood.

They said, "Yes, well, you're young. You don't have a clue, Lou. You don't know what you are into. Will he know you when you are downtown or in his neighborhood?"

The same old suspicions, I thought. I know you've heard it before, but Chauncey was not a typical white boy. He loved life and was eager to enjoy it. He was a true friend. We were friends because we were different. When we were together, we made a statement. Jazz was now taking over. We had white bands playing jazz music all over.

Benny Goodman had a mixed band and that changed everything. Now jazz was America's music.

"Oh, so you are going to a dance mister smarty," they said. "You can't dance."

I said nothing, knowing they were right. "I will enjoy the music. I will see and be seen, and I will feel myself a part of this great new movement. Yes, Chauncey can dance at colored Greystone. There will hardly be any white girls there. Chauncey alone will integrate the place. The only place where truly mixed dancing is seen is in the Savoy ballroom in Harlem, New York. I would like to see my hometown be a part of or lead these changing times."

"Go ahead, little brother," they said when hearing sounds of Chauncey's horn outside.

I rushed to the front. I saw a car standing on the opposite side of the street. It was Chauncey sitting behind the wheel of the sleek, new Oldsmobile. He was dressed more dapper than I expected. On entering the car, I quickly noticed that rare odor of fresh new leather. Wow! This was the jazziest. Nobody but Chauncey had got it like this.

"It's my daddy's toy. He's pretty good about letting me use it." Chauncey sat waiting while I put on my tie.

"Your family must do pretty good," he said, looking up at the house.

"Oh yes, we do fairly well. My daddy works regular. We have a rathskeller, plenty music, and sometimes we have a party." I did not want to say too much. I did not want him to come there alone, although he probably would. I had great respect for Chauncey. I knew his daddy from coming to the barbershop. I knew about his affluent lifestyle. To Chauncey, however, everything was taken as circumstances. I knew his daring way with people. He wanted to be friends with everyone. As if he had something to prove.

"Just turn left at the traffic light, or do you know the way from here?" I asked.

"Oh yes, I do know the way to the Topper," he said. My mind lingered with the anxiety of this new car with the nearly pungent smell of new leather.

"I like this car," I said. "It's great, it's sharp, it's the lick."

"Dad trusts me. He's good about letting me drive. I'm insured and all. I just don't have my own, but that will come at least by graduation. How's things at school with you?"

"I am okay. I have no problem at all, passing grades, no detentions or any of that."

"Me," he said, "I'm doing better than good, especially with some of them because they know my dad. They don't want to ruffle his feathers. He's so much into P.T.A. and then he has friends on the school board. I have no problems there."

Approaching the ticket taker, we heard loud and clear the local group headlining the show. A trumpet blasting imitated the featured Erskine Hawkins, who would later blast away the audience with a superb performance. I wondered how Chauncey would play out the night in this atmosphere so different from his norm. What would he do? I had never given it a thought until now. My usual thing was to get as close as possible to the bandstand, right up to the restraining rope facing the stage. There I would stand throughout the entire performance, only going to the restroom at intermission, if necessary. I loved music and wanted to hear every word of the lyrics. From a glance and at a distance I once or twice saw Chauncey. Then I would lose him but knew he would be there at the end.

Within the huge crowd, leaving just before that sea of humanity where all would be jammed shoulder to shoulder, I saw Chauncey. We seemed to see each other simultaneously. He had a smile indicating he had enjoyed the night, and I was glad. We walked together to the car. It was a great performance. We both expressed our feelings. "I had a great time, so many different people, and super dancers, like I've never seen. I learned a lot," he said. I knew him to be a good communicator and a persuader. It was clear he only wanted to join in.

Chauncey seemed to have a maturity beyond his age as he maneuvered that new car from the tightly-congested area of the ballroom to Gilbert Avenue, downtown, and onto Montgomery Road. Then the straight shot to Pleasant Ridge where he lived just off Montgomery Road. He pulled onto the drive where a detached garage held a canopy to the kitchen area of the house. As late as it was, there were no other cars on the driveway. His parents, Pierre and Kitty, were likely somewhere still partying like the newlyweds they were. We entered the kitchen.

"I'm pouring me a drink," he said. "Want one?"

"No," I said, "I'm okay."

"There's enough, one or two won't be missed," he said. Then he called out, "Come here Deb." He was speaking of course to his younger stepsister. He wanted only to show off or show her his privileged position. His daddy, Pierre, had married that top beautician, Kitty. He wanted to show his stepsister he had position, he could do what she could not. She came to the kitchen or at least to the bottom of the steps. Still in a nightgown, Deb was clearly not happy to have been awakened just for Chauncey to show off.

"Run and tell Deb, like I know you will, but it's okay, you will never stop me, we are in control, me and Dad. I don't care what you say or do," he said.

Deb looked hard at each of us, showing her distain, and uttered, "Okay, Chauncey, but you . . . well, you . . ." She turned and went again up the stairs.

"I'm ready to go home, Chauncey. Take me home," I said.

"Okay, Lou, I'll be ready in a minute. But you see the life I live. What I go through?" Really, I did see what he was going through. He was used to being the only child. Pampered by the notable Pierre. Now he had a stepsister and didn't know how to deal with it.

"Take me home, Chauncey. Take me home."

Vivian

Late in 1939, Loby came to Cincinnati from North Carolina along with his sister, Lois, and brother, Justion, known as Jet. They now lived two doors from Aunt Hattie, Mama's sister, who lived at 3539 Irving Street. This house was still owned by Grandpa Williams and the birthplace of most of two generations of that family, including the Gardner's. At first Loby and I saw little of each other because of the walking distance and the need to transfer when having the funds for the streetcar. Loby came over one day wanting to go to Stone's bowling alley with me. He wanted a job. "Great," was my response. He fitted in well with the work and people. However, again the traveling distance and meager wages made things difficult. Loby gave no thought of schooling in Cincinnati. The family of three sought employment and soon found jobs that would sustain them until something better came along. Meanwhile I visited on Sundays after church and dinner.

These houses on Irving Street had lots running to Forest Avenue. On two of the lots stood one-car garages accessible from Forest Avenue. One garage was converted and used as a church. The folding entry doors were permanently closed, then covered with a draped cloth inside. A pulpit was fashioned in front of the drapes. A raised bench stood along the back wall.

"Come on," said Loby while I followed, coming from his house on the adjoining lot. "Let me show you something." He stopped just outside the church. "You want to go in?" he questioned.

"No!" I said.

"Then just wait a minute," he answered. Abruptly the door opened, showing a lighted view of the small church. Two girls stepped out. Loby introduced me, and the four of us walked the several feet to the corner of Forest and Irving Street. From there the older girl said goodbye, and turned to her house on Irving.

Then, as the younger girl said goodbye and continued up Forest, Loby turned to me, saying, "Talk to her. Say something, just talk to her. I dare you, Louis." I had said nothing to this point and having great difficulty with shyness, I took my cousin's challenge. Loby, seeing me fall behind, cupped his hands to his mouth and said, "Her name is Vivian."

I quickened my step, catching up. "Vivian," I said. She stopped abruptly and looked directly into my face with the most engaging smile I had seen. Warm and beautiful, but I could see she was far too much younger than I to be a girlfriend. I was seventeen. More the reason to walk her home at a mere fourteen. This little sister figure will never be a girlfriend.

"Loby is your friend?" she asked.

"He's my cousin," I answered.

"I like him a lot, he's funny. I love the way he talks." She had an accent that spelled Kentucky, while Loby had that North Carolina drawl, as Papa would say. I asked how far she lived from where we were. She answered with an unexpected maturity and assurance. "You can make it to my house and it's okay." Soon I was into the longest conversation I had ever had with a female other than family. I was enjoying this. We reached the last house on Dick Street where she lived. At the sidewalk before her front porch, I stopped, said goodnight, then waited to see her open the unlocked door. Then it was that long walk to Norwood. The weather was gorgeous. Darkness would not overtake me on this late summer evening. We repeated this scenario until cooler weather when Vivian's mother noticed our standing just inside the gate, nearly shivering, and told us to come in. I then got to know her family, her father, mother, and one brother, George Gazzaway, who was one year older than me. Vivian, however, maintained that little sister status to me. Vivian and her parents were the Moors. George Gazzaway was the child of a previous marriage. Mr. Moor was a janitor at Douglas school. He bought a car just one week after I bought my first car, for their transportation, mainly his job. On one occasion I was there when

George went to pick Mr. Moore up after work when George was told to attend evening adult classes while waiting. I was greatly surprised to find George, along with the adult class, could not do simple arithmetic.

One Sunday Mr. Moor gave Vivian tickets to Carthage Fair. We went and walked the entire grounds, observing everything that piqued our interest. We sat on a park bench. I gave her the cost of a hot dog and soda, explaining I had dinner at home before leaving. She went to the concession stand while I waited, sitting on the park bench. After standing in line a considerable amount of time she returned, empty handed. Before she reached the table where I sat, I asked her what happened. "Oh," she said. "There was this little boy, and he seemed to want some food so bad and I just had to give it to him. You should have seen him. He was cute." This impressed me greatly but not enough to spring for another snack, which I later regretted.

While we sat the subject of school came up. "You are in eighth grade, tell me about your school," I said.

"It's okay, you know it's Avondale school. All Jews, well, you know, mostly Jews. We have some white teachers. Some are good some not so good. I'm onto what they are about, though. Those Jewish kids have so much. They come to school with everything, most have allowances. They have the clothes, rings, watches, they carry candy, chewing gum sometimes, even cigarettes." She chuckled. "They come to school by car, some chauffeur driven. I'm not the only colored in my class, though. There's that silly Billy Bowens who sometimes makes me sick with his silly remarks in class. As far as grades go, I'm satisfied just keeping up, but my parents always want more. George, my brother, hates school and has not been to school since we came here from Falmouth Kentucky. Where we used to live. He's been working at that dry cleaners but I hope he finds something better and so does Mom and Dad. He drives pick up and delivery and only gets paid when driving. That's not fair. The Avondale school is our school. There's no other school when you live in Avondale. Mom and Dad they think it's great, better 'n Falmouth, where they went. Even before me."

With great passion for her and her past, I interrupted. "My mother went to your same school, Rockdale and Reading Road."

When I tell her of some of my experiences at Norwood High she said, "Yes, I went to a school just like yours, Avondale." We laughed. "Now that you have a car, you know where my school is, you can take me home sometimes. We get out at three. George gets me sometimes, but he is not dependable at all. Sometimes I am almost home when he comes. Then if I wait he doesn't show. He has excuses, oh yeah, but I don't know his problem."

When saying goodbye, I said, "I'll see you after school tomorrow." A great and sincere promise.

As I sat in that 1935 Ford Convertible directly across the street from the Rockdale entrance, I could see her break from the crowd. She noticeably held back that great smile, which I was anticipating. We went directly to her house, with little conversation. When we arrived I got that great smile, tied in with a feeling closer than in the past. As fate would have it, that day would long be remembered.

Spring 1942

"Suddenly I hear singing just outside the door.
There goes my baby with someone new.
He sure looks happy and I'm so blue."
Hank Williams.

I heard a tap on the door. I didn't see her as she passed the window.
Likely I was too busy selecting just the right recordings I wanted
to hear before catching my ride to work on the four to twelve. I
knew who it was right off. Hazel Lackey, she's a younger, white
hillbilly girl my sister Della's age. *Don't she know Della's not going to
come downstairs for a visit with her?* I thought. I heard her low voice
singing again. I could hear her snap her fingers.

Bye, bye love.
Bye, bye happiness.
Hello loneliness, think I'm going to cry.

I opened the door. She stood still and erect, as she knew I would
stand in the doorway to talk. Her attempt at a smile did not convey
joy or sadness. She truly was a sad person who tried to spread some
kind of joy. She was from one of the two Lackey families from way
down in Kentucky, though she herself was born here in Norwood.
They were the least-respected families in the neighborhood, avoided
by most and rejected by some. With only one house between their
house and ours, we could often hear loud conversations and knew
the atmosphere there, though we never visited. There seemed to be a
pecking order at her house, and she, being the youngest, was picked
on the most. Though they say Kentucky is the state of fast horses

and beautiful women, there was no beauty among the Lackeys. Hazel was persona non grata.

"She's not the same as the others. You have got to know her," is what my sister Della said.

She went on telling me of the new hillbilly songs. She even sang the first line of two of her most liked country songs and then a church song. "All music is good," she said. I felt she would lift herself if she knew how. While I vaguely listened and thought back on her family's standing within the community, I wondered how could she have come from such a vile and prejudiced family and be any different. I remember how she came to the door one time before. Her father called and she answered while he went on in profanity as to what would happen if she did not get her ass home where she belonged.

Suddenly, Hazel seemed to see my lack of appreciation of her conversation. She took a deep breath. "I might take a lickin' for coming here, by God. But so be it. I just always liked you guys," she said. She never returned and I never saw her again.

Desperado

"We'd like to speak with Louis Gardner."

"That's me," I said, before they went any farther.

"No, we want you to go to the station just for a minute we want to ask you about just a few things." Fully assured I had no knowledge that would interest them, I walked with confidence between the two officers to their cruiser. Then we went on the short distance to the fourth district police station on Beecher Street in Walnut Hills.

"Who is George Gazaway, and how does he happen to be driving your car?" was the first question.

"He's my girlfriend's brother," I answered.

"Then who is Ronnie Evers to you?"

"I don't know him," I answered.

The fourth district police station was housed a modern building on a mostly residential street. A gravel driveway led to a garage at the rear end of the lot. The two officers stepped from the car and opened the door while I stepped out un-handcuffed. Was this an attempt to charge resisting arrest? I was ushered to one of the two holding cells. Then came that unmistakable sound of the cell door closing.

These guys are serious, I thought. *What's this all about? Why me? I know nothing. If they had questions why didn't they ask?* George Gazaway could have told them more than I could about anything. I was only visiting Vivian. I let George use my car, but I had got a job. I didn't hang out. I had no need to steal. *I make more money as a janitor at that Wright Aeronautical plant than you guys do*, I thought. I don't steal. It was hard to believe George would steal.

The jailor's conference was over. They came to me, saying, "We need you to identify someone for us. We will only take a few minutes." They drove to a house on Irving Street. One of the many which I had no knowledge of who lived within. "Stay put," were their threatening words as they left the car.

"I will shoot," the other said. The house was dark and no one answered the door. We returned to the holding cell.

Jail cells are constructed in such a way as to restrict their occupants to only straight away vision. You can see the blank walls directly opposite the cell itself. Going to the barred doors you see more walls. You begin listening to sounds. You quickly learn to identify sounds and connect those sounds. This building was one floor and slightly larger than a service garage. The windows and doors were screened and open because of the heat, thus the sounds were not restricted.

Again I questioned myself as to what was really happening to me and why. George used my car on Friday and came back with some used fog lights. He had attached them to the front bumper of my car. He did not explain. He just thought they were a nice addition to my car. "They look good," he said. Unable to see any of the actions of those who controlled this place, I again went to listening intently. Between the cells and the side door by the driveway was the officer's locker and exercise room. Not all, but much of the conversation was audible from the cell.

I heard them say, "We are going to have a roasting. Oh yeah! Fresh meat. He don't know anything. I'm going to give him something to make him remember. He'll know something. We're going to make him sing just like all the others. Oh yes, he will sing."

I heard their words yet they seemed so far removed as to refer to someone else. Yet there was none but me. I alone was the subject. A deep, chilling feeling consumed me when I realized all the talk and their intentions were their plans for me. I had heard many stories of how many African Americans had been severely beaten right here at this police station. They used rubber hoses to prevent visible scarring. They said the screams were ungodly. I attended the Beecher Theater just down the street every week, where many stories were told. We all knew them to be true. *Oh my God!* I thought. *How could this be really happening to me? How would I ever overcome?* I was weakened to submissiveness. My heart pounded and I began to sweat. Painfully I paced the cell and pondered the situation, putting together and reliving the events of the day, still in my Sunday clothes. I had been to Sunday school and church. My thoughts were in turmoil. With one hand I held that great spirit just this day uplifted by the Reverend Young at Mount Zion, United Methodist Church, who so elegantly preached forgiveness by faith. That song, "Hold Onto God's Unchanging Hand." It was still a part of me. *Oh, spare me Lord or help me endure.* My thoughts were now pitted against each other. I knew which one I wanted to prevail. I now know which one would prevail.

I remembered the words of my mother, "the truth shall come to light, and the truth shall set you free." So confidant was I that now I could feel for those who went through this before me.

I listened more intently. I did not hear a car pull onto the gravel driveway. I did hear a screen door slam shut. Then I heard the voices within the room go to whispers, then a complete silence. I realized it was the captain and commander of the station checking in on a Sunday. He immediately sensed the mood, posture, and intentions of the on-duty officers.

Loudly he stated, "You guys have a lot to learn. You take too much for granted. You don't know. This man may not even be eighteen. Gilbert! Take this man to headquarters and have him booked right now." As instructed, Gilbert came to my cell, handcuffed me, and took me to the basement of Cincinnati City Hall where I was booked for possession of stolen goods. I would face the judge the next morning and likely be released if my statements were correct. I felt somewhat better.

Later in the evening I heard a door open and shut. Then whispering voices. It was my sister, Mabel, and Mama trudging alongside. Oh, what a relief it was to see them. Mama was not as disturbed as I would have thought. She certainly had prayed and she knew I was not one to be involved with the police. They now knew I had been charged with possession of stolen property. They needlessly advised me to tell the truth and they left, seeing I had been comforted by their show of support.

When morning came I somehow had managed to get at least some restless sleep. This dreadful cell had cold running water and a towel, which I feared using. An officer came to my cell, loudly calling out my name. Again I was handcuffed in a matter of fact manner. Still wearing those now wrinkled clothes from Sunday, I must have looked as miserable as I felt. The officer directed me to the elevator, then down the hall to the courtroom. Surprisingly there were few people in the halls or courtroom on this early Monday morning, which eased my tension. We stood inside the courtroom's door, in the middle aisle. From this point on I was unaware of the court's procedure. When ready for me to appear before the judge, the prosecutor beckoned the officer to bring me up. We approached the bench, stopping just before the judge. Sitting on the witness stand was Ronnie Evers. This was my first time to put a face to the name I had been questioned about on the night before.

"Who is this man and how do you know him?" the judge asked Ronnie Evers.

"I don't know him," Evers answered. With a backward move of his right hand, the judge gave an order for Evers to be removed from the bench. On his way, Evers could be heard saying, "What you all trying to put on me now?" There was a muffled sound of voices in response to Evers's remarks. This almost comic sneer at the justice system could have caused him additional harm. He was asking for trouble. I then was directed to the bench Evers had left. At this point I felt some relief, yet had no inkling of what to expect from here on. The judge swore me in. Then the judge, wanting to quiet the room, raised his right hand with two fingers extended like a third grader wanting to go to the bathroom. The sparse crowd in the courtroom went even more silent. He turned toward me while setting aside the papers he held in his hand. I saw a broad-shouldered man with a face similar to John L. Lewis, the head of the United Mine Workers Union, who had been in the news a lot lately. Very heavy graying brows, somewhat squinted eyes, huge jaws, and a wide, thin-lipped mouth. There were no microphones. His heavy voice was quite sufficiently controlling the courtroom. Even with the hum of the electric circulating fan placed at the side door, he could be heard throughout the small room.

He beckoned for me to come even closer. Looking down with a grim face, he said quite loudly, "Look at me! Listen up. State your name." In a quivering voice, I answered. He continued, "Where do you live? Do you have a job? Where?" Things he already knew. "You are charged with possession of stolen property. That is something serious. Your problem is hanging out with the wrong crowd. You had better learn who you are associating with. Listen, get rid of every one of them. If you don't and you ever come here again, you will be facing some serious consequences."

When he finished he did not give that same simple one-handed brush off motion he gave Evers. Instead he turned toward the officer and raised his heavy eyebrow and tilted his head toward the exit door. The meaning was the same in a kinder, gentler way.

Standing before that judge while handcuffed was an overwhelming experience of humiliation. Nothing I can imagine could be worse. His judgment was yours, not to defend against, but to live with, without compromise. Painful yes, yet so real. No recourse. A done deal. No more associating with my new friends in Avondale. Hard. No more of my "little sister's" companionship, not even that unforgettable smile. Even harder. My cousin might visit at my house, but I would not be going to Avondale. The hardest.

I soon met Mabel and Mama in the hall. I took the back seat in the car out of respect. I expressed my sorrow for having so inconvenienced them and embarrassed the family.

"I will overcome this," I said. "I'll do the right thing."

"That's what I want to hear," said Mama. "You look okay." Mama knew the stories of horror in the city following the arrest of Negroes. She had likely heard more than I could relate.

A quick bath, then while still in my robe I threw myself across my bed. Many troubling, provoking thoughts consumed me. The new aircraft engine plant called Wright Aeronautical where I worked. The unusually high wages put me in an unbelievable position of means, yet there was so little time to enjoy. Ten hours for five days, then a mandatory eight hours on Saturdays. Quite miserable at times for a barely eighteen year old. I had to carry on. This was what set me apart. It's why I was looked up to by the younger children who were so happy to run to the drycleaners for me. They like the opportunity to have their own just as I did. Wonderful!

I greatly missed my only brother Ralph, now away at school. He somehow would have advised or warned me of this predicament. I was proud he was going for a higher education and I'd be proud when he finished. He would be smart, I knew. Certainly tops in his things. Whatever. Why? He competed with the best, always. That's what makes the best. Where's Mama? At times like this she vanishes. She entered one of the rooms and closed the door. On days like this we all know she is likely praying. When she shuts herself in you don't disturb. God, I loved my family. What would Papa say? My agonizing thoughts drifted away, allowing sleep to intervene, overtaking my troubles.

Mildred

You promised me love that would never die.
That promise you made was only a lie.
Hank Williams

"That's Carlotta going to an old hillbilly song trying to put a cap on John and me" said Mildred The girl can sing but not that song. It's not getting her anywhere. She's no better than I am. John's in jail and can't, her man's on the street and ain't. She should have shut her mouth then but she went on. "I saw you coming from the hospital, your little one all wrapped and dainty. It wasn't John, it was your sister who your mother had to send to pick you up from the hospital." She went on, singing, "And when I was down, you just left me there. I needed you so, but you didn't care."

I turned away, tormented. I nearly called my best friend what rhymes with witch. Let me tell you about my new friend, Carlotta. "Who Louis? I already heard about him. Big eyes curly hair, don't sing, can't dance guy. What are you going to do with him? He's from way out in the sticks. Your mother likes him. He's got a J-O-B, he's mannerly. What's mannerly gonna get you? Another baby if you're not real careful."

"Oh, Carlotta, please. Where do you get all that stuff?" I asked.

"I get it from your sister, Bunky, that's who. She's no icebox. She can't keep a thing."

"Let me tell you, Carlotta, just let me tell you," I told her. "He was working evenings. I didn't remember him telling me that. I called his house. The phone was off. I called the neighbor's number he gave me. I could not get him, so I got concerned. I went to Leon. He said he would take me there for the minimum bootleg fare and he knew how to get there. I had never been there before. Nervousness

227

hit me as soon as I tapped on the door. One little sister came to the door. She must have been shocked. She just stood looking without words. I only said, 'Louis.'

Then she turned and went calling, 'Louis, Louis.'"

"I think his mother is the greatest—she has that great smile. I don't know how she feels about me, but I could really like her. When he showed me the basement party room, his two sisters and the brother were there. The brother danced with me. He was somewhat quiet, too, but not shy like Louis. I liked him. I don't know about the sisters, though. They seemed to stand off. They are all so different. They live in Norwood, of all places. A group of colored, much smaller than here where we live. Then an all-white school you might as well say."

Weeks Later

"When one day he drove to the park by the swimming pool in Middletown I liked it. We picked up a bag of food at the grocery store on our way there. We did not go to swim, he just wanted to show me the place. John did not have a car and we never went far, yet he was entertaining and he always fit in. He was always a big part of our little neighborhood group. You remember, Carlotta, when we would skip school together, you, James, and John? We danced and had fun upstairs at the Parker house. Mother liked John, maybe not as much as before he went to jail, but he was trying to provide and she knows that. All these mothers want their girls to marry for money you might as well say. I don't know if that's good.

"Louis sat quietly and patiently while I made sandwiches from the bag. I wanted to show my appreciation for the times he had given me. That's when he began to tell me a story while waiting. He was coming from the sixth street market with his sister Cecelia, his brother Ralph, and their mother. They were all carrying bags. A man stepped in front of his mother begging for anything she could give him. He was hungry and needed food, badly. His mother reached into her little snap purse, and gave him some pennies, and said that was all they could spare. The man repeatedly thanked her and while doing so they caught the odor of alcohol. The words of an old song came to Louis and he sang as best he could, 'What's the use of getting sober, when you're going to get drunk, again?' They looked at their mother and saw a smile then they all laughed.

'He should be ashamed,' Cecelia said.

'Yes,' said their mother, 'but when you're down and out you lose your shame.'"

Later in the Summer

Louis still worked at the aircraft engine plant until twelve nightly. Since Pearl Harbor he had worked eight hours a day, seven days a week. He was also 1-A on the draft list and his job could not save him from the military.

Because of his job, Louis met me at the club very late. He took me across the river to Cincinnati. I like going out with him. There was always something new, like after-hour joints as they call them. Places where people really get loose. I love dancing but he don't dance. Then I was ready to go back to Kentucky's Newport where I felt more comfortable dancing with strangers.

On the other days, he comes in the morning, wanting to go to one of the colored lunch counters in Cincinnati. I'm so into sitting on the couch, dinner plate on my lap, eating with my fingers. Sure it's just a habit, but when I'm out I feel like I'm being watched and become very uncomfortable, especially with him. Again, he came yesterday. I was shocked when he said he would be off all day and we would spend the whole day together. He claimed that would be his first day off since Pearl Harbor.

So again early in the day he wanted to go to a park. We stopped at the store again. It's okay. This time we went to Devou Park, which overlooks the river from the Kentucky side. It's just up the hill and has a spectacular view. The sun was bright and warm, the squirrels were running around, and the trees showed signs of fall. We walked to the viewing area then to a choice table where he removed his sweater and I unbuttoned my button-down. He had already told me he came to my house on Thursday and I knew he did. He even went to Henri's Tavern to look for me and my mother. "I'm sorry," I said to him while preparing our flat meat sandwiches. "When you came to the house, mother and I were just inside the house coming

230

from Henri's saloon. We had washed the front glass, cleaned the spittoons, cleaned the toilet rooms, and mopped the floors. We were tired. Not wanting you to see us, looking the way we were, we told Willow Dean to answer the door. She did and told you where we came from and not where we were." He gracefully accepted my apology and went quiet. At times like this I wondered what he was thinking and how much did he really care. He seemed not impressed by my dancing. He complimented me on two occasions about my style and dress, then often on my hair. He loved my baby Patricia just like everybody else did. He told me about his family and wanted to know more about me and my family. Today I'll tell him all I can. We will likely become closer.

Mother came here with two of her four children, Willow Dean and Marietta, leaving behind one boy and a girl. We hope to go there one day to see them. Tom, an older cousin of mother's, came along with her for protection and assistance. It's what her mother wanted. You will surely meet Tom soon, I'm sure. Tom comes and goes. Doesn't stop anywhere too long. Cleveland, Pittsburgh, Chicago, he travels all over, never staying anywhere, really. Even when here he's sometimes at our house and sometimes somewhere else. When questioned where they came from, mother or Tom have little to say. "Small town, crazy people, hard times, and jealous husband," they would say and often laugh.

We've had some hard times, too, I told Louis. Mother went on a riverboat and we were all alone. When she came home, she had some money but promised to never go again. She told us never to go on a riverboat, either. Too much, drinking, gambling, and even prostitution by those white folks. Later she went to the racetrack in Lexington. I was young but I do remember. I think she helped care for the horses. Each time she promised not to go away again. She took the extra money and bought whiskey in large and small bottles, which she would sell. Then Mr. Harrison came (that's Bunky's daddy) and he helped us. You don't want to know how horrible it was when Mr. Harrison was killed. We all were there and we knew it was time for him to come from the distillery. We heard loud screams, then we saw the horror of his limp body folded across our front gate. Mother went into a panic and had to be restrained by the police. Then she was taken away. We did not see her for something like ten days. She'd been confined to a rest home. We survived by caring neighbors. Tom was away and we could not reach him. Then Marietta went away with that door-to-door silk stocking seller, Mr. Underwood. She called him Chuck. Those stockings were so cheap they would run quicker than a rabbit, said Tom. Mother said they'd run if you looked at them hard. They came by the house in an old car I don't know where they got it. It was strapped down with belongings all packed and tied to the car. They said they were going to Detroit. Jobs, they said. It really hurt mother because Marietta was old enough to help and she was without a child.

Then it was my daddy who did not deny me. But once called me stray oats, which made me very angry when I found out what it meant. I questioned him as to why he did not marry mother and why he did not take me to his house. Everything he said angered me. I was so upset I wanted to run away. Then John Chappel came, promising things would be better. I got pregnant. For a time things went well even though I found out he had another baby girl by that girl in Newport, Bobette. Louis, you will see her too someday. They look too much alike. Mother was disappointed with me not being able to help out and she showed it. Then John went to jail. Breaking and entering, they said. I don't know why. I don't know what she thinks about you and me together, but she does like you a lot.

After telling my history he went silent again and so did I. Right now, I'm not so sure of anything, I thought, as I turned away from him. I cleared the table and went to the trash can while he simply looked. I wondered what he was thinking. I don't see him often as I would like. He gets me away from my family and the hard times. Mother's problems. Patricia needing things. Each time we go out I feel good and have a great time. He don't dance but he continues to take me. I won't complain, ask too many questions, or face him with my daily needs until I must. I'll just live for the day just see what happens.

Mildred and Carlotta

Mildred and Carlotta went to the new government program under the President's New Deal public works program. There they were introduced to electric industrial sewing machines. Mildred said one time she sewed a button on her finger while trying to sew a button on a man's shirt. The factory was called Mack Shirts in Camp Washington. They eventually worked limited hours and sporadic days at the plant. Before World War II the top pay was fifty cents per hour. Lunch and a double fare of nine cents to and from Cincinnati to Covington reduced one day's pay from three twenty to a meager sum. Mildred and Carlotta both had one child at home and constantly debated the benefits and their options of working against the need to be with and care for their child. They both lived in single parent homes of mothers who on some occasion found some days or half day's work away from home. Though Mildred had three sisters at home, she felt uncomfortable leaving her child with them while her mother, Pinkie, was away. Her sisters, Willow Dean and Vivian, called Bunkie, both loved Patricia and laughed hilariously when playing with her on the couch, yet felt no obligation to burden themselves with the responsibility of caring for her.

They went to the Cincinnati garment district where they worked to buy clothes. They bought one dress each. After wearing the dresses, they traded. Then they attempted to sell the used dresses. If unable to sell them, they attempted to trade them for anything of greater value. They often scored. They worked together to gain what they needed, such as a babysitter or tickets to a dance. They were schemers of the highest order.

Rose Calloway

As I approached my car, parked one-half block from the Sportsman's Club, I saw my number-one friend, Julius. I had not seen him in more than a year. He stood waiting by my car, dressed by the book, as I often described him. He wore a light gray fedora and a chesterfield coat with matching scarf and gloves. *Someone must have told him*, I thought. He would not have been here without being told. He had not seen me with this car.

The season was late February, and a chilly wind drove us to enter the car, whereupon Julius exclaimed, "What's going on, what's happened? I've been told you were involved."

"Well, I have a friend, Mildred, who meets me here on weekends. She was at a table with some of her friends when I arrived. I entered the club in my usual flamboyant way, removing my coat and folding it across my arm, when that Rose Calloway stepped in front of me. She pushed out her purse at me and said, 'Here, hold my purse.' Knowing her character, I stepped back and she nearly lost her purse. Without a word, I went to the table where my girlfriend was sitting.

"Rose, filled with anger, pushed people aside to stand before me and in front of my friends. She grabbed the chair and said, 'Don't you sit here.' I was thoroughly shocked. She had no reason to do that. I braced myself to be calm. I walked out the door. She followed. Rose is the one I told you who lives by my church, Walters and Altoona. She plays the piano to entertain and gets possessive and even demanding with those she draws. Outside she agreed to take a cab home if I would give her the fare. I did then, returned to our table. My girlfriend Mildred was gone. I went in the direction of her home and eventually met her at the bridge to Covington. We talked and she said she would meet me here next week. I believe her. We're getting to know each other real well now. I'm truly sorry for her problems. In fact, I am beginning to like her a whole lot. She doesn't know I feel this way. I don't dare tell her. We can't get married. I'm sure that would be the next thing on her mind."

"Louis, you met Lucille, she and I are having much fun. We have parties at my brother's, either Bus or Joe's. They both are married, you remember, and have cars and apartments. Maybe you and your friend could join us sometimes. Lucille and I will soon be married. It's the thing now. You and I are soon going to be in uniform. Those Japs bombed Pearl Harbor more than a year ago and we have got to make them pay. We will need someone to come home to." "Well, Julius, you know I work to twelve every night. That's why you have not seen me, it's so late when I hit the streets. I wonder what she does when I'm away and can't call. I wonder what she is thinking when she dances so much with others. No, I have to be sure. I will not get married. I will wait. The time is not right for me. I'll walk alone. It's my promise. I'm blind and deaf to all else. It's a family thing."

The Few, The Proud

The end of boot camp came with little fanfare. There would be no so-called graduation as in peace time, except for a group picture. We were instructed on preparations and what would be expected of us during and after our upcoming seven-day leave. On our return we would all be assigned, meaning all or most would be assigned overseas duty. The constant reminding of an unknown future burdened us. Yes, we had spent day after day pounding the hard earth of a drill field from daybreak until evening. We did the obstacle course, bayonet training, and judo. We fired the range. We practiced amphibious landing. We survived the extreme tests of endurance, the heat of the southern sun, the dust, the night treks into the river. With backpack and rifle we walked twenty miles through the forest of North Carolina and survived.

Ollie Brunson, the only boot from Arkansas, came into the tent. He offered me the use of his tailored Marine Corps blue uniform for my one-week home leave. "How much," I asked? "You are my size more than anyone I've seen and you seem to be a pretty good guy. I want nothing. Use it, take care of it, enjoy your vacation. You only get one." I thanked him in the best fashion I knew how, knowing this was a blessing. The blue uniform was not government issued. They were tailor-made and expensive, and would take more time than we had to get one made. Now this boot camp leave was not just routine leave for relaxing and recreation. It was a chance of a lifetime to do some showing off. To walk proudly in that uniform before all you might survey. Seemingly a reward, a payback for what we had gone though and all we were likely to face in future service.

I landed at home on a beautiful mid-June day to find my family well. We rejoiced while I heard remarks on my deep and early suntan and having grown. I don't know if I had grown taller in less than two months. A few pounds, maybe, but more muscle than fat I'm sure. As usual the little sisters were ready to help. A trip to the store the drugstore and the dry cleaners. Yes, my blues to the cleaners for a press. They handled that well.

Shortly after dinner I walked the several blocks to Hopkins and Montgomery to a phone booth as I wanted a completely private conversation. I inserted the nickel and dialed the number. The phone should not ring so long. Ms. Silverman was the wife of a deceased politician, well kept and secure. She or Mildred should answer. After more than the usual five or six rings I hung up the phone. I stood back outside the phone booth contemplating my next move. What had happened?

I was sure she still worked there. What could be the problem? She could have told me something in her last letter. She stayed on the place. She went on weekends to be with Patricia, her baby, but it was early Friday evening. She should be there. In frustration I held off as long as my patience would allow before I called again.

On the second try, after only a few rings, Ms. Silverman answered. "Hello?" she said.

"Hello! I'm Louis. May I speak to Mildred?"

"Oh Louis, oh I'm so happy to hear from you. I know Mildred would be so happy, but she is not here." She hesitated while I waited. "She is not here. She, uh, went to a boat ride. Yes, she will be so happy to know you are here. She will be here in the morning."

My feathers dropped. This was not at all what I expected. A child at home with her mother and sisters and she's gone on a boat ride? It took some effort to hold onto the phone. "She'll be here tomorrow, I'm sure. Call her or you might just come over. She'll be here and she is free to be off since you are here. By the way, how long are you home? She'll be so glad to see you. I've not yet met you. She talks of you constantly."

"I'll be there tomorrow," I said. I did not want to be so brief and nearly rude, but I had nothing more to offer.

Mildred had our neighbor's phone number and she reached me there. We changed plans. I would not get to meet Ms. Silverman, I would meet Mildred at the terminal on Fourth Street. I got off the streetcar at the Square, at Fifth and Main. While proudly wearing the Marine Corps blues I was stopped, greeted, and questioned by many of the whites along Fifth Street In front of the great Albe Theater, where months earlier with Mama I had remembered seeing the movie, *Gone with the Wind.* I was at one point saluted by some white soldiers because of my uniform. When I said I was a private, he rushed back to tell his friend of their mistake in thinking I was some kind of officer. I continued to Fourth Street's Dixie Terminal where I would meet Mildred on arrival from Covington, under the curious eyes of the many people downtown on this late June day. I saw her first before I reached the gate that separated us. She walked directly and confidently toward Fourth Street, with a noticeable neatness in her dress. She was gorgeous on this day as she easily strolled ahead of the other passengers. She wore low heels, stockings, and a form-fitting, knee-length skirt with a short-sleeved, high-collared blouse. As usual, her long hair flowed to her shoulders, thick and shiny in a modest pageboy style. I could not hold back the feeling of pride on greeting her. The feeling of disappointment left me. This was my real joy; this was my future, though my promise of no marriage to Mama stood. This was my future. Hopefully the time is short.

As we walked, I felt she knew how I felt. I thought or hoped she felt likewise. We passed the row house on West Eight Street. Nothing had changed. I remembered parking in front of that building, not knowing if I had the right building. I had walked cautiously to the front door, as this was my first time. I rang the bell at a very early hour of the evening. The cordiality and look on the face of the woman who answered the door assured me I was at the right location. With a little fear and much anticipation, I asked, "So, you have a room to let?" I asked as I had been told by my friend Julius.

When seeing Mildred in the car she responded, "For you and the lady?"

"Yes."

"Well have her come in."

On we walked now along Mound Street. I felt that my body had changed to a more muscular structure during boot camp. I swelled with pride and confidence. Now squarely into colored West End, the curious became bold. They approached me, attempting to shake hands. They called out from first- and second-floor windows, causing my face to redden. This was unexpected. I saw Mildred losing her composure, so I stepped closer to hold her hand. We walked onto the corner of Sixth and Mound Streets. At Sixth Street, suddenly standing before us was a young man casually but sportily dressed, motioning for Mildred to step aside in his direction. We continued. When the light changed he said something, and she stepped aside while I continued across the street. Mildred turned from the young man and hurried to catch up. When she reached the sidewalk I looked into her face and saw a most disturbing unsettling expression, after which she looked away. This would have been an invitation for many a serviceman to show any pent-up feelings or resentment. I shelved my recently trained warrior mentality. We continued to the door of the club without words between us.

The doorman spoke first, "Well, well now the marines have landed. We have all branches of the military here tonight. I don't remember this ever happening before." When I tried to pay, he said, "No! Oh no, the night is on us, we are just thrilled to have any of our military and the both of you."

I put my money back in my pocket. He pointed to the tables in front of the stage, saying, "Sit wherever you'd like." On regular occasions, Mildred would have taken a down-front table close to the dance floor. This night she pointed to the raised section just to the right of the stage. We watched the warm-up band, as we were early. Before the show began others joined us until every seat was taken. I did not dance at any time, though Mildred loved to dance and would have on any other occasion. As the tables surrounding us filled with young women I could see her expressions of uneasiness.

The MC announced "We have all three branches of the services represented here. I would like all of our servicemen to come to the stage to start this session. Now come on down, you marine. Yes you, you are the only marine in the house. We're so happy to have you and your lady. Please come on down complete the circle." I continued to sit while shaking my head when the MC looked my way. He finally relented and the dance and music went on. The girls surrounding us began to openly pass bits of paper notes, mainly addresses or phone numbers. I saw Mildred in tears. I moved closer and assured her there was not time enough for me to spend other than with her. Soon the night became a bore, and to prevent an embarrassment, we left. We went again to our old haunt. The row house was seemingly awaiting us. This night's lodging was not for the cover of sin only. It was to patch and preserve a relationship that was faltering badly.

On the following morning I rode a streetcar then transferred to the Lockland bus to the Wright Aeronautical Plant. Before pulling onto the concrete turnaround, the driver said, "This plant is all that's here."

"I know, I used to work here."

"Oh well then," he answered, "you look so young, you must have friends there; I'm sure they will be glad to see you. Will this be the first time for them to see you in uniform?"

"Yes, certainly, including my family members who work here."

At the front office a large visitor's button was pinned on me by a cheerful young man who was assigned to escort me to any part of the plant. I first went to what had been my station. There I was greeted by all who recognized me. They came forth to shake my hand. Many said they'd never seen a marine before. All seemed happy and cheered me on. The young escort led me into the north shop, knowing it to be the shop where all AA machinists were assigned. Mabel and Cecelia worked here. The Marine Corps dress blue uniform with the corporal stripped pants caught all attention. I heard, "Who's that fine hunk of a man?"

"He's my brother," said Cecelia.

I heard someone say, "Shiiit." Then I was mobbed.

Traveling at this time was hectic. Travel time could not be estimated due to the large number of travelers, business vacationers and the military. To arrive late on return from vacation could mean a day in the brig, and knowing traveling in the south your seat could be given by a white mandated early departure. Out of seven days of leave I would only spend three full days at home, so we went to that brick row house again. This time we felt better about our visit. We were not just hiding our sinful act we were patching up our relationship which was strained by the events that so shortened our time together.

Mildred was permitted to escort me to the trackside where we would board the train. We held our last embrace and last goodbye on the last minute. Before sitting I glanced out but could see nothing. The glare of lights hid those leaving the tunnel. I placed my bag beneath the seat, then dropped myself wearily on the padded seat. I leaned back, weary of it all, and with a mixture of pleasure and wonderment. My thoughts went to reliving the past and attempting to survey the ominous future.

As the train sat I relaxed into a melancholy mood. Then, strangely, I could hear Mama's voice. "Walk together, children. Walk together, children." As her children we knew the next line. "There's going to be a great camp meeting on the other side." We recognized this as one of those old songs representing that great time of transformation from slavery. A time when our people used these songs to motivate and guide our people from that hated past. This had not the same meaning for us but it somehow hit hard on our consciousness and we responded in every way to what we thought expected of us by our parents. We wanted to be a part of progress. We wanted to correct things.

Double Jeopardy

I lay across my bunk bed in the middle of the barracks, fully dressed, anticipating. What would it be on that Saturday evening? There was a movie to see, as always. Some say it's good. They always say that. Probably a shoot 'em up cowboy thing. I've seen too many of them. I have read my most recent letters from home again. Even the one from Vivian, which Robert Horn says was scripted from *Reader's Digest*. I read every page of last month's issue. I would go to the end of the barracks and ask Robert Horn if he had anything new to read. He sometimes did. He was the one who said he is a cousin to the great Lena Horne. He certainly looked the part. But he was not there. Likely he was at the movie.

This coastal North Carolina weather in early July was scorching with nearly unbearable humidity. The once grassy drill field was a dust bowl. We sweated through every maneuver and each class session. The classes were held in tents, giving us plenty of that hot and humid air. Any activity simply drained the energy. This was Papa's beloved North Carolina. He could have it. He did grow up in the northwestern part of the state's mountainous area, however. That one big circulating fan just placed at the first barrack's door made some difference, but only when there was some lessening of either the temperature or the humidity. There was only slight relief when a storm came through at night. I arose from my bunk and walked to the open door, hoping to find cooler air and to gaze at the sky to see if relief might be coming in the form of rain. Instead, I saw marines coming from that steamy laundry room across the company street. Wet clothes tied in bundles carried in many odd ways. That's what I needed to be doing. No, I must. There would be no movie or search for something to read. I needed to be washing my dirty uniforms.

I pulled my dirty clothes from my footlocker piece by piece. I bundled them under my arm all the while wondering the many whys. Why was I separated from those who came from my hometown? Why had all but myself and six others been set aside to be assigned to this fifty-first defense battalion? We were told we were much better off than those who were now somewhere in the South Pacific. I must accept my fate, yet I would like to know more. I don't think those at the top really know much. Our Negro leaders in the NAACP and all want us activated and in full participation, yet those who make the decisions for us are holding back. One day they want to give us certain training then there's another order. Are we needed at the front? Then prepare us. Are we not wanted because of race, even at this juncture in history where one ideology is so desperately trying to overthrow or destroy the other? We drill, we do the obstacle course. We do karate. We do maneuvers. Our equipment is forthcoming. We will eventually fire our guns. Those 155 millimeter cannons.

It was late, but there were several hours before dark. The crowd at the laundry had thinned some and I would not have to wait too long for a washer. That's all there was, just washers and rinse tubs. Gosh, it was hot. Without any effort sweat poured. "Are you finished?" I questioned a marine as he pulled his clothes from the washer.

"Oh yes, and darn glad to be," he answered. I quickly loaded my clothes and then stood back, arms folded,

"Where are you from?" he questioned.

"I'm from Cincinnati," I said.

"What? I'm from Cincinnati. Madisonville, that is. What part are you from? West End?" "No," I said. "I'm really from Norwood."

"Norwood?" he said loudly. "I didn't know we had people in Norwood. So you are one of the new guys?"

"Came in just last month."

"I'm Tommy Daniels," he said. "When I came here I admit I did not know the lingo. I once introduced myself as T. S. Daniels, which is my name." We laughed. Here instead of saying too bad, they said tough shit. "Now I'm known as Tough Shit Daniels." We laughed again. He told me proudly how he 'turned out' the Manhattan Club on Madison Road near where he lived. Then he terrorized Mount Auburn. He questioned my experiences while on that one vacation following boot camp. I had had no stories to tell compared to his.

"We need to keep in touch," he said. "There will be news from time to time, especially from my buddies, some of who, are still there." With that, he bundled up his clothes and left with a thumbs up. *It's getting late*, I thought, rushing to get my clothes rinsed and wrung out sufficiently enough to carry the load. Now I hung them on the line beside the barracks while I could still see what I was doing. The heavens cooperated with a moon that semi-illuminated the night. I was finally finished.

Daylight and early Sunday morning came. The sun shone brightly. I heard the loud voice of one corporal. "There are clothes out there on the line and somebody better get them. Captain DeFossi will be coming through like he does every Sunday, and he don't want clothes hung out on Sunday. Your name is on them. You better get them in." With that, I went with another I and another marine to get our clothes. When we finished, two pairs of trousers were still on the line. I grabbed them and stuck them into my locker along with my own, to avoid the captain's indignations.

After a heavy day of drills and classroom instruction on target training, I was greeted with some hush-hush talk. There had been some pilfering. We had a locker inspection. The culprit would be caught. I went about my business, getting dinner, thinking the matter did not concern me. After dinner, I was called to report to Captain DeFossi's office just across the company street. After the proper salute, I was asked to have a seat before his desk. He squared himself into a more dignified look and posture. He then directly accused me of thievery. He said I had taken what was not mine. The clothes I removed from the line belonged to Sergeant Thomas. I was dumbfounded to think he was accusing me of stealing someone's clothes. The sergeant was clearly two or more sizes larger than I was and his name was clearly stenciled as required. What foolish person would attempt to sell such as that and to whom? When after giving him a full and clear explanation of what happened, Captain DeFossi looked at me as if I had said nothing. I could clearly see he had made his judgment before I arrived. I would be an example.

"If this were peace time you would be thrown out of this Marine Corps. We would not stand to have a thief among us. Do you understand that? I've requested and seen your record, you do have a past. Now take a pencil and paper as much as you need." He went on. "Write down the whole story as best you can of how you were accused, your charges, and the outcome. When you finish your regular duty tomorrow, bring me those papers."

If, as he said, he had the record, then I'm sure he knew what happened. But I'd show him I could write what happened and explain it exactly. I had nothing to hide. This half-baked southern cracker could hardly do what he was asking of me, but I'll show him. I went to my barracks and to my bunk. I spent as much time and paper as needed to tell the story as accurately as possible.

When I returned the papers he read them while I sat. Then he expressed his disbelief. He had gathered the facts from both sides. Was he God? I didn't believe this.

"I'm giving you thirty days extra duty," he said. You will report to me each day, morning noon, and night. That means before going to your regular duty. At lunch, when and if you return to your barracks, and evenings you will report to me. Evenings after training classes, you will do some menial tasks such as picking up cigarette butts along and in front of my office." Captain DeFossi fixed me with a stare and said, "Do you understand?"

"I—I, Sir," I said, then answered in the natural manner of a marine, meaning, "I do understand and will carry out your order." I was stunned to the quick. I walked alone to dinner at the mess hall. I would walk alone for days. No one person could know how I felt. I carried out my duties. I reported, I picked up cigarette butts. I sat on that hard chair before the captain's desk with much pain, but with a subsiding anger.

Had I read of the news more closely—though very little was available to us—I would have known the racial policy of this Marine Corps. They had not accepted any African Americans since its re-establishment in 1798, and they did not want them now. Less than two years prior, in 1941, the commandant, Major General Thomas Holcomb, declared that blacks had no place in the organization he headed. "If it were a question of having a Marine Corps of five thousand whites or two hundred fifty thousand Negroes," he said, "I would rather have the whites." Then as a doctrine, African American troops would be disciplined by southern whites, who by experience could better lead them. This is what I and the others were up against, unknowingly. Captain De Fossi was a prime example of the bigger problem.

It's like my big sister Lillian would say, "You have had a great experience. Chalk it up to that. Sometimes you think you know someone. Chalk that up, too, and underline *think* because that's all that's there."

Jacksonville, North Carolina

It was the first evening after Mildred arrived in Jacksonville. We went to the little movie house, which was the only one in Jacksonville. Colored people didn't get tickets at the front window—they paid at the balcony stairs. The balcony was crowded. From that point we could see a nearly empty lower level. The feeling so depressed me to be segregated in such a small space I vowed to never return. We looked at those leaving the movie inquisitively. We saw two young boys, about nine or ten years old, coming from the matinee. They had just seen the newsreel that President Roosevelt decided should be seen by all citizens, of the retaking of Tarawa by the marines. They saw footage of the destruction, the carnage on the beaches, and bodies on the sand and floating on the surf. The young one spoke, saying "We glad we livin'."

We passed the railroad station with its small room for colored passengers, where Gross, Richardson, and I first arrived four months ago. The young attendant at the counter sat bug-eyed in fear of these three well-dressed (nigger) recruits from up North. At four in the morning he would likely have to endure our presence at least a few more hours. We were the beginning of a flood of colored marines who were greatly and rapidly changing this town of Jacksonville. We watched the young white employee call the police and Camp Lejeune for advice or someone to pick us up. He stayed on the phone fearful without cause. We later laughed at his foolish actions.

Jacksonville was somewhat larger than Union Mills where my daddy was from. A short block from the center of this colored and completely separated section of Jacksonville stood a frame duplex with two floors. The only other two-story building was the theater, because of its balcony. All others buildings were one floor. Only the highway that ran by the train station was paved.

The people attempted to be cordial with their natural southern hospitality, yet they were fearful of what was happening to them and their town. An unforeseen restless generation away from home and ready to contest would be taking over the streets, bus load by bus load. We watched as the places that served only beer were filled to capacity. On her first day there, Mildred found friends, and with a great stroke of luck or divine intervention found a place. It had one room on the first floor, and was one block from town center in a small house. Very few young men were seen. The few young women living in Jacksonville worked for R.J. Reynolds Tobacco Company and avoided the marines. Seldom did they venture outside after five o'clock. Often I would be followed to our room by a couple begging for the use of the one room for just an hour. "No, I can't do that." I said. Certainly I could make good, but I couldn't do that. An elderly couple who own the place would be offended and I could not forgive myself for doing it.

On weekends things worsened the business owners left their Negroes in charge. There were no whites, police, or city personnel beyond the railroad tracks. The streets flooded with young leathernecks, a majority of eighteen and nineteen year olds, mostly from the northern cities. They wanted any type of action to relieve their pent-up frustrations of boot camp. The two beer bars were filled and overflowing. They mingled in the streets making it unsafe for cars, but thankfully none of the few residents ventured into the street at this time. Suddenly there was mayhem, ungodly screams that stirred compassion within anyone who heard and most would. Then all who resided in colored Jacksonville feared the next move.

The colored Marine Military Police, having stood by, observing from a distance, came as if to the rescue. They came in their new jeeps, two of them. They judged and they executed their form of justice. They beat many more than they arrested. The streets had belonged to the evil. Those who wanted to rob or rape had their time. Now it was the MPs who had their hour. Luckily they were the only ones armed.

When returning to camp at dawn, the streets revealed the violence perpetrated over the night. Broken glass, shrubs broken down by bodies that had been thrown into them. There was blood on the sidewalk from those who had resisted. Wigs, hair, shoes, and pieces of clothing showed that some marines had exerted their will on some unsuspecting female. Lawlessness prevailed. A field day for the Military Police. A battleground existed for the evil on both sides.

The Orizaba

In the early days of World War II there came a sudden and great need for fleets of seagoing ships of every description to move masses of materials, troops, and supplies of every description to wherever was their greatest need. Seagoing ships from across the globe were bought, leased, or conscripted for use by the military. The USS Orizaba, bought from Sweden, had been an old cruise ship, which enabled its quick change to a troop carrier. Stripped of its ballrooms, its bars in the dining halls, game rooms, and anything having to do with pleasure cruising, the ship was refitted to carry as many troops as possible. This ancient riveted steel plate constructed ship was fitted with two six-inch guns and three twenty-millimeter cannons. These guns bolstered the morale, which might have been their original purpose. They would have meant nothing in attack by any plane, sub, or even a gun bout. Thanks to the fleet commanders of the Navy, only one troop's ship was sunk during the entire war,

On December 7, 1943, two years from that fatal day, Pearl Harbor day, I saw my name on a bulletin board as having been transferred to the Fourteenth Marine Depot Company, which would be leaving Camp Lejeune on December 10 for overseas duty. What a shock. What was this sudden change? I would never know. This was a serious time in the war. There were meager successes, but the nation longed for some decisive victory that would boost moral on the home front.

We arrived by train from Jacksonville at 10:00 AM. There she stood, this huge ship patiently waiting by the dock. We boarded her at eleven o'clock. This vessel had the capacity to transport three hundred troops and military personnel, yet the capacity to feed them three times daily was impossible. To feed them two times was a stretch. The chow line never really ended. They closed down for two hours between the first and second or last meal. We were the last to board this ship, Orizaba. Two depot companies, the fourteenth and fifteenth along with one Ammunition Company and Headquarters Company, completed the list of colored troops from Montford Point, North Carolina. Single file with backpacks and rifles, we climbed the gang plank and to our assigned quarters. These colored marines were in the majority aboard the Orizaba and were assigned the complete lower deck and sleeping quarters. All commissioned officers were white and were not seen by their troops during the voyage. Having been assigned to the Fourteenth Depot Company only four days earlier I did not know any of my fellow marines.

On December 11 at about 11:00 AM, the ship pulled its anchor and its mooring and began to slowly move from dockside to the open sea. Cheering erupted when it was finally on its way. Happiness abounded as all men aboard were excited to be on their way to play a part in the struggle to end this war which had by now lasted too long. They were leaving loved ones, wives, children, and parents. They hoped to return in months. Not one expected to be gone two years or more. Discipline training, physical conditioning, and weaponry training had prepared these men for something about which they could only speculate. Separated from commanding officers, they could only question themselves and each other. We wondered where we were going, when would we get there, and what would we be doing?

On day two we noticed we were in a small convoy of ships, three ships somewhat like the Orizaba, likely carrying troops. One destroyer and a smaller destroyer escort circling as we traveled southward from Norfolk, Virginia. It was a beautiful sight on a clear day under a lightly-clouded sky watching the speedy destroyers splitting the waves as they circled the convoy, protecting against possible submarines.

On day three there was a sudden attack of sea sickness that had nearly all passengers vomiting, starry-eyed, and holding their stomachs or on their hands on knees throwing up puke. "Attention all passenger-troops." It was the voice of the commanding officer, not heard or seen since before our embankments. The public address system lifted his words, "I'm Captain Richard Ronheisen, he said. "What you are experiencing is sea sickness. An experience we all face on our first voyage aboard ships. It's caused by the ship's motion. It is unavoidable. It is also untreatable. It will last only two days or less. I can only advise to eat light and try to relax."

I noticed him as I came from a late breakfast. He was leaning on the ship's rail. He held a Bible in his hand. He would read and then close the Bible with his index finger between the pages. He would look to the sky and contemplate. As others did, I walked the ship deck after meals for exercise as well as relief of the boredom that arose daily. *I'll have to avoid this man, he is likely a religious fanatic wanting to convert people*, I thought. I had my own religion. I'd been a follower of the faith. I had my mother's prayers, my family, and others. He was going to confront me, I knew it. Dinner lasted from early afternoon until nearly eight o'clock at night as it took this long for all the passengers to be fed. After dinner the marines would wander helplessly around the ship's deck until far beyond dark before retiring to their sleeping quarters below deck. It was late afternoon on the third day when I failed to change my route. I was confronted! He raised his open hand in my direction.

"Young man," was his call. I stepped toward him.

"Yes?" I asked. "Excuse me," I said, as I was confronted by another who I recognized immediately as the marine who had sat behind me on the train from Jacksonville, North Carolina.

"Here," he said "I want to give you what is rightfully yours. I don't want blood on my hands, so to speak. I want to be clear of wrong doing. We're going somewhere for a purpose we don't understand and I want my conscience to be clear." He handed me that handkerchief with the one dollar and some change still intact.

I thanked him and said, "I hold no animosity toward you or anyone. I'll see you later." "What was that about?" asked the man with the Bible in his hand.

"Well," I said, "you remember when we boarded that train in Jacksonville, the women standing on the hillside waving and blowing kisses just as we were leaving? Well, being that I had been in the

Marine Corps since April, I had been into that town of Jacksonville many, many times I know many by name and many have served me in the bars and restaurants. This one young lady I did not recognize but who likely recognized me threw this handkerchief intended for me. That fellow marine you just saw reached far out the window enough to grab it before I could. The lady screamed, 'No, no him,' pointing to me, but my friend ignored her call. Today his thoughts have changed."

"Oh!" said the man with the Bible in his hand. "What's your name?" I told him.

"Where you from?"

"Cincinnati," I replied, nearly saying Norwood, which he of course would not recognize, thus requiring another question. Seemingly to test my knowledge of the Bible, he read a passage from his book, then asked my interpretation. What I gave him he liked. I looked at his dark-skinned face. It was square, robust, and sturdy looking. He had a large scar on his left cheek. He was more muscular than most. His face, unshaven as we all were, showed some gray. He had come through boot camp an older man who would add stability to those young and restless comrades, yet he had not for some reason been given any position of rank. While admiring him I wondered why. "Are you married? Do you have children?" he asked.

"No and no, but my girlfriend is expecting," I said.

"How did that happen?" he asked.

"Well, I told her my mother said we, my brother and I, should not get married until we returned. She then came to North Carolina and went home pregnant."

"Did you ask her to come to North Carolina?"

"No, in fact I sent her a letter telling her why she should not come, but she arrived, saying she did not get the letter."

"Well that's on her," he said. "She will get an allotment for the child when it's here. Ohio is a state that recognizes common law marriages. If she gets a check and can get a babysitter and work she's better off than you."

"What about you?" I asked.

"I'm Nicholas Battle. They call me Nick. I'm from Jersey, Newark, on the east side. Street gangs, robbing, break-ins, you name it, my early life was hell. At fourteen I was supporting my mother and two brothers. The gangs got me nowhere, so I joined the Civilian Conservation Corps. I was sent upstate. I had little connection with the family I was supporting. No news was good news. They received the money I sent. I assumed all was well. Then after two years I went home and I found my little brother left dead. He copped a fix on a rusty needle and was gone. Dead! Yeah, dead too young, he was much, much too young. My family had been abused by a pusher and I knew just who he was. Full of rage, I went to face that lowest of the lowest dogs. I cannot tell you exactly what happened and how. I was so enraged and things happened so fast I collapsed in the hallway, heavily bleeding. I heard sirens and screaming. I was told later I nearly bled to death. Then I was charged with nine counts of attempted murder. Luckily no one died.

"Now Nick," I said, "do you really mean they charged you with nine attempted murders? Why would you try to kill nine people?"

"Because they were there," he answered.

"Then what?" I questioned.

"Nine years one on each charge. Luckily I went to the state prison. After six and one half years I was given amnesty for volunteering to be here, in the Marine Corps. That's my past I have changed, I'm a new man."

After his confession he looked different, a more docile person. Never did he attempt to deny or justify what he did nor did he attempt to blame others. I saw a man converted. There was a long pause. He reached into the left pocket of his dungarees and pulled out an old, worn book I immediately recognized as a Gospel Pearl song book. From this book he pulled a folded page from a prayer book or book of poems. The page had been used as a spare bookmark. He urged me to read:

> I trust in God.
> I trust in God wherever I may be
> Upon the land or the rolling sea.

For come what may, from day to day
My heavenly father watches over me.
I trust in God I know he cares for me
On mountains bleak or on the rolling sea;
Though billows roll, he keeps my soul
My heavenly father watches over me.

I know his intentions are to calm people's fears, I thought. He must have prepared himself for this. Again a pause in conversation, and he said, "We are on our way to some unknown destination. What will we be asked to do? What's our future?" I listened but offered no answer or remarks.

"It's getting awfully late, I'll see you later," I said. I had no real fear of the future at this time and felt no need to discuss these concerns.

On day four boredom set in full square. There was no library aboard the ship, no post exchange except for the sale of cigarettes. There were no radios, no movies, no entertainment of any kind. We had to entertain ourselves, which became extremely distressing. Walking the deck after meal number one I heard those conversations of young men from the big cities. If you believed them they were all male dominant controlling pimps.

"If I don't get another day on the streets, I've had mine, I've done it all," they said.

"This world don't owe me nothing," they would say. Boring, so boring. This bitter earth that takes a man in the prime of life for unknown reasons. To defeat an evil dictator or for greed? I had to find an isolated spot, sit down, and contemplate these things. There by that rolled up canvas cover by the hatch. I couldn't lean back, but I could lean back on my elbows. Immediately my thoughts went to my last visit home. My sister, Della, walked me to the bus stop.

She told me that she would be leaving home, she wasn't happy. "I'm not allowed the privileges some of my friends enjoy," she said.

"You are seventeen," I told her, "and you are not ready or able to support yourself." My advice seldom lasted long with her. I wish I knew her whereabouts. I watched the sky and the horizon, then my thoughts turned to home, I would return a father. That's okay, but there was much work to be done. Soon as this is over we would get married. Mom and Pop, they're okay. My little sisters are okay, too. I miss all their fussing, then they turned on me. I have come from fifty dollars a week to fifty dollars a month. Nothing to spend, though, just stamps and smokes mostly. I can save some, just leave it on the books. There will be no letters for a while until Orizaba gets us wherever. No post office on these high seas. My brother was fine in West Virginia State when we last talked seven months ago, he could be anywhere by now. I'll question the family in my next letter whenever that will be. My older sisters Lillian, Mabel, and Cecelia. I'll joke with them and their husbands when I return.

The clouds had long ago been burned away by the intense sun. It was early afternoon when the burning heat from the heavy metal deck penetrated the seat of my dungarees. I leapt to my feet, stretching my legs and arms. Suddenly there were loud screams from the crowd. I rushed towards the screams. One ship, a troop carrier, had lost its steering and was headed directly toward the front of the Orizaba where I was standing. All passengers on deck of both ships were shouting, screaming, and waving, attempting to gain attention of those navigators at the ship's helm. The Orizaba turned sharply in an attempt to avoid a collision, but only caused the point of the collision to be farther to the rear. A gaping hole appeared on the ship's bow of the other ship. The Orizaba, however, was hit closer to the waterline and aft of center. This was frightening to the crew and more frightening to the passengers. The large hole in the side of the Orizaba was taking in water. All aboard ship were ordered to stand on the ship's starboard side, raising the damaged hole above water level.

On the morning after the ship's collision, the crew gave an announcement there would be a funeral and burial at sea that day at eighteen hundred for private Richard Gains at the spot of the collision. All passengers were welcome. Most, as well as I, had not known there had been a death or even an injury in the collision. We could see the other ship and no one appeared close to the point of contact. After questioning man to man, there soon came one who had witnessed seeing several marines standing under the ladder leading to the upper deck and before the door to the mess hall. This was the location of the impact. Where I stood I could see the ship coming directly toward where I was standing, then the Orizaba turned in an effort to avoid the blow from this ship, which had apparently lost its steering. This ship hit the Orizaba, first raising and tilting its deck, then seemingly raising its bow above the deck, then sliding back into the ocean with a large, gaping hole in its bow.

Their hole was much above sea level and not taking on water. I remembered seeing men running in different directions attempting to distance themselves from the impact. I could not see a frightened comrade beneath the steel ladder, frozen in fear. He was crushed between the steel cabin structure and steel ladder. He died moments later. Burial at sea was the quick decision, as the ship had no means for embalming. The body of Richard Gains was wrapped, weighted, then taped and placed in an open-end box. At the end of service the flag-covered box was tiled, while the body slid into the ocean. Our first casualty was so close to home. We were saddened that he could not have returned home, as close as we were. The ship's crew caused some of the ship's compartments to take on water opposite the hole. They then placed mattresses over the holes. This huge ship in this way limped from its location between Miami and Cuba back to Charleston. The crew was furloughed. The colored marine passengers were quartered at the nearest army camp. Because German submarines were at this time on the prowl in the Atlantic, secrecy of ship movement, especially troop movement, was of the utmost secrecy. All personnel aboard the ship were quarantined and no phone calls of any kind were allowed and no mail was to be sent or received.

Day two at Charleston brought disaster again. Two inches of snow fell on Charleston. Residents related as how they had not seen snow for twenty years. Some of the marines themselves were from the area and admittedly had seen no snow before this. Sergeant Bostick, however, was determined, if given permission, he would perform a close order drill into the streets of Charleston. I knew

Sergeant Bostick to be likeable and well respected but a thorough disciplinarian as all drill instructors must be. At about six three he stood tall and erect, a perfect picture of what a platoon leader should be. He could make anyone aspire to his level of perfection. Having just transferred to the fourteenth depot company I had forgotten some of what I learned in boot camp. I did not want to embarrass Sergeant Bostick or myself. There was no way out of this, so I practiced with some others the night before. When morning came, Sergeant Bostick divided the company into two units. The first were those he knew would perform well. I was overjoyed with these arrangement, because I could watch the performance and observe the reactions of the people of Charleston as well. The people saw a great performance. They cheered from crowds along the streets as well as from open windows. Most had never seen colored marines.

Upon returning to the barracks, Sergeant Bostick gave us a pep talk of which we would not forget. He praised our performance, encouraging us to continue to perform wherever we would go or whatever our assignment, and that we would be a credit to our country and our race. He said we would be honored in due time for our sacrifices. He tried to tell us some of the problems we might face and how we would deal with each of them. Then, in a sly way, he put in a plug for his home town of New Orleans. "It's a wonderful city, it's the best," he said. "If ever you are there, be sure to go to Rampart Street and visit my dad's place, he has a club there. Just say Bostick, anyone will know. Tell Dad you served with me his son and I guarantee he will see that you have a great time."

In just five days we were back at the Charleston dock waiting to again board Orizaba. I had contacted a severe cold in Charleston and was sick when the Red Cross came with sweaters, having been informed we carried no winter clothes. I did not receive one. I was the happiest person as we climbed aboard, knowing we would be headed south. Portside we could see the patched work; a heavy steel plate had been welded over the hole surrounded by the original riveted sides. A very noticeable condition. Back again were we to our familiar surroundings, happy to be back to our future yet not really ready for the smelly sleeping quarters, the two meals per day, or the terrible boredom that was bound to return. Nazi submarines were being seen in these waters so we had a destroyer escort. By day we watched the sky and the sea. By night we watched the same. The days passed the destroyer left us. Now the only life we saw were those sea birds following us, eating scraps from the galley. Otherwise we were alone. We could not see life aboard the destroyer when it was following us, but we knew there was life. Now that was gone as well.

While standing in a group waiting for chow time in the location where the Orizaba had been struck and damaged, I recognized the one person who had been in this location when the accident occurred. We questioned him. What happened and how did he escape? In a effort to show us, he attempted to climb to the deck above without use of the ladder. His several attempts failed. We laughed and asked him why he couldn't do it no? "I'm not scared," he said.

Boredom again set in. We longed for some kind of change. I lost count of the days. We were close to Christmas. At nearly nine nautical miles per hour, we should be somewhere by now. We had been told when we saw land in the form of hilly outlines on the horizon we were at least twenty miles away, or several hours, away from landing. Suddenly we saw land for the first time since Charleston. It was the Panama Canal.

The design of the canal put the Atlantic entrance on the north. On the north are the cities of Christobal and Panama, the capital, nearby. We entered there on Christmas in 1943. We had our Christmas dinner while on Mira Flores Lake, a beautiful, elevated lake at the Pacific end.

Panama City and Christobal were said to be run by business people, venture capitalists and the like from far and wide. Panama hats and cigars were made here. We stopped at Balboa city on the Pacific side to take on water and fuel. While this took place we were given leave and as planned we went into the city. We marched from the docks to a large school. Along the way we observed the beautiful, spring-like weather, here close to the equator. The small frame homes and lawns were neatly cared for. A mixture of races was clear by the looks of the people and especially the children, as they were the descendants of those who came there to build the canal. They were Africans, African Americans, Caribbeans, Indians, and Caucasians, many of whom still work for the canal management. We entered the school and went to the basement gym and occupied one side. Several classes of students filed in, occupying the opposite side of the gym. We were welcomed by one of the teachers, informed of the age groups, and urged to sing along. There were about sixty marines and many more than sixty children. They sang loud and they sang very well, surprising us all. They sang in English, their second language. Their first language was Spanish. They sang "Jingle Bells," "I Wish You a Merry Christmas," "La Cucaracha," "Pistol-packing Mama," and then a song that shocked us all, "Swing Low," a song that was sung by our own Fisk University that surprised and so greatly touched and lifted our weary hearts. As they left the gym, each one in leaving gave a final wave of the hand, causing sniffles within the ranks of those colored marines who were so moved by this event.

On the evening of the same Christmas Day, the Orizaba passed from the last locks of the Panama Canal into the vast Pacific Ocean. Away from the danger of submarines, we sailed un-escorted, wondering where those other troop carriers might be. And again we wondered where we were headed. We had not yet been told anything. We watched the rising sun to determine our direction. As the days drew on, the heat became more intense as we unknowingly grew closer to the equator. The poem of the ancient mariner came to mind. "Water, water everywhere and all the boards did shrink. Water, water everywhere and not a drop to drink." The ancient mariner's problem was much like ours. This ship's mass of steel was sun scorched by day to an untouchable temperature. Water was rationed to about two cups daily, enough to wash face, hands, and shave. We had to wait in line for water, which meant there was a good possibility we would get none. Void of any kind of entertainment, the Orizaba ushered these marines into a melancholy sadness. There was only this ship churning its way across this the largest of oceans, destination unknown.

After several more weeks of travel, boredom again took over. The sounds from the engine room were constant and repetitive. The ocean waves striking the bow, the ship's wake, and the sounds coming from them.

In order to stave off madness we had to placate our thoughts to other things, places, and times. We had loved ones at home giving us determination to endure, survive, and return. However, we had boarded the ship on December 11, 1943. It was now at least two weeks into January. We had received no mail due to the quarantine at the army base, and our morale was at its lowest.

At midday, ship's crew rolled out water hoses with pumps. They began to hose down all passengers who had not crossed the equator before. This was a ceremony honoring Neptune, the god of the sea. They read some kind of chant over the speakers. The cooling effect tempered our bodies, but the drying saltwater was irritating to the skin. We questioned the sailors as to our destination. They claimed no one knew. The skipper received teletype messages once daily with navigation and other instructions. They said in that way nobody knows and nobody tells. A slip of the lip might sink a ship. We were now below the equator. We were out of imminent danger, but the captain maintained no smoking on deck after dark. "We must keep vigilant," he said. This was all the information we could get from the sailors. They again disappeared into their assigned duties aboard ship.

Days after the crossover day, as they called, it boredom set in again like never before. I went to my spot to sit and lean back with my elbows on the rolled-up canvas. Someone was there, so I wandered along the deck to the ship's broad fantail. While watching the late sunrise, the trailing wake from the Orizaba, as well as anything observable in the sea, I heard voices in conversation. I listened and I turned and looked. Standing behind me was a private first class who I remembered was called "school boy." School boy had been coaxed to join the marines. He was told it was a great outfit.

"With your college experience, you will do great, don't be drafted," people told him. "Then you will be a cook, mess man or in construction." Damon Carruthers joined the marines. He was ridiculed in boot camp as there were few from any college among the enlisted men. Damon should have been in Headquarters Company or quartermaster, where his skills were needed.

"I volunteered for this, fully expecting to be something to this Marine Corps," he told me. "I fully expected to play a big part. Everywhere I'd served I did my very best. But you know we who are from those big northern cities are suspects, not to be trusted in the ranks of the segregated. All commissioned officers and nearly all noncommissioned are white. They don't like our style, we are not rightly submissive. We do not fit in. Our 'yes sir's' don't ring niggerish enough. It's our colored troops on the drill field and in the officers club it's those and them niggers. They don't want to be assigned to one of our units. Fifty-first defense battalion or a depot or ammunition company. They are bitter and feel degraded. Only one, only Captain Bobby Troup. Captain Troup was the greatest. He had the best band in all the Marine Corps and he was the sharpest dressed. Remember he told us—well, you were there—how he and his wife were returning from an overnight trip to one of those big jazz band halls.

"His wife said, 'I like this highway, it's beautiful. I would write a song about it if I could write one.' Then he said he would write one about Route 66, it's longer and better. She said go on and get your kicks on Route 66 then. The thought continued with him as they traveled. When they got home he went straight to the piano and did not quit until he had written that song. How he wanted no one but Nat King Cole to sing it. Nat made it a big, big hit. He's now with us, at least there at Montford Point with our band. Captain Troup accomplished a lot in organizing recreation groups and shows. He liked what he did. Although forced to play a segregated role, he did his job seemingly happiest when with his band and bunch of sports figures, many of whom had been at the top of their age group in sports."

Reluctantly, with a "See you later," I parted the conversation with Damon, knowing he and I were on the same page. I ventured again to my sitting spot up at the ship's bow. First kneeling, then sitting on the steel ship, I wanted to think of more pleasant things.

My first car. I parked in front of Hughes High just before the last bell. When no females I recognized came, I left, not taking a chance with someone I did not know. I'll get married when I return.

That's going to be different. I must, I promised. I was going to be a daddy. Yes, I went going overseas with a bunch straight out of boot camp. No experience whatsoever. Just officers six weeks out of basic training and a short furlough. I couldn't complain, I really didn't know what would happen. I was in the Fifty-first Defense Battalion Seacoast Artillery, first control room, then base end station, observer.

As they say, all must serve a month's duty in the galley. I served six weeks, emergency. I did guard duty at the brig. I returned to the fifty-first when they went to fire the coastal range. I operated at one of the base end stations when we set a record. I was assigned to communication classes, was promised a promotion after completion. I was reassigned and denied a promotion. I don't know if anyone was promoted. I was later sent to malaria control from which I was placed with this Fourteenth Depot Company. Had I gone with my boot camp group, I would have been one of the first colored marines overseas. Big deal, being in the marines was not hard, Jim Crow was. Darn there they go again. Those slicks from the streets, fakers, falsely proud yet not indoctrinated. When will they be, the few, the proud, real leathernecks. They were talking about women in a vulgar way under their clothes and all. Sinful and proud of it. Mama always would say, "Don't make a fool of yourself." There are enough words in the English language to tell someone how you feel without using profanity. Profanity has never been a part of my life. Not at our isolated home, our church, or school. Did I have to deal with this? The expression "cussin' like a sailor" came to mind. I would hear this for the duration. God, when would we land somewhere?

Yet another day came just like the rest—until morning. Land was sighted. We were thrilled to see the low outline in the distance. We rejoiced like never before, anticipating a landing and visit to this Pacific island. The Orizaba dropped anchor, the skipper's boat was lowered to the surf. He went ashore with his aids. Natives from the island, Easter Island, came in row boats filled with fresh fruit.

These heavily-browned men of mixed ages pantomimed that we should throw coins into the boat. They then tossed a line onto the Orizaba deck from which we could pull in the fruit. This was a normal practice for them when tourists arrived. They gained few takers from these leathernecks. After a few hours of refueling by tanker we again sadly watched the other ships, the palm trees, and then the total Easter Island fade from our view.

Now again this ship alone was steadily pushing its way across this vast ocean. The Pacific Ocean is said to be the more peaceful one. At times it rages. The surface was like a mirror. We had seen the latter mostly since the canal. The stop at Easter Island entered our thinking. Perhaps we were close to our destination. Yet we saw no sign of land, day after day. Then we were told by the ship's crew that we were passing over O-Deep, the deepest point in any ocean. We were only seven and one half miles from land, straight down. A sobering thought. The world most certainly is two thirds water. I could feel the despair those ancient sailors felt having to spend so many months crossing any ocean. On and on we went, seemingly without direction. If the captain found that little Easter Island he must be on his target.

Another night, another day, another night, another day. They came, they went, they came, they went. I descended the ladder to my bunk below deck. I felt the intense, stuffy heat surround me. Then there was that stifling odor. Snoring, bad breath, as well as all the other odors unwashed men could produce. Stifling, putrid, sickening, so bad as to burn the nostrils and upset the stomach. I returned topside to gaze at the sky and the open sea. The sky darkened, then an occasional light gust of wind. Then came lightening and thunder, first in the distance then closer. Suddenly we were into a storm. I retreated back to the funky sleeping quarters. I had to bear the worst. The storm continued, creating a tense atmosphere within the ranks of men below deck. As the ship fought back at these enormous waves that attempted to engulf her, there could be heard from below the stress and strain of the powerful diesel engines. From the sounds heard below we could identify sounds as waves covering the deck, causing the entire ship to vibrate from the force.

Winds whistled through the ship's steel superstructure. This went on for hours, while the wind, rain, and enormous waves pummeled the ship again and again. The men below were in a somber mood. They were apprehensive. Young men as they were, some barely nineteen, they were drafted from the streets, unprepared for such a long, arduous nerve-wracking, and extremely boring sea voyage. Then someone bellowed out an old song so familiar to all. "Hurry down sunshine see what tomorrow brings." Then suddenly there was a realization. But for the stormy sea it was daybreak.

The first meal was late, very late, due to the storm. All aboard were weary. We saw land again. It was New Caledonia, a French-occupied island. We were extremely happy to see land, a land that also had experienced the same storm of the past night, palm branches strewn about. We watched as we approached, recognizing this to be a much larger island than Easter. When we pulled along the dock and realized we likely would get off, we were excited. Our sea legs hit the ground happy. We stayed in tents three nights. While there, an explosion of ammunition dumped at the beach two and one half miles from us. Our tents nearly were blown away by the force.

Soon again we were back at the docks. The Orizaba was gone without fanfare or celebration. We would forever remember her. Standing where we had left her was another ocean liner, not quite as big, but more modern and somewhat faster. We left this French city of Noumea, New Caledonia in a French-named ship, the U.S.S. Rochambeau. Now more knowledgeable about sailing the seas, we watched for birds following the ship as well as the color of the sea. Water would darken going out then get lighter closer to land. In only four days we were seeing land again. This time it was Guadalcanal the first island we reached that had been renowned for its battles and finally capture by marines. The Rochambeau moved into what was called Iron Bottom Bay. The bay had been invaded and re-invaded by sea battles so many times, it was called Iron Bottom Bay. Many ships could be seen from the beaches or aboard ship. Many were partially sunken with their hulls above or partially above the surface. The ship anchored, large nets were thrown over the side, and we climbed to waiting landing-craft boats. Observing the beach and the dense vegetation bordering it, we could clearly see how a nest of fifty-five millimeter guns could have been completely invisible to an approaching ship. When all were ashore we were told we would spend the night there on the beach by the bay. We walked to a location high enough to be safe from the tide. Here and along the way we could see signs of the past, more than the ships we could see shell holes and trees with their tops blown out. There were leftover campfire sites, articles of clothing, and shell casings. Definitely we were now at journey's end or very, very close. As far as the ships Orizaba or Rochambeau were involved, this was the end. All who wondered what would be their fate when boarding her knew no more than they had at the outset. The doubt and the uncertainty returned. There was no trust in a system that separated its leadership from its personnel in times and situations like this. Morale was at its lowest. We each in our own way had to cope. When I left home, many had said I would be in their prayers. I believed them. I was loaded with faith. I was alone yet not afraid. My upbringing had not forsaken me. When you can't call Papa for advice and sympathy and you can't call Mama for her uplifting words, then you call upon the Lord. A simple prayer was all that was needed. A spiritual uplifting, An uplifting of the faith, and a brightening of spirit.

With my head on my backpack as a pillow I gazed into the open sky. I loved blue. You could color my whole world blue. Here it was above me, every shade of blue fringed by black and lightly streaked with white. Suddenly a white parrot soared from the towering palms to another tree on the skyline. I watched as he floated from the treetops. Lying face up and staring at such a beautiful star-studded sky, that same bird reappeared from the highest palm. As if searching for the best place to roost for the night, the bird glided into another treetop. I stared at the treetop waiting for his reappearance, as if I must see a repeat of this spectacular display. As my eyes got heavier and heavier I strained to hold the view. At a point I didn't know if I had dozed or maybe missed the sighting. Would the beautiful bird fly again into a sea of splendor in the blue? I waited.

I wondered if this dispassionate bird would return. I watched with an intense stare that I could not hold. I could see the stars and stripes of old glory backed by the blue skies and I thought one day it would be. My great grandparents believed in it. I believed in it and it would come to pass. We had nothing to lose and everything to gain. Justice and equality was something we had to work on. It would be long coming, but it would come. This nation would rise mightily after this war to be a world leader, to be scrutinized by all other nations and it would respond with justice for all of its citizens, I was sure. Yes, we are Americans first. This land is our land, let's sing it, and believe in it, be a part of it like never before. We are a long suffering people of the worst kind of deprivation, beatings, lynching, yet a people of pride and dignity. A people determined to rise in the face of opposition to be an integrated part of this vast society that teaches justice and humanity to the world. We will show ourselves to the world a people of survivors. We are a people with no bounds or limits, equal or above any others throughout history. Yes we have as much right, perhaps even more right to loudly sing, America the beautiful.

Well went the night, pleasant was the morning. I was rejuvenated.

The Blackberry Pie—Betty

We sat around that big dining room table in the kitchen on Hopkins. It was a Sunday. We had all been to church, which was not quite normal in these days of World War II. Papa was taking a needed day off from his plant. Mama had somehow managed to prepare a complete meal and very tasty dinner around her own efforts to make it to church. Still at dinner, Papa pushed away his empty plate with a satisfied look, while holding onto his fork with his right hand. This, we all knew, meant Papa was finished and waiting for dessert.

"What is it you want, Ralph?" asked Mama.

"Oh, I'll take whatever there is. I'm not choosy. If you really want to know, it's blackberry time, how about one of those cobblers?"

"I've got everything but the berries," answered Mama.

"Oh yeah," shouted one, "we can go pick some".

"Get the kitchen cleaned up now," said Mama.

Only Della, Jeannette, Gertrude, and myself, Betty, were at home. Lillian, Mabel, and Cecelia worked in war-defense plants, Frances at the hospital. Neither now lived at home. The boys were in the military. This wartime prosperity allowed money for needs at home—things not rationed, that is. Except for movies, there was not a lot to do now that all those who did work with youth were now full-time employed or in the military. Why not go pick some berries and have a late night snack? But where? Oh, Papa knows.

Della, the senior of the four, was exempt from duty in the cleaning up of the kitchen. It was not her turn. She retreated to the *rathskeller where she turned up the music, "Straighten Up and Fly Right" by Nat King Cole, while she relaxed with one of her copies of *True Romance*.

"Didn't Mama tell you about those magazines? They are just trash, something to get your money. You need to listen; don't be a dumb-bunny." With a clear show of resentfulness, Della turned to join us. We wore pants, and we tied them around our ankles and sprayed our arms against those dreaded chiggers we knew we would face. Papa took us to Grove Road. We noticed Grandpa's farm as we passed. The memories of past summers and the grief of losing our grandparents saddened us all. We went beyond the farm and to nearly the end of Grove Road. There we saw many blackberries. Papa pulled the car clear of the road where we set out to get sufficient berries for a great cobbler. Each with our own pail, we joyfully picked berries for maybe twenty minutes.

Then suddenly the words rang out loud, "You niggers get off my property." Frightened, we turned around, and were even more frightened when we saw a man holding a long shotgun. We had the presence of mind to hold fast to our pails, not spilling or dropping them. Papa, when seeing this, rushed from the car to face the man. With open palms stretching from his body, he walked directly toward the man with the gun, approaching him in a submissive stance.

"We only came to pick wild berries; we did not know we were on your property. We are the children of Washington Williams down the way who passed away two years ago. We are not intruders. We will not take any more."

Now seemingly with a sudden change of heart after getting his point across, the man replied, "You seem to be respecting people. I'll let you get a share of those berries if that's what you want. Go ahead," he repeated, while turning toward a big farmhouse in the distance partially hidden by huge oak trees. Papa had showed his daring and caring protection for his family. This day would be forever remembered.

At this time music to dance to in your basement was called a rathskeller. A tongue cheek reference to an affluent place of entertaining.

THE TEXAN

The end of the second monsoon season came suddenly on the island of Bannika. Three months of daily rain had finally ended. The sun woke me up this morning. On my way to breakfast at the mess hall, I saw the wet, marshy fields. The bushes and distant palm trees were all giving up their moisture to a brilliantly rising sun. In a short time, the whole horizon would dry. Lizards would dot the surrounding vegetation, followed by those pesky mosquitoes, for which we all must take cautious protection from their deadly malaria. I joyously watched the changing scenery, mess gear in hand while walking the well-worn path to the chow line. Spam, then some eggs, formerly dehydrated now brought to edible condition, were plunked onto my G-I issued gear. This happy day is not one I want to isolate myself. I take the first table with space. As usual, Tex was one occupant of the table. This great change in weather brought out conversation.

"Podna," said Tex, "This is going to be a beautiful day."

"Yes, but that sun and humidity is going to be terribly hot and stifling."

"This is our second season here. We should be used to this by now," said Tex.

"No, never," I said.

"Look we've got the next seventy two hours off. What are you going to do? That is a long time to sit here in this camp. I'm going to the brig and visit Neal Bush. Bush was in my boot camp platoon. I want you to go with me."

"No," I said. "Why do you want to visit someone who is a criminal? Just don't want to do right," I said, to provoke more conversation from the slow-walking, fast-talking Texan.

I wore a pith helmet. Tex wore a sweatband under a helmet liner. We walked quite briskly down the hilly drive to the road that led to the beach. We rarely referred to the roads by their given names. Roads were named after ranking officers, Army and Navy, after people we did not know. The roads were poorly posted and each went to a designated place—the beach, the airport, the ship dock, or landing beach and that's how we referred to them. We wore no gun belts, carried no rifles or packs. We were hands free except for Tex, who carried a Bible wrapped and strapped in a belt carried slung over his shoulder like a school boy.

I began telling Tex about the one all-night party we had just two days ago, which of course he had missed, as he was not a beer drinker. In the Navy all enlisted men were entitled or allowed two bottles of beer daily. We had no place to buy beer. We received beer after five months on the island for the first time. Each marine was sold one full case at two dollars and fifty cents, then reminded it could be the last. Two days prior we received our second case of beer while going into our second year on the island. Sergeant Hendricks one day at the dock was asked, by one of the skippers, if his troops ate mutton. We had no Jews aboard our ship. Hendricks not only ate mutton, he loved the stuff, and knew well how to cook it, even outside grilling. Having little, if any refrigeration complicated things and two marines walked six miles each way for ice, which lasted a very short time. Though the mutton seemed to have missed some of its seasoning, the meat and the beer made for much of the merriment. I took a whole case. We first played cards for a while. We were beside the last row of tents where the field began, just before the tropical mass of trees. The moon gave us light through the night. James Oscar Dotson, who we called J.O., took over the entertainment. Some people told jokes, some pantomimed. J.O. then told about his life on the streets of Detroit. How he would go early to the clubs to beg enough money to get his suit out of the cleaners. His stories of life on the streets of Detroit touched us because most of us were from the larger northern cities.

"You should have been there, Tex." I said. "They sang church songs, too. They sang that new spiritual, 'Take My Hand Precious Lord.' You know that one.

"That's not for me," he said. "You go along to get along."

"Well," I told him, "we are a mixture. It's what we do, it's what we are."

"It's not what I am," he shot back while walking faster with a more erect posture. I accepted the truth. I kept quiet.

Together we recalled an overnight guard duty trip on a landing ship tank. Early into a star-studded night the ship's skipper came out to question us. Did we know we were sitting on a canvas-covered cargo of explosives and one of us was smoking? "I can't sleep with that," he said. He showed us a stairwell location where smoking was allowed. I assured him I was the one smoker and I would obey the rules. We really were not informed we were to be guarding explosives. He then questioned our rank, noticing we had none by our uniforms. We were privates, I told him. "Given this kind of responsibility you should be at least corporal, if not sergeant," he said.

"The Marine Corps is stingy with promotions," I told him, repeating what I had heard. On our return trip aboard a small ship, a faster and more maneuverable one, we were spotted by a Japanese light bomber on the prowl. We zigzagged while the pilot likely decided this small, fast mover was not worth his effort. Thankfully the trip was over for Tex and me.

Reaching the road to the north shore, we thumbed a ride on an empty four-wheeler. I grabbed the seat. Tex stood on the running board while holding onto the canvas top. Shortly we were there. Hidden behind the roadway, palm trees and thick shrubs stood the jail, really a stockade. A small guardhouse consisting of a bamboo frame and palm leaf thatched roof stood beside a twelve by twelve foot area fenced in by a ten-foot-high wire mesh fence. While hidden from the road, this seemed not to be the most miserable place to be on the island except that it was open to the elements. There was no escape. How could anyone endure this intensely burning sun? Water and bread was the one meal brought from our own kitchen, the same as all marines. I watched the two in sadness, the only jailbirds on the island. Tex confronted his friend, Neal, then introduced me as a friend and a follower, as he described me. They had a lengthy conversation while I stood by. The second prisoner was uninterested in us and annoyed only by the heat and the misery of it all.

The intense rays from the sun forced me to retreat to the nearest tree for a smoke. Palm trees are poor shade trees but that is all that was there. I watched as Tex attempted to talk to the one other prisoner who just turned and walked away from Tex. Tex persisted by raising his voice. The space was so small the prisoner could not get beyond his voice.

"I just want to be your friend just to talk. I know how you feel," said Tex.

"If you know how I feel then let me alone," answered the prisoner. Now with a conversation came at least a verbal contact. Tex pressed on. Their voices slightly lowered while the conversation continued. Tex was now delivering his message with fervor. I watched Tex as he held his unopened Bible in one hand while pumping his hand and gesturing with the other. He stared into the prisoner's face from outside the heavy, laced wire fence. Being unable to hear the conversation I lapsed into my own private thoughts. Then noticing how much time had passed I began to wonder how long would this take. I watched the road. An occasional vehicle went by. I looked out toward the ocean for its scenic beauty and calming effect. A patrol plane slowly passed my view.

The sun now bore down relentlessly, heating the tropical air to temperatures of one hundred degrees or more. I could tell even the wire fence was hot because Tex and the prisoner no longer touched it. I had noticed a large piece of twisted steel against the tall fence when I arrived. Neal Bush was sitting on the ground beneath it, sheltering himself from the intense rays of the sun.

Tex came to me asking for just one cigarette. I took one from the pack then gave the others to him along with the matches. I knew what this was about but cared not to ask. Neither did I ask how much longer this was going to take. This was draining my patience. I could not imagine a full day under that intense unbearable tropical sun.

On leaving, I glanced back to see the two prisoners who never talked before, now in conversation. I suddenly felt a warming within, though I had done nothing but be there. I watched Tex, his head held high swelling with pride, and rightfully so. He had fulfilled the greatest of callings. I was proud for him.

THE RETURN HOME

It was my birthday, July 28, 1945. I was twenty-two. I had been hearing music coming from a tent only a short distance from our company's location. I ventured to see what was happening and was met by marines who were more recently from the states. They were jubilant. They had somehow found a way to get a record player and some recordings. They had the latest. Like most, I had been practically ignorant of what was happening in music. The whole experience was uplifting. I left with a new spirit, feeling our longest days were behind us. In the immediate following days, we were hit with news that a newly-discovered bomb had just been dropped on Japan. For months, we had been sleeping in tents just below the airfields on Guam. We watched as those huge B-29 bombers roared overhead on their missions over Japan. We watched as they left for their targets. We watched as they returned. Many limped in, heavily damaged, resulting from enemy fire. We continued our daily task of handling supplies. We made trips to the U.S.O. seeking any information we could gather on the progress of the war. We learned this new atomic bomb was so powerfully destructive as to bring a quick ending to the war. The bomb had been dropped on Hiroshima, Japan on August 6, 1945, and was so powerful as to destroy an entire city and kill seventy thousand people. We only waited and anticipated. When the second of such bombs were dropped only three days later on Nagasaki, we felt the significance immediately. On August 9, Japan offered to surrender. On September 2, 1945, (V. J. Day) the Japanese leaders signed a formal surrender aboard the Battleship Missouri in Tokyo Bay.

This horrible, devastating war that had compromised the lives of this entire world had finally come to an end. The hopes and prayers of all had now been answered. Now all the marines wondered how soon we would be going home. We gathered and we talked. What would be the procedure? We cannot all board one big ship. We would not be flown out. It was September. Oh how I wanted to be home on Christmas Day or before. What a joy to be home with all the celebrating. The news was there would be a point system. Married with children would go first. Not married, but with one child, I would be in the second category. I was happy and now one of those who expected to likely make it home by Christmas. That's what we all hoped for. We now had time to reflect however on how we would be moved. It took months to get here. It would take the same to get back, barring a miracle, meaning Christmas was a remote possibility. Our daily routine now consisted of routine makeshift work. Inventory seemed so useless. What a waste of time. All this material would become waste, wartime waste. The food would rot, the rolling vehicles would rust away. We were going home. There was talk that a native woman school teacher here was a graduate of Wilberforce University. I wished somehow I could have met her to ask did she know my sister Lillian, who likely attended while she was there.

"All those who have twelve points please report to your company commander for assignment," the voice on the loudspeaker said. Quickly as possible I made a list of names and addresses of all I wanted to keep in touch with, then went on to the headquarters tent. We were instructed how to prepare and given a time and place for assembly. On November 18, 1945 we broke camp with a joyous farewell to all. We boarded landing ship transport which was to carry fifty troops each equal to three times its normal capacity. In a convoy of such ships, we set sail. On the second day our ship suddenly seemed to just float without any power. Sailors aboard explored the problem, finding the ship's propeller had dropped off completely. With no replacement possible, the captain radioed for help. Two ships in the convoy pulled alongside then rigged us to be towed by one of them. This meant that we would be towed seven and one half days to our destination of Pearl Harbor. We were late arriving on November 24, taken by trucks we called cattle cars, to the large park beside Waikiki Beach, another tent city. I stayed well within the confines of that tented area for fear of being left behind. The food was the greatest for four days. Then the big wood-framed cattle car trailers carried us back to Pearl Harbor. We boarded an aircraft carrier, the USS Kalimin Bay. Officers occupied the former pilots' quarters; we had the huge hanger space as all planes had been removed. To relieve ourselves from the severely crowded conditions, we went to the flight deck by day. On day two fierce and relentless winds prevented anyone from even crawling aboard the flight deck, forcing extreme crowded conditions for two days. On December 4 we landed at San Diego, California, in what it seemed like good time for a Christmas arrival home. The U.S.O. welcomed us on a huge dock with donuts and coffee. Most troops were hurried and did not accept the hospitality. We arrived by train in Oceanside, California. After a long wait, again we were trucked to Camp Pendleton, California. This Marine Corps camp trained no colored, thus we were camped for two nights far from its facilities. We saw no other marines while there.

On December 8, we boarded a train for the final lap to Camp Lejeune, North Carolina. Aboard we meet a captain who had been designated our conductor when we landed at San Diego. Let us call him Captain "C," as his purpose was to see that we were fed daily. He saw that we were on our appointed time when changing trains. His job was an easy one, because seldom were we served aboard a train. We stopped many times and many times, we had layovers, some overnight some even more. "C" had vouchers for our food, which was a problem when we found our designated place closed because we were late. We traveled through Arizona, where American Indians served us. In New Mexico we saw Indians and Mexicans living in shanties along the tracks. We saw vast fields of discarded airplanes, mostly trainers no longer needed by the Air Force. Aboard the train we gathered around "C," the friendliest officer we had ever had. He was white, as all commissioned officers were. He told us he was from Houston, Texas and we would be going through his hometown in two days. We questioned him as to the racial climate in his hometown. How would we be treated will "y'all speak" in public places? Must we eat in the kitchen, by the back door? Captain

Louis Gardner

"C" laughed and said he would guarantee we would be served just as anyone else in his hometown. It turned out we were to have lunch in Houston. We arrived at one of those semi-fast food restaurants that served double deckers, hamburgers, and chili. We stood on the sidewalk for a long time. "C" said we were early. We stood closer to the building. The shades were drawn to keep out the Texas sun, was "C's" logic. One white couple sat at the counter, which was likely the reason we waited. When the door was finally unlocked, there were only two employees in the place—one colored man who served us and one white who stood by the cash register, hands folded. Though the food was as expected, the service was extremely slow. There was no trouble like "C" said, though we expected this restaurant, like all others, did not usually serve colored. They needed the money, or it was just too much to turn down.

Now about halfway to Camp Lejeune, we boarded a train headed for the big city of New Orleans. This was exciting to many who were from the South, but to those anxious to get home by Christmas it was but another likely delay. The scenery was beautiful, with many lakes as well as distant views of the Gulf of Mexico. Suddenly, through the windows of the train, we could see a light December rain blocking our view. Then, Chas Gaspard, a marine from New Orleans, stood in the aisle bubbling over with excitement, urging everyone to look out.

"See, you are now headed right for New Orleans. See that water we are riding over, that is Lake Ponchartrain, you see. We are going over a trestle that is just above the water. Doesn't it look scary?" We all agreed. Riding as fast as we were just above a large body of water was much like the first amusement park ride.

The word from "C" at breakfast was we were to have a great dinner, the best we ever had. We would defer lunch; however, the night will be ours until 8 AM sharp, when we were to be at the train station. Great cheers erupted, except from the few who still held out for a Christmas at home. We again assembled at the terminal and walked toward town. We waited in front of a large, two-story building. A plush-looking restaurant occupied most of the first floor. We waited a short time, then we were signaled to ascend some stairs

278

to the second level. There we found a huge empty hall with a stage and dance, floor. We were told this was the famous New Orleans Cotton Club. A grouping of tables and chairs were placed next to a dumb waiter where we would be served. In minutes, the dumb waiter opened with plates of hot food that filled the room with its aroma. First shrimp salad on lettuce, then plates with jambalaya, chicken roasted or fried, one half baked and stuffed baked potato, greens, candied yams, buttered dinner rolls followed by desserts.

"'C' you have won again," someone said.

"Yes," echoed the others.

Then "C" said, "I will call the maitre d so you can thank him." The huge Creole came and was heartily thanked and applauded for the fabulous meal. We went to the pullman porter's room to shower while some went to a Y.M.C.A. Then it was a free evening until the next morning.

We went to the nearest club where the crowd flowed on to the sidewalk. Half the place and more were in uniform, and the civilians were so outnumbered they felt threatened by the military. Our group of four gathered outside. While in conversation someone remembered Sergeant Bostick saying, "Go to my dad's place in New Orleans."

The cab driver knew where it was, so we went and Mr. Bostick was there. He favored his son very little. He was short and Sergeant Bostick was tall. "Stick around," he told us. He asked if we needed food, and we told him we had eaten at the Cotton Club.

"Well then, we will party at about 10:30," he said. Some of the patrons, who were aware of Mr. Bostick's parties, opted to hang around until he approached them. "Allow me to honor these men who have served overseas for us all the past three years," Mr. Bostick said. Shortly afterward he was on the phone with the police department. He told them what he was doing. He then addressed the crowd of about fifty marines, thanked them for their service, and asked that they not be rowdy this night or while in the city.

"When we close if you need transportation, ask the bartender. He will be glad to help you." The bartender locked the front door while Mr. Bostick set several bottles of the stronger drinks and two boxes of cigars on the bar. The police came and peeked into the window, but there was no trouble whatsoever. All parties were on their way home and wanted no interruptions. When the night ended those cabs never stopped until all were safe and on time.

Again, we were given a short leave while in Southern Alabama. Four of us hailed a cab and went to the first and only place mentioned by the driver. The place was a dud, packed with military and again we stood outside and talked. Our driver told us this was the only local place women would not stay at a place filled with soldiers, marines, or any military.

"All in uniform, man that's intimidating," he said. "Would you want your wife or sister there? Even with a man they would rather get up and leave," said the driver. My friend Roger and I were ready to give up the night and go back to the train, so we left. Our two companions, however, were called to the side and were influenced by another driver who told them he could take us all to a place where there would sure enough be some girls. That driver didn't know what he was talking about. The three tried hard to convince Roger and I to go. The four of us had hired the first cab for the night. We could not go our own way. We paid the first driver and he left us. The second driver stopped after a fifteen- or twenty-minute drive and pulled out some condoms and insisted we needed at least one. Roger and I by now felt we were being duped. We were not fearful of being physically harmed. We were government protected. We gave in to even buying a condom. *Now what*, we thought. After about thirty minutes of foolish talk by the driver and our companions, who had completely bought into the driver's hype, the unmarked cab pulled through a farm road while he said, "We are almost there. It's a nice place, everything you want." The driver pulled off the gravel road directly toward a well-lit barn. Inside was a makeshift bar at one end. Except for the man behind the bar, there was just one couple sat at a table and left upon our arrival. Roger and I by now were so curious that we wanted nothing to drink. We held a conversation while watching what little was going on. The man at the bar called out he was ready with the drinks. We ignored him while wondering what this place would be like on its best day. Our two fellow marines stood outside along with the cab driver, awaiting the arrival of the girls. Someone called out, "The girls are here," but we ignored them.

Later we desired to know when we would be leaving this hapless place. We went a few feet beyond the barn door to see. Outside was the cab, and beside it was the car the girls arrived in. We looked up the hill and could see the two drivers and the fellow marines standing beside an abandoned pickup truck. It looked like they were negotiating. Then Roger pointed there was a girl, her legs sticking out the door, she was lying on the seat.

"God, did you ever see anything like that? Those are what you call heathens. I'd call the police if there was a phone, I'd call somebody. Something should be done about those guys. This is us, man raping our own, what the hell is this? Those guys have no guts, no feelings. They will be home in a day or two, there are plenty wherever they come from," said Roger.

"I'm with you," I said, "those are some of the ones who talked about women in a vile and vulgar way when we were aboard that ship Orizaba." I had heard of such but I never believed I would ever see this. Soon we were back in the cab, headed for the little train station.

"You all are bastards," Roger said after we exited the cab, with a scowl on his face, loud enough to be sure all those he had accused could hear. All went to their assigned train car.

"Jacksonville!" cried out the train's conductor. We could feel the train slowing down. "Jacksonville," repeated some of the marines, while gazing out at their surroundings. This was not the Jacksonville they had known. There was a real train station large enough to accommodate the fifty marines. No longer would they board the train from the outside yard. Almost every building outside was replaced or drastically remodeled. Nothing was the same, except you could recognize that side of the railroad tracks that separated the white from the colored part of town. We boarded buses to camp. The roads were now blacktopped and the gate and guardhouse had been replaced. There was housing for visitors; the original drill fields as well as the first barracks buildings were gone. The tents where we took boot camp were gone. We had been the pilgrims. Thousands have passed through since. We had to be shown our way to the place of the discharge process. Nothing was as we had known it.

We were given an option of taking four days to go through the process of being discharged, or take a thirty-day vacation of which we were entitled, then return for actual discharge. I, like many, opted for the vacation, thinking it would mean that much-anticipated Christmas at home. We were given our final allotment of money, clothing, and several options, indoctrination, and a leave of several hours, thus a head start. First, we went to the post office for money orders to secure safety for what pay we had accumulated. We then bought tickets for our first destination. Leaving Camp Lejeune on December 19 and before the evening should assure an arrival in Cincinnati before Christmas.

Leaving Jacksonville later than expected took a day not planned. We finally arrived in Richmond, Virginia early on the second day without much hope. Many civilians were traveling for the holidays, making travel problems for all. First we heard our train would be arriving in Richmond, Virginia early on the second day, then we were told our train would be arriving at 2 PM. We waited patiently. When the train arrived we were told that all seats were taken and we would have to take the next train at 9:30 PM. We waited angrily. Why had they not told us? The train finally arrived and we told again that all seats were taken. Returning troops had been declared a priority by the government. We boarded the train regardless, somewhat in desperation and much more in defiance, though we had been warned.

The conductor said, "You are occupying someone else's seat. I will have to call the law if you don't leave. Go back to the lobby." We sat and we waited defiantly. Soon we heard sirens, and we left the train. Knowing we were in danger of being delayed further and likely being arrested or worse, we left the train. We heard more flashing lights and heard more sirens. We left the station. We saw more flashing lights and heard more sirens. We went in a direction away from the station along the railroad tracks. We walked briskly to distance ourselves from the now evolving police search. Along the railroad tracks we went past many freight cars, some standing with open doors, some closed. Roger and I watched the two ahead of us who found and entered an open car ahead of us. We followed by entering another open freight car close by. We could hear fading sirens. We entered a freight car, stood behind the door, and vowed if an officer entered we would have to attack before he called for help. We must escape arrest. We would not and could not give any chance they could call for help. We watched. We waited. We saw officers with flashlights searching several cars. Knowing they could not see the two of us without entering the car, we felt sure we wouldn't be detected.

Even though we had vowed we would take an officer by storm if he climbed aboard the boxcar, we stood with our backs to the sidewalls of the boxcar, positioned where an officer would have to enter the car to see us. We stood silently as long as there were flashing lights. Hours later and just before daybreak, we regrouped far down from the station. A curious young Negro, who offered us help, approached us. He suggested we go to the bus station, a long walk, then catch a bus to Washington D.C. Better still, he could get a cab driver who would take us to Washington for a reasonable sum. Four people dividing the cost would not be so bad. We did, avoiding a police search in so doing. We arrived without problems at the train station in Washington D.C. in a few hours. We were ready to accept our fate; we would patiently wait on the next train. Washington D.C., our mighty capital, was no better than Richmond, Virginia. We waited while others we knew or expected were white filled our expected seats. Why were so many civilians traveling, and why were they given priority over us? We watched and we waited. Finally, we were called. We boarded our train to Charleston, West Virginia. Maybe this train was to Cincinnati, non-stop. No there would be another stop in Charleston, West Virginia. Likely another layover of at least another day. What day was it? December 23? We arrived in Charleston very early on December 24, past midnight.

We met a thirty-five-year-old Negro, who intended to con us for a donation. His legs were taped, forcing him to walk as if disabled. Then, while still in the early morning, he admitted he had pretended to be disabled throughout the war, thus gaining sympathy while begging. At midnight, we finally boarded the train from Charleston to Cincinnati. It was just Roger and me now. I would walk from Union Terminal to Sixth and Vine to catch the streetcar to Norwood.

Roger, who lived in Addison, Indiana, would walk to the bus station on Fifth Street to catch a bus to Addison. Now the best of friends, we vowed to keep in touch, made convenient by the close proximity. Cincinnati and Addison were near neighbors. It didn't happen.

I looked into the store window and the clock on the wall said 5:10 AM. This would be much too early to awake Mom and Pop. *I'll take my time, I'll walk slow.* It was a cold December morning, with snow in leftover pockets along the thoroughfare. I waited for the number nine streetcar. My thoughts ran wild in anticipation. Who would be there at the house? Mom and Pop for sure. What other family members will still be at home? Oh, did I beat my brother home? He was in the Philippines last, I heard. Where was Pop working? The defense plants where I worked were long closed. Where would I get a job? I certainly need one. Could Mildred be here? No, she was in Madisonville with the baby. What did she name it? Lois Mae, that's right. No picture was ever sent. Cincinnati really looked dead. Is it that I'd been gone so long? Everything looked depleted and neglected. Was I expecting too much? The war effort caused all other upkeep and improvements to be put aside. Make ships, make airplanes, and make bombs.

Now it was over. The people who started all this were gone, as well as their country, destroyed. A street corner away I could see and hear the screeching sound as the number nine Norwood streetcar turned toward my stop. *Finally*, I thought as I climbed aboard. Looking into the conductor's face, I saw a fifty-ish white man, more like a robot operator than a representative of the transit system, saying nothing, only watching and waiting. *Oh, I got a dime,* I thought, *got more too.* Had I been white he would have been all over me with conversation and likely would have said, "It's okay about the fare." That was ordinary at this time, a uniformed marine or any other coming from the war. Maybe I looked too young, likely not. Did I go to war for rednecks? That thought would gain you nothing.

Mom would say, "Put it behind you, son." What would I have done without those guiding words and prayers while so often in harm's way? Determined not to fall asleep in the warm streetcar, I fidgeted. At Hopkins and Montgomery I rang the bell, waited, then stepped out into the cold December air. Knowing I would be waking my parents on such an early arrival, still I could not, due to the cold and slightly windy morning and my anxiety, refrain from a fast-pace walk. I noticed as I walked streets in disrepair, homes in neglect, cars with damaged bodies, only neglected by lack of people in the service. It was the war and we had to work eight hours a day, seven days a week to defeat the enemy.

What had been the toll on my family, my cousins, and my friends? Where were they? My younger sisters would be home. The others were working, making airplane engines when I left. That place was now closed. Only Della, the one closest, to me I did not know. I'm sure I'd see my one brother soon. Like I, he would return home to be with the family first. I knew him as well as he knew me.

I rang the bell. I looked around. The home was seemingly in neglect like everything else. This was far from the glorious Christmas homecoming I envisioned. Not at all. This was the day after. All my rushing in anticipation had gotten me home one day after Christmas and nothing could change that. When the doorbell was answered, it was mom in her gown. I had broken sleep of all in the house. I gave mom my love. She returned to bed, explaining as the time and conditions. Christmas was over.

I spoke to Pop. He said, "So great you are back, I'll talk with you in the morning." He never left the bed. Suddenly feeling the mental and physical pressure from the extremely long trip from the Island of Guam to home, I fell upon my bed, where I had not slept in two years and eight months. Practically sleepless over the many months, I could hardly hold back as the thoughts continued. Were the record player and the records still in the basement? Would Mom cook and bake as before? When would I see my child and future wife? Tomorrow, for sure, as soon as I found how to get there. I had the address. Gosh, I didn't know I was so devastated from that long trip. Many nights without really a night's sleep. I could and likely would sleep for hours. Home again, home again at last. Truly there is and nor will there ever be any place like home.

I closed my eyes in a prayerful mood while the events of the past years paraded my mind. Yes, I would always be proud to say I was a marine. Once a marine, always a marine. Along with all the others, I had returned a drastically changed person in a drastically changed world and did not swell with pride when reminded of what we did. The war had affected all citizens across the nation as well as nearly all individuals around the planet. The war brought more death and distraction than all the wars to this time. By mass production on our farms and in our un-bombed factories, we overwhelmed Hitler and his forces of evil. Now we were the superpower. Need there be skepticism? This was where the Native Americans were driven from their land and nearly eliminated. This was where a nation of people who were brought from Africa to be slaves for centuries. This is where the atomic bomb was developed and used on the Asians. I did not believe its devastation would have been used on a European city. Yes, we were the good and yes we were also the bad.

We went, with and for love of our family, love of our race, our God, and our country. Either volunteered or drafted, we went willingly to serve our country's best interest. For whatever the reason, we dedicated ourselves and accepted our fate as ordered by whoever were our superiors to the best of our abilities. Not having been given an opportunity to make the greatest sacrifice does not mean we were not dedicated, it only means we were not given the chance. However, many did make the greatest sacrifice while serving in the supply lines and services. To those who were blown to bits, burned away in a plane, or entombed beneath the sea, my heart goes out to them. I sincerely share the pain of those who came home lame. So, I declare all who came home whole are blessed to be and are equal as I.

Will Gardner and Susan Francis Gardner (adults)
Along with their children Bill and Lucy. Standing
behind is Ralph (Papa) and Lola, children from Will
Gardner's first marriage to Della Forney.